BEAUTIFUL EXILE

THE LIFE OF
MARTHA GELLHORN

BEAUTIFUL EXILE

THE LIFE OF MARTHA GELLHORN

Carl Rollyson

Originally Published by Aurum Press

Copyright © 2001, 2007 by Carl Rollyson

ISBN: 978-1-5040-2996-4

Distributed in 2016 by Open Road Distribution
180 Maiden Lane
New York, NY 10038
www.openroadmedia.com

CONTENTS

ACKNOWLEDGEMENTS

WHERE DOES A biographer begin? After reading Gellhorn's work, I turned to Jacqueline Orsagh's informative Ph.D. dissertation on Gellhorn's life and work. Orsagh had the inestimable advantage of having interviewed Gellhorn, so I could draw on Gellhorn's own words. Similarly, Bernice Kert, (*The Hemingway Women*) not only interviewed Gellhorn but was given access to letters which Gellhorn later sequestered in her closed archive in Special Collections, Mugar Memorial Library, Boston University.

Of course, biographies of Hemingway also provided leads and documentation.

I got help at just the right time from a friend and fellow biographer, Ann Waldron, who gave me the address of Delia Mares, one of Edna Gellhorn's close associates. Mrs Mares, in turn, provided me with the names, addresses and phone numbers of several people in St Louis whom I was able to visit and interview: Mrs Virginia Deutch, Mrs Aaron Fischer, Mary Taussig Hall and Emily Lewis Norcross. Mrs Hall suggested I see William Julius Polk and Martha Love Symington, both of whom were very helpful on Martha Gellhorn's St Louis years. Mrs Deutch provided an invaluable tape recording of Edna Gellhorn and helped me to secure an important early photograph of Martha. I was fortunate enough to record all of my interviews, which are now deposited in my archive at the University of Tulsa.

When I visited St Louis, Carol O. Daniel, Director of the Library of the John Burroughs School, took me on a tour of the school, provided me with Gellhorn's publications in the *John Burroughs Review*, and assisted me in obtaining several photographs. Patricia Adams, Associate Director of the Western Historical Manuscript Collection, University of Missouri–St Louis, was especially helpful in locating information on the Gellhorn and Fischel families. Charles Brown, Reference Librarian of the St Louis Mercantile Library, retrieved from clipping files a number of important items. Noel C. Holobeck in the History and Genealogy Department of the St Louis Public Library, patiently dealt with my inquiries about the Fischels and the Gellhorns, and put me in touch with Mrs Coralee Paull, who did some of the genealogical investigation for me and turned up several items that proved useful. Beryl Manne and Kevin Ray of the Washington University Archives, John M. Olin Library made available files from the Edna Gellhorn Collection and Katherine Burg sent materials from the Mary Institute.

Outside St Louis, several librarians and archivists have supplied me with invaluable information: Fred Bauma, Manuscripts Reading Room, Library of Congress, Washington, DC; Denison Beach, Houghton Reading Room, The Houghton Library, Harvard University, Cambridge, Massachusetts; Mary Burkee, Norman B. Brown, Anne E. Champagne, John Hoffman, Special Collections, University Library, University of Illinois, Urbana-Champaign; Ned Comstock, Archives of Performing Arts, University Library, University of Southern California, Los Angeles, California; Megan Floyd Desnoyers, John Fitzgerald Kennedy Library, Boston, Massachusetts; Fiorella Superbi Gioffredi, Villa I Tati, Florence, Italy; Alan Goodrich, John Fitzgerald Kennedy Library, Boston, Massachusetts; Cathy Henderson, Harry Ransom Humanities Research Center, University of Texas, Austin, Texas; James R. Hobin, Albany Public Library, Albany, New York; Patrick Lawler, Rare Books and Manuscripts, Butler Library, Columbia University, New York City; Jane Moreton and Jean Preston, Firestone Library, Princeton University, Princeton, New Jersey; Caroline Rittenhouse, Bryn Mawr College Library, Bryn Mawr, Pennsylvania; Dean M. Rogers, Special Collections, Vassar College Library; Elizabeth Shenton, Arthur and Elizabeth Schlesinger Library on the History of Women in America, Radcliffe

College, Cambridge, Massachusetts; Andar Skotnes, Biographical Oral History Collection, Butler Library, Columbia University, New York City; Audrey J. Smith, Humanities Reference Services, New York State Library, Albany, New York; Raymond Teichman, Franklin D. Roosevelt Library, Hyde Park, New York; Ann Van Arsdale, Firestone Library, Princeton University, Princeton, New Jersey; Patricia C. Willis, Beinecke Rare Book and Manuscript Library, Yale University Library, New Haven, Connecticut.

Lisa Middents and Stephen Plotkin at the John Fitzgerald Kennedy Library in Boston, Massachusetts were especially diligent and prompt in searching out items that might be of interest to me in the Ernest Hemingway Collection. Similarly, Hilary Cummings in Special Collections, University of Oregon Library, Eugene, Oregon not only did a thorough search of the Joseph Stanley Pennell Papers, she also put me in touch with two researchers, Mary Anteaux and Sally Hague, who found more material. It was my good fortune that Sally Hague, having returned to New York City, was able to do further research in Special Collections at the New York Public Library, where the *Collier's* magazine archive, which had been under my nose, had been located by Rutherford Witthus, a librarian at Auraria Library in Denver, Colorado contacted by my old friend Joan Fiscella. Eric Neubacher, who is known as the genius of inter-library loan at Baruch College, saved me many hours of time and trouble in securing hard to find books and articles. Similarly, Diane DiMartino went out of her way to conduct successful searches for information that I could only define in the vaguest terms.

I have often found it profitable to call upon my fellow biographers for information and advice. Bernice Kert was very generous in giving me background information about *The Hemingway Women*. Jeffrey Meyers suggested several avenues of research, gave me a quick sketch of Gellhorn and directed my attention to a stimulating article he had written about researching his Hemingway biography. Michael Reynolds wrote me a very thoughtful letter. One of his suggestions led me to the discovery of a cache of material at the New York Public Library. Similarly, Kenneth S. Lynn suggested an archival source that was of immense help to my biography. Blanche Cook shared with me her formidable knowledge of Eleanor Roosevelt and the part Gellhorn had played in Roosevelt's life.

When I wrote to Genevieve Dormann inquiring about the life of Bertrand de Jouvenel, she recommended that I consult his associate, Jeannie Malige, who in turn gave me the address of John R. Braun, who sent me a detailed letter about his biography of Jouvenel. Marion Meade shared her Gellhorn correspondence with me and alerted me to a Gellhorn item in the Houghton Library at Harvard. Richard Whelan answered a letter of mine with a friendly phone call about his impressions of interviewing Gellhorn for his biography of Robert Capa. Other biographers, Joan Peyser, Robert Newman, Eric Gordon, have been great sources of inspiration, encouragement and advice.

Frederick Vanderbilt Field patiently went over his reminiscences of Gellhorn and Hemingway for me that are included in his autobiography – as did Stanley Flink who had only a passing but vivid recollection of Martha Gellhorn and T. S. Matthews when they made a handsome couple. Robert A. Martin respected Gellhorn's injunction not to co-operate with an unauthorized biographer, but he wrote me a charming letter conveying a sense of his friendship with her. I also thank Cornell Capa for a brief phone conversation about his impressions of Gellhorn and her friendship with his brother Robert. Richard Cohen discussed his friendship with Gellhorn while I was at work on my biography of Rebecca West. Sydney Knowles shared his Gellhorn correspondence and his sharp memory of their meeting. Dan Brennan, Dr Heinz Richard Landmann and Ernie Sibley provided vivid vignettes of Gellhorn in action. Frances Saunders alerted me to the existence of David R. Meeker's fine Hemingway collection. I am indebted to Mr Meeker (Nick Adams & Co., Rare Books) for allowing me to examine the superb materials he has collected. Similarly, Rob and Abby Mouat allowed me to read the Gellhorn and Hemingway letters in their collection. I regret that I cannot name all of my sources, many of whom knew Martha Gellhorn well but who preferred anonymity.

I am very grateful to all my interviewees who are listed in the Notes and Comments section. I would especially like to thank Alison Selford, Raleigh Trevelyan, Francis King and Pauline Neville for making the last period of my research so stimulating and rewarding. Julie Burchill was very kind to send the letter I quote in this biography. Veronica Horwell and Maggie O'Kane were also very helpful in supplying me with the names of interviewees to contact. Victoria Glendinning has been more of an inspiration than she can possibly know.

Minnie Magazine of the Time-Life Alumni Association tracked down several of T. S. Matthews's *Time* colleagues for me, including Mrs Joseph Cowan (Content Peckham), who treated me to a memory of her first meeting with Gellhorn and to a rare glimpse of the inner workings of the magazine. Randall 'Pete' Smith provided what he called a worm's eye view of what it was like in Spain during Hemingway's and Gellhorn's sojourn there. Pauline Gadd put me in touch with her uncle and aunt, Ron and Beryl Gadd, whose hospitality and helpfulness made my trip to Wales and the search for Martha Gellhorn's cottage such a success.

At Baruch College I have found colleagues eager to hear about my work and to help in a variety of ways. I am indebted to Martin Stevens for his recollections of Germany in the 1930s and to Martha Kessler for the glimpse she gave me of Gellhorn working in the McGovern campaign. Several members of Baruch's staff helped with the countless tasks involved in producing a biography. I thank them all: Denise Cascini, Connie Terrero, Marcia Laguer, Eileen Leary, Ken Liebowitz, Joyce Marrotta, Violet Parnass, Carmen Pedrogo, David Thomas, Marlene Thompson, Jacqueline Gathers, Tessa Rougier, Debra Dorry and Alison Wong. My thanks to Dian-yu Yu, the best research assistant I have ever had. Norman Fainstein, my colleague and good friend, provided strong support during a period when I was balancing the demands of scholarship and administration. I am also grateful to several former Baruch administrators: Joel Segall, Paul LeClerc, John McGarraghy and Louanne Kennedy. My secretary, Lenora Rock, performed more services for this book than she knows – as have Katherine Curtis and Miriam Allen.

An American Council of Learned Societies grant-in-aid provided the assistance and recognition that made it possible for me to complete my research more quickly that I had anticipated.

My agent, Elizabeth Frost-Knappman of New England Publishing Associates, has been a joy to work with in shaping the original idea of this book. I am greatly indebted to my London agents, Gloria Ferris and Rivers Scott of Scott Ferris Associates, for their persistent faith in my work and their sound suggestions for its improvement.

My editors, Sheila Murphy and Piers Burnett, helped me locate interviewees in London and significantly improved the shape of the story I wanted to write. I have been buoyed by their enthusiasm for this project. In the day-to-day existence of the writer – when I have needed the right word – I have always turned to my wife, Dr Lisa Paddock. I have never felt the need of another muse.

INTRODUCTION

WHEN MARTHA GELLHORN died on 15 February 1998, just shy of her ninetieth birthday, the press reacted with shock: to her many friends in journalism it seemed that she would go on for ever. The redoubtable Martha – as the newspapers called her – had reported on wars from Spain in the 1930s to Panama in the 1980s. She had beguiled H. G. Wells, with whom she lived for a time in London. He wrote a preface to her short story collection, *The Trouble I've Seen*. Married to Ernest Hemingway, she was the only woman ever to walk out on him. She smoked and drank and travelled with abandon. In a single article in *Paris Review*, Gellhorn cut down Lillian Hellman at the height of her influence, demolishing the playwright's pretensions to being a witness to war in Spain and an anti-fascist courier. Gellhorn seemed perpetually young, a voice filled with outrage raised against the perfidy of governments and the posing of phoneys. She had outlived most of her generation. She was planning new trips. Nearly blind, she persevered, gallant and without a shred of self-pity. Indeed, she would say she had had it better than she had any right to expect. Who could not admire such an intrepid personality?

Reading about Gellhorn in the Hemingway biographies would not tell you that she was the better journalist – and funnier. She took on life with an exuberance that had her still snorkelling in her eighties and charming men half her age. It was the feisty, outspoken Martha who provoked me into writing the only biography of her, published in 1990. She opposed it – 'nothing personal,' she wrote to me, she just did not want it done. Yet when she claimed to have an authorized biographer – apparently a ploy to disarm me – I renewed my biographical quest. If she could have one biographer, why not two?

While interviewing friends of Rebecca West for my biography of her, I found that many of them knew Gellhorn. Then I discovered that library collections of West's papers also contained Gellhorn's correspondence. Her friends wrote to me, enclosing letters and photographs. And so I began to collect material for a new biography of increased scope. I discovered a long suppressed Wells manuscript in which he spoke candidly of his love affair with her.

Wells numbered Gellhorn's letters among the liveliest he ever received and the specimens I have collected recently bear him out. She often sounds like the wisecracking women of 1930s screwball comedies – but one that is uncensored, who refers to herself as a 'bitch', a 'girl-author' who sometimes writes 'on one foot' for money that will support her trips abroad. This is the uncensored Gellhorn. To another of her intimates, Alexander Woollcott, Gellhorn describes a fellow writer as a 'little man with a mouth which I like to think looks like a hog's ass in fly-time'.

Gellhorn was not the first female war correspondent – as some naïve obituaries put it – but she might as well have been, for she had a way of erasing other women from memory. In *A Stricken Field*, her novel about her experiences in Prague on the eve of Munich and World War Two, she seats her fictional surrogate in a room full of men, giving as good as she gets but never losing her charm. (One woman covering the recent war in Bosnia took *A Stricken Field* along as a kind of primer.) Although brought up by a feminist mother, Gellhorn disdained special pleading for women and bashing male chauvinists. She grew up with two brothers, and early on she learned how to enjoy and often best the male competition.

A handsome woman who never lost her sexual allure, Gellhorn kept her chaps (her word for them) in thrall. She knew how important sex was for most men, and she used it not only to please men but to get good stories. She slept with generals; she had one-night stands with ordinary soldiers who might not survive the next day. She dressed elegantly, used make-up skilfully, flirted and coaxed men to do her bidding. If employing a bit of glamour helped her on her way, Gellhorn played along – whether it was modelling French designer dresses in Paris when very young, or posing like a Hollywood starlet for the jacket of an early novel, or playing the *grande femme* in her later years. She hated publicity and the world of self-promotion that her second husband, Ernest Hemingway, succumbed to, but Gellhorn used the machinery of celebrity when it suited her. She thought she could turn it off and it always perturbed her when others still wanted to play the fame game with her long after she had tired of it.

What is missing in the British obituaries of Gellhorn is an acknowledgement of her ambition and of her refusal to reflect on the implications of international affairs. One would suppose from reading the encomiums that Gellhorn was fired only by outrage at injustice – whether it was Margaret Thatcher putting down the noble miners, or America bombing North Vietnam (as was often said at the time) back into the Stone Age. Outrage plays well, especially in the press. Gellhorn got rave reviews for saying trust no government, suspect all politicians. In the context of her melodramas of good and evil, such statements have enormous appeal. The trouble is that they also shut down thinking, allowing reporters to withdraw from a complex reality to report only what they see. And this was Gellhorn's advice: 'Write what you see. I never believed in that objectivity shit.' Well, she was a remarkable observer, but the testimony of the eyewitness is never enough. Reading all of her reports on Spain, for example, with their impressive evocation of events on the ground, one would never suppose that the Stalinists were systematically eliminating all opposition, that the brave Spanish Republic that Gellhorn so loved would have been swallowed into the Soviet maw if the fascists had not devoured it first.

The Spanish Civil War broke Gellhorn's heart. She never forgave the United States for not intervening to save the Republic. She never believed in the 'free world' rhetoric of the Western powers or in the perfidy of the Soviet Union. 'If one wants to be depressed, I think the US is subject number one', she wrote on 21 April 1990 to Milton Wolff, her friend from the Spanish Civil War days. She confessed to having no interest in the USSR – she 'thought it was their problem to solve'. It posed no threat to Western Europe or to the

United States, although she had no illusions about the tyranny of Soviet life: she 'could not stand living there even ten days'. She was no 'ideologue but a simple soul'. She hated the US government. Hate is, of course, blinding, and in her case it accounts for many instances in this biography when her views will seem simplistic for such a well-travelled writer.

Biographies are necessary to remedy the sentimentality that creeps into obituaries and the lionizing that inevitably follows the death of a figure as legendary as Martha Gellhorn. It takes nothing away from her achievement to document how cannily she made her way in the world. Her fierce drives were every bit as political as those of the politicians she deplored. Her careerism was just as intense as Hemingway's, even if she rejected the idea of mythologizing her life. Indeed, she went to the opposite extreme, supposing that she could threaten and sue (if necessary) anyone who produced a version of her life that did not accord with her own. It is a very strange position for a reporter to take. And it is a very controlling attitude – one which is understandable in writers who want to command the narratives of their own lives. Gellhorn's success in writing her own story is demonstrated in those obituaries and memoirs that flooded the press. She is always pictured as an opponent of cant, always in the right place at the right time. What the obituaries never ask – what her friends fail to note – is how Martha Gellhorn got there.

In her old age Gellhorn made her friends – mostly adoring males half her age – think that Bertrand de Jouvenel (her first husband) and Hemingway (her second) were her youthful follies. Poor Bertrand, poor Ernest, these yearning males wanted sex with her and she obliged. What she omitted from the story was her overwhelming need for a male hero, a need that made her gush over John F. Kennedy and take the dashing paratrooper general, James Gavin, to her bed. Men were a *huge* disappointment, but Gellhorn still went after them like Hemingway after big game.

Though Hemingway found Gellhorn enticing in Key West, he did not pursue her. Instead, he left for Spain. Gellhorn expected an invitation to the war and safe passage there. Hemingway proffered neither. So she showed up on her own, angry at Hemingway, but determined to snag him nonetheless. Hemingway was not a fool; he knew this was a woman intent on goading him into action. Although he responded to her gambit, he also – well before they married – set down the conniving side of her character in his play *The Fifth Column*. This portrait has been treated as sour grapes, but it was written before the couple married, when Hemingway was smitten but no sucker. He was neither as self-involved nor quite as needy as Gellhorn made him out to be. In retrospect, with a hoard of Hemingway biographies treating him as a boor, it has been far too easy to accept Gellhorn's denigration of his character.

Hemingway once told Gellhorn in a telegram that she should stay at home and be his wife. The truth is that she could never settle down and that she despised people who did so, including her third husband T. S. Matthews, a literary man who had started well at the *New Republic*, but later was beguiled by an offer from Henry Luce at *Time*. Somehow Matthews managed to convince himself that he was a prince of rectitude and not just the managing editor at *Time*. He persuaded Gellhorn to marry him and then set himself up as an English gentleman in 1950s Britain. But right at the outset Gellhorn wrote to Bernard Berenson clearly signalling her boredom with the stuffy Matthews. She thought she needed a secure home for her adopted son, Sandy, and Matthews admired her so, as all the men did. She thought she would have enough freedom in the marriage to drop everything for a story. Matthews, like Hemingway, assured her of this latitude, but for Gellhorn marriage – any sort of bond – was bondage.

A new biography of Martha Gellhorn has to cut through the bromides and eulogies to reveal a tough, sexy woman who lent journalism a sense of immediacy and responded to human suffering with an alacrity that startled her readers out of their complacency. She had a unique ability to register the suffering of others. It can even be said she had a professional eye for it. Personally, however, compassion often failed her. She could tell writer Sybille Bedford to her face that she bored her, thus ending a thirty-year friendship. Other friends would be cut off instantly for raising the wrong subject (usually Hemingway). She would show them the door. She went through a kind of courting procedure with young female academics interested in writing about her. First, she welcomed them, but then she turned sour as these women began to ask questions and probe sensitive areas. Many of them called me to share their dismay, bewildered that Gellhorn had turned on them. It is not − as the obituaries had it − that Gellhorn could not suffer fools (Bedford was no fool), she simply could not suffer most people. As Hemingway said, she loved humanity but hated people. She could only abide them in ones and twos, rarely allowing her friends to meet in her company. By rigidly adhering to certain protocols, she controlled her image with as much assiduousness as Hemingway massaged the media.

Not only did Gellhorn regulate what was said about her − she drove a friend to frenzy by omitting almost all biographical material from his BBC programme about her career − she *never* addressed certain key facts about herself. A number of the obituaries pointed out that she had a fanatical devotion to the state of Israel. To many of her friends this seemed odd, if not downright reactionary. She had no sympathy for Arabs, not even the Palestinians. She supported the Gulf War − again a very strange position for a liberal, indeed, an avowed socialist − to adopt. Gellhorn was a Jew, but in the 1930s world of internationalism, in which the Left looked forward to a world where ethnic and religious distinctions would not matter, she kept silent about her own Jewishness. (Hemingway, with his usual shrewd but loutish acuity, fastened on her Jewishness to the verge of anti-Semitism.) But this suppressed side of herself came out strongly in her unremitting hatred of Germany and in her adamant refusal to entertain any criticism of Israel.

Living in London for half her life, Gellhorn played the role of a cosmopolitan expatriate, disparaging her home town and deprecating America. She could not abide talk about her origins. She wanted to conquer other worlds, very much like the two female reporters in her play, *Love Goes to Press*, which was a hit in post-war London − as was Gellhorn herself.

After divorcing Matthews, Gellhorn remade herself in the 1960s, befriending reporters, newspaper editors, and later writers such as Victoria Glendinning, Bill Buford and Paul Theroux. When not making her periodic forays abroad, covering the US invasion of Panama and exploring the slums of Brazil at a time when cataracts made her nearly blind, she was campaigning at home for Labour, greeting Blair and company as the dawn of a new age. Gellhorn welcomed anyone who might open up the world for her, as she had done for generations of readers. Wells called her a writer of 'instinctive directness and vigour'. It was a quality she never lost, a quality that also made her an arresting personality, a quality I hope I have captured in this biography.

I

THE SPIRIT OF ST LOUIS
1860–1923

MARTHA GELLHORN was the third-generation offspring of a family that had helped to establish their city's tradition of community service. She bore the name of her maternal grandmother, Martha Ellis, whose family was descended from English settlers. Martha Ellis's father, Turner Morehead Ellis, born in Kentucky in 1808, had been a commission merchant (travelling salesman). She herself was born on 25 May 1850 in Jackson, Mississippi. Only five when her mother died, she accompanied her father in 'memorable excursions on river boats' to St Louis, where he settled in 1860, becoming one of the city's solid citizens.

In the heady milieu of a frontier capital and border state full of the remnants of its founding French families, Southern sympathizers and reform-minded immigrants, Martha Ellis launched her first act of public protest: defiantly displaying a Confederate flag, she picketed a federal prison. But she soon abandoned the lost cause, influenced by German liberals who had fled Europe after the failed democratic revolutions of 1848. Instead, she shrewdly subverted her genteel society and the institutions of a segregated, conservative city. She began by becoming a teacher. As one newspaper reported, she became 'one of the first of social standing to earn her own living'. She did it gradually – taking care not to embarrass her family, finding her first position in a small country school teaching English language and customs to Russian refugees. A superb public speaker with a commanding platform presence, she served as principal of

Howard College, the female auxiliary of Central Methodist College in Fayette, Missouri, and taught in the St Louis public schools.

In 1876 Martha Ellis married Washington Emil Fischel, a St Louis native whose Jewish family had come from Prague. He soon established himself as a distinguished physician known for his liberal convictions. A professor in clinical medicine at Washington University, he organized the medical staff of the Barnard Free Skin and Cancer Hospital. Dr Fischel died in 1914 before his granddaughter's sixth birthday, but Martha Gellhorn remembered that her grandmother revered him as much for his humour and good temper as for his devotion to his poor patients. People liked to confide in this youthful man Martha Ellis called 'Wash'. He brought gaiety to everything he did.

Martha Ellis promoted self-improvement and conscience; that is, she and her husband were part of a liberal generation of Jews who had forsaken orthodox Judaism for a more modern, secular progessivism that emphasized individual responsibility. Many Jews of her generation became Unitarians, finding in this tolerant version of Christianity a home for their cosmopolitan and radical politics. But Martha and her husband belonged to no church. Wash's parents, Ephraim and Babette Fischel, were members of B'nai El, a small but very active Jewish congregation, and are buried in Mount Sinai Cemetery in St Louis. Their son and subsequent members of the family did not practise Judaism or identify themselves with specifically Jewish activities although, like many Jewish families, they became active in the St Louis chapter of the Ethical Society, founded in New York City in 1876 by Felix Adler, to promulgate 'the supreme importance of the ethical factor in all relations of life, personal, social, national, and international, apart from any theological or metaphysical considerations'.

Even among broadminded Jews and other liberals, however, Martha stood out. There were no social workers, so she had to invent her own 'home-making classes' for the poor. She visited schools, picking out the students who seemed 'most neglected'. From the teachers she obtained parents' names and addresses. When she found a student's mother lying about in a 'dirty house', she asked permission to send the child on Saturdays to the settlement house, the neighbourhood welfare institution, where educational and recreation facilities for the poor were provided. The mother usually consented, grateful to be relieved of family responsibilities. Then Martha Ellis engaged her female friends to teach these children and to treat them as they would their own offspring. In borrowed premises (a room over a bakery) she set up a stove, kitchen equipment, and bedroom and living-room furniture, so that children could be instructed in how to prepare and serve meals, and how to make an attractive, well-planned home. Eventually, these classes became the basis of the home economics curriculum in the St Louis public schools.

In the early 1880s Martha Ellis established the Shelley Club, thirty-two women devoted to analysing the poet's life and work, including his atheism and radical politics. In St Louis, such subjects were judged not 'fit for discussion in polite society'. She also organized the Wednesday Club, a group of one hundred women who began by discussing cultural and literary topics but soon became involved in welfare projects.

Before she married, Martha Ellis attended suffragist meetings. She believed in 'equal pay for equal work', but she 'deferred to my husband in not flaunting my views on the subject. Dr Fischel admitted the principle of the thing, but he feared results that might lead to the lessening of home ties.'

In 1939 Martha Gellhorn wrote a memorial tribute to her grandmother. She recalled the epitaph Martha Ellis had put on the gravestone of her dearly beloved husband, '*Ich Dien*' – I serve. That was her grandmother's credo, Gellhorn explained: you should help others, especially if you are safe and secure, and well-sheltered and educated. Martha Gellhorn saw herself in her grandmother's image, for she used virtually the same words in *A Stricken Field* to describe Mary Douglas, the foreign correspondent modelled on Gellhorn herself, who feels she must 'pay back' her privileges and good luck by helping refugees fleeing Hitler's persecution.

Edna, Martha Ellis's only child, was born on 18 December 1878. She quickly became her mother's pride, a beautiful child who grew up to carry on and extend her mother's liberal campaigns for social and political reform. As Martha Ellis put it, 'My light shines through my daughter.'

In 1894 Edna's mother boldly decided to send her east to the Baldwin School in preparation for the following year at Bryn Mawr College. To all but the most liberal families in St Louis Bryn Mawr represented a radical choice for a proper young woman. Founded in 1885 by Quakers, the college was dedicated to obtaining for women the right to a full and equal participation with men in public affairs and professional life – hardly a conventional goal at a time when women did not even have the vote. Bryn Mawr educated individualists and activists.

Four years later Edna returned as a suffragist, an ardent advocate of women's rights and with an accent 'clear and unstrident and quite un-Midwestern'. But she behaved with such 'natural and unconscious pride' that she won many people to her side. In 1903, visiting the Bryn Mawr campus for her third reunion, she was 'trailed' by a group of sophomores who were immensely taken with 'this gorgeous creature. With her masses of golden braids and her blue eyes, she was like a tall, slim Norwegian princess.' T. S. Matthews, Martha's third husband, observed that Edna 'wasn't the embattled clubwoman or the crusading social worker type at all'. In fact, organizations per se did not appeal to her – even though she ran them and shook them up. She once said to a neighbour, 'Political science will not get you very far.' Better to model yourself after 'priests and gangsters' who knew their own people well and got things done.

When Edna travelled the state in milk train cabooses conducting voter education classes, she struck a proper ladylike pose by pretending to knit. Public work, she implied, need not negate a woman's domestic life. Male politicians ridiculed Edna's zeal for social reform – but not to her face. They wanted her good opinion and courted her support. A legislator who did not vote her way asked mutual friends to 'square me with Edna'. He knew and she knew that there would be occasions when they would help each other out; neither one could afford to offend the other.

In 1908, the year Martha Gellhorn was born, her native city was undergoing a campaign of moral and civic renewal. The impetus for much of this improvement came from more than a decade of discussion and planning for the St Louis World Fair of 1904. That year Edna became involved in one of her first major projects: cleaning up the city's water supply in preparation for the Fair's Louisiana Purchase Exposition. St Louis wanted to celebrate a century of growth and to commemorate President Jefferson's acquisition of a territory that stimulated the settlement of land and the development of a new civilization.

In fact, the city had been seriously damaged by the Civil War. It took more than a generation to recover its position as a major trading centre, and by the turn of the century it faced stiff competition from Chicago, which had surpassed St Louis in population, industrial output and trade. The World Fair, then, was a bid to recoup some of the economic strength St Louis had lost, to regenerate the glory of its role as the gateway to the West and to deliver on promises of progress that had never been fulfilled.

Thus Martha Gellhorn grew up in an era of reform promoted by her own mother, who would achieve a national reputation. During World War One, she would be a Civil Service Commissioner and regional director of the food rationing programme, and later she would actively involve herself in the American Association of University Women and in the United Nations. In 1920 she became a founder and first vice-president of the National League of Women Voters. Through her many efforts on behalf of civic reform Edna made important friends, including Eleanor Roosevelt, who would become Martha's friend, supporter and adviser.

Early on in her career Edna staged big demonstrations for causes that also entertained the public. Raising funds for a new hospital, she paraded eight elephants through town while she herself sold peanuts at a concession stand. The herd got separated and the event turned into a 'big game hunt'.

Edna included Martha in marches for women's suffrage. Martha rode on floats festooned with slogans championing the cause and pointing to her as 'the spirit of the future'. For the Democratic Convention held at St Louis in June 1916, Edna organized 7000 women decked out in yellow parasols and sashes proclaiming 'Votes for Women'. They lined both sides of the 'Golden Lane', the streets that led to the convention centre. 'We had a tableau', she told a reporter in 1963. Different groups of women dressed in white, grey and black (the black ones dragging chains) symbolized states that had suffrage, partial suffrage, or no suffrage for women. Seven-year-old Martha Gellhorn, in the right-hand corner of the front row, represented a future voter.

Edna's husband George liked to accompany Edna to women's suffrage speaking engagements and 'nod approvingly'. A distinguished gynaecologist and obstetrician, his work seconded hers when he established free prenatal clinics and other medical services for the poor.

Born in Breslau, Germany, George Gellhorn had studied at the Gymnasium in Ohlau, received his MD from the University of Würzburg in 1894 and served as an assistant in clinics at the Universities of Berlin, Jena and Vienna. Respected as a bright young man in the German medical community, Gellhorn also had ambitions as a scientist and for a time he served as an assistant to Wilhelm Conrad Roentgen, a Nobel Prize winner (1901) noted for his research in physics and famous for his discovery of X-rays.

George Gellhorn, an anti-militarist, opposed the rise of Prussianism. Possessed of an overwhelming desire to travel and with letters of introduction to distinguished professors in the American medical establishment, Gellhorn embarked on a trip of exploration. He sailed the world for a few years, becoming a ship's doctor, before landing in the United States in 1899.

Gellhorn did not plan to stay in St Louis, but he had a letter of introduction to Washington Fischel, who had studied at the Universities of Prague, Vienna and Berlin for two years after obtaining his medical degree from St Louis Medical College in 1871. Gellhorn and Fischel shared many of the same convictions; more important, they admired each other. Fischel urged Gellhorn to stay. St Louis needed men like him.

Martha romanticized her parents' first meeting. Edna glided down a centre stairway, the beams from a stained-glass window showering her golden hair with highlights. Bewitched by her charm, George resolved to woo Edna. But it took him three years to win her (a telling part of the story for Martha, who always had her doubts about marriage).

Martha liked to recall that she grew up with her three brothers, George, Walter and Alfred, in a 'loving, merry, stimulating' home. But Martha was less fond of George and Walter, the two oldest children in the family, than of Alfred, the youngest, with whom she would sometimes travel in later years. At the dinner table they listened to distinguished guests like Herbert Hoover, who visited the Gellhorn home during World War One when Edna became prominent in the War Food Administration. Walter remembered being taken to hear Senator William Borah, Woodrow Wilson and others, who were stumping the country in favour of the League of Nations. If there were no guests for dinner, if George Gellhorn had no night calls or evening surgery, he studied and wrote at home in the evening, with his children often emulating the example of this well-read man with a command of five languages and a deep appreciation of music.

George Gellhorn 'set icily high standards', Martha recalled. 'Isn't there anything *better?*' he asked her when she brought home a report card with all As. Educated in Germanic precision and politeness, he found his children a little too forward, even though he had encouraged their candour and enjoyed their informality. They enjoyed his attention. He liked to drive a car on his medical rounds while listening to Walter conjugating Latin verbs. He helped his son with his algebra, but he never scolded him about homework.

The Gellhorns were permissive parents and their children seemed to behave well without overt discipline. Edna emulated her mother's 'substitution plan' for training children:

> Instead of telling your child to stop what he is doing, suggest something else which he would like to do, instead. When he has picked up an article you do not want him to have, hold out to him something else which will engage his interest before you try to get him to relinquish what he holds. In this way, you will get through the day with as few 'don'ts' as possible.

Edna could not have been a more encouraging mother. According to Martha, she made her children feel they were 'wonderful'.

George and Edna forbade the use of racial or ethnic epithets. They did not gossip. They did not talk about money. The children had to base their opinions on what they had observed, not on what so and so had said. Family discussions followed Robert's Rules of Order, with George Gellhorn as Speaker. Disputes were resolved by consulting reference books.

Children of reformers often decry their parents' fanatical devotion to causes, but Edna's children saw the sporting quality of her

civic campaigns. 'Peels of laughter' emanated from her meetings, her
son Walter recalled. 'She made it fun', one of her friends said. Everyone had a part to play. Indeed, each of her children thought that 'she
or he had virtually single-handedly achieved woman's suffrage and
had founded the League of Women Voters', Walter remembered.

Martha's best friend, Emily Lewis Norcross, understood early on
that Edna was an outstanding, powerful person, a 'doing woman'.
Martha seemed to be on her own much of the time. 'Marty's mother
was away an awful lot,' Emily recalled. 'So Marty was very independent as a child.' She did not have the 'governed' home life Emily and
her friends enjoyed. 'We all grew up in this little protected community, going to our debutante parties, having our fun, and Martha was
not about to do that', said Mary Taussig Hall, a schoolmate and
friend Gellhorn would continue to visit years after she left St Louis.
Martha Love Symington, another schoolmate and lifelong friend,
remembered that 'Martha went along with her brothers, doing anything they did.' By the age of eleven or twelve, 'she knew the whole
city. And we weren't allowed to put our *feet* in buses – unless we
were going to school and back.' Already a strong personality, and a
'hell of a lot of fun', the well-read Martha had an impressive vocabulary and ambitions to be a writer. Emily realized that by this time
Martha was 'turning terribly against St Louis'.

'Marty's family was half-Jewish,' Emily said pointedly, 'but they
were accepted in St Louis as gentiles.' Delia Mares, who came to St
Louis in the mid-1930s and began to work closely with Edna Gellhorn, remembered that people were conscious of the family's Jewish
background. Martha's oldest friends agreed with Emily Norcross's
delicately phrased comment that being Jewish was regarded 'with a
little more feeling in those days':

> For instance, our Jewish girlfriends did not go to our dancing
> classes. They had their own thing. We had a couple of friends who
> were *intimate* pals, whom we were devoted to, and Marty would often
> talk to me about how 'isn't it sad that because they're Jewish …' I
> knew that Marty was part Jewish –
> [Rollyson]: She never talked about it?
> [Norcross]: *Never!*
> [Rollyson]: Never?
> [Norcross]: *Never!* This was a very telling thing.

Martha Love Symington also noticed this troubling element in Martha's background.

George Gellhorn could not square his scientific research with religious belief. But he had no hostility towards believers. On the contrary, his children often found themselves in the company of a great-aunt, Sister Miriam, a former Episcopal nun notorious for her fierce, narrow-minded piety. Born Susan Mary Ellis, Sister Miriam (Martha Ellis's sister) had done missionary work in Baden, 'instituting Sunday School classes for children of laundresses at the school' and establishing a 'Peace Mission' in St Louis. She had a rugged dedication the community admired: 'I have encountered her far from home at all seasons of the year, all hours of the night. Dark alleys, miserable hovels, lonely county roads, river front jungles, held no terrors for her. She was never afraid', a doctor said of her. Frequently at the Gellhorn home for Sunday dinner, present through the courtesy of some member of the family who had driven far out into the country to get her, this zealot remained devoted to the Gellhorns, as they were to her. She once admitted to Walter that his parents led such sainted lives that it was a pity they were not Christians.

Walter and Martha did attend an Ethical Society Sunday School for a few years and their brother George quickly gained his parents' permission to join his friends at the Episcopal Sunday School. Neither Walter nor Martha seemed especially interested in ethical instruction; sometimes they would play hookey and buy candy with the donations they were supposed to make to the Ethical Society.

Martha sensed how peculiar her parents were in comparison to their contemporaries. Her mother had not only gone to college – unusual in itself for a woman in her era – she was a Bryn Mawr graduate. She had been east and that alone provoked gossip. Martha's nonconformist father refused to join a country club, which he considered undemocratic. Martha claimed the Gellhorns were the only important family in St Louis not to join.

Of course, the Gellhorns were upper class, Martha admitted, but they were singular. At classical concerts in his native Germany, George Gellhorn relished the food available at intermission. A pastry fortified the concert-goer and enhanced the pleasure of the remainder of the programme, he contended. Alas, St Louis concerts did not provide such nourishment, a deficiency he rectified by bringing his own provisions. This deviation from community norms embarassed Martha, but it was a family principle 'not to do something because everyone else did it and not to condemn something because no one else did it'.

In their early teens Emily and Martha whipped around to 'gassy little Friday night dancing classes', but they were not popular girls, Emily recalls: 'Marty was overpowering to those little boys.' She did not make a debut the way most girls did, since her family 'were really sort of above that, and didn't want it, but she missed it. *Really.* She missed it', Emily insisted. Martha's parents were distinguished citizens of St Louis, but they certainly were not in the social mainstream.

Martha attended Mr Mahler's dancing classes once a week in the winter season. William Julius Polk, one of her companions, could not vouch for her attitude then, except that he suspected that she viewed places like the Fortnightly Club askance:

> It was an exercise in deportment and ballroom behaviour. Everyone in the sense of being everyone one knew went to Mr Mahler's dancing school. I think it's in Alexis de Tocqueville's study of the United States – when he comes to St Louis, he says that in order to understand St Louis you have to take into consideration the influence of the religion of the sacred heart and M. Sarpi's dancing academy.

'Nice girls' dreamed of pretty social affairs in Mahler's ballroom. 'Every girl wants to have a ball, and many of them will have their desires granted', a social column observed. This kind of niceness did not have appeal for Martha, 'slightly rebellious and slightly nonconformist. ... When we were growing up we felt that St Louis was somewhat Midwestern and provincial. And she thought it would be more interesting to belong to the big world', Polk concludes.

Children her own age often found Martha peculiar. She disliked St Louis, and dreamed of living in France and seeing the places her father loved to reminisce about. She read constantly and had little use for small talk or socializing. She was a doctor's child whereas her contemporaries came from families in business. The Gellhorns were not snobs about the world of commerce, but children could not help but feel less cultivated than Martha. They could not identify with a girl who came from a family so conspicuously devoted to the general welfare. Martha's parents hosted their share of parties for her and her friends, but the Gellhorns did not indulge in many purely social affairs. Martha noticed this and developed a 'slight chip ... well, a sensitivity', Martha Love Symington recalled.

Martha Gellhorn felt ostracized, eating her lunch alone at Mary Institute, her elementary school. Even the self-reliant Martha found it painful to be regarded by classmates as 'the kiss of death'. During the Great War feelings ran strongly against a child with a German last name and a family engaged in 'scandalous' activities. What is more, the Gellhorns employed a German housekeeper who helped to look after the children when Edna was away from home working on her public-welfare projects. Martha Love Symington, who lived a few blocks from the Gellhorns, remembered that she and her friends used to march up and down the street singing: 'Kaiser Bill went up the hill to take a look at France. And Kaiser Bill came down the hill with bullets in his pants.'

Martha, a resourceful child, overcame this prejudice. She trusted in close friends like Emily Lewis Norcross, although she noticed that her very freedom from restrictions isolated her. 'On Saturday let's go downtown on the streetcar and have lunch', she proposed to Emily. They were twelve or thirteen at the time. Emily said, 'Marty, I can't. I'm not allowed to go downtown alone.' A week or two later at Mary Institute, a girl they did not know very well came up to them at recess and said, 'Listen, tomorrow, Saturday, let's take the streetcar to town.' 'I'm not allowed to go into town alone', Marty said.

The first time Martha Gellhorn ever felt truly content and comfortable was during her vacation in Grenoble, France. She was sixteen and chaperoned by a female companion. The boys from Paris and from Oxford appeared to be more mature and refined. In St Louis, it did not take much to be popular – just hum one of the popular tunes while you danced. Only in France did she feel comfortable in conversation, discussing ideas freely as she had done in her parents' home. In France, it was as if she had been welcomed home. What a delight actually to watch people weighing her opinions.

Martha also found European topography more appealing. The way city and country seemed to blend into each other was preferable to America's enormous discontinuities, its mountains, plains and plateaux juxtaposed against cities Gellhorn considered ugly. Back in St Louis, Martha bided her time, wondering when her life would really begin.

2

A WINDOW ON THE WORLD
1923–1926

B Y THE SPRING OF 1923, when Martha Gellhorn, now fourteen, completed the ninth grade at Mary Institute, Edna Gellhorn had founded a new school for her daughter to attend. It would reflect 'the new spirit in education'. Unlike Mary Institute, it would be co-educational and emphasize the practical side of education. Unlike the public schools, it would not discriminate between the kinds of subjects boys and girls could learn, and it would not emphasize learning by rote. If Edna and others had not established the John Burroughs School, Martha would probably have been sent east to the Baldwin School, where Edna had been prepared for Bryn Mawr. 'In the 1920s,' remarked Delia Mares, who came to St Louis in 1933 to teach at the John Burroughs School, 'we came to call it progressive education and learning by doing.'

Beginning in 1921, Edna and her mother organized a committee to gather support for the new school: 'Each time we would bring a new guest to inoculate him!' she later recalled. The public received similar treatment: distinguished educators were invited to St Louis to present lectures on the modern school. Dr Otis W. Caldwell of Columbia University, for example, was quoted at length in a two-column report in the *St Louis Globe-Democrat*:

> If we teach children to confer with one another on their subjects of study, we stimulate their understanding ... They can teach one another much faster than we can teach them.

Then we are too apt to consider the school plant as existing for the excuse of arbitrary adult techniques. We should permit the children a co-operative part of the school management. I do not mean a pupil-governed school, but a co-operatively governed school.

Edna knew how to build constituencies for her causes, but she could not finesse everything, and soon the community of supporters split over the proposition that boys and girls go to school together. Civil war broke out, 'dividing family against family, children against parents, friend against friend', Edna recalled.

Edna and a strong group of supporters persevered. By 1922 they selected a site in the country 'close to nature and free from pollution', and guaranteed the purchase money. The school was named after John Burroughs, the naturalist who had died a year earlier. As one of the founders said, 'He loved personality for its own sake … He coupled the appreciation of beauty with a rugged spiritual sturdiness. He radiated self-reliance, usefulness, brotherliness. Particularly he admired leadership founded on high motive.' Edna became an officer of the school and served as its Secretary.

After successful fund-raising campaigns, the school opened on 2 October 1923 with ten teachers and seventy-five students. Martha Gellhorn was the first girl admitted to the school. Each day she boarded the 8 a.m. streetcar with its sign in front announcing 'Special: John Burroughs School', and travelled from the city to the countryside, out across open fields and through a small village to a narrow paved country lane, full of potholes, from which she would climb a footpath to the school.

In 1923 John Burroughs was a handsome, compact, L-shaped building still under construction. The Spanish-style architecture, the white plaster walls and red-tiled roof evoked 'the thought that St Louis had always been the gateway to the Southwest'. With everything new and no precedents, it was 'pretty heady living' for the fourteen tenth graders who had to take the lead in school affairs. They were evenly divided by sex. Boys and girls had separate athletic activities, but they ate together in a handsome dining room with palladian windows, a fireplace, long wooden tables and straight-backed chairs. Classrooms were odd sizes and shapes, with low or sloping ceilings and windows of varying dimensions, white plaster walls and dark wood trim. The original library had heavy wooden beams, beautiful chandeliers and a fireplace.

Along with many other distinguished visitors who addressed students on special topics, Edna Gellhorn would periodically come to John Burroughs to give talks. In Martha's senior year, Edna spoke on Lincoln's birthday about 'personality'. This 'great man' had an 'ineffable and attractive quality ... greatly influenced by environment', she observed, striking a balance between the individual and society – not for a moment denying genius, but suggesting everyone had a share in shaping it.

These pioneering students had a sense of solidarity and pride in a school that by any standard was unusual for its time. Since students contributed to making the rules, rule-breaking took on added significance. They were accorded a degree of autonomy and responsibility that made their school experience more intense, 'every joke the epitome of wittiness'. Girls found it a 'strange and exhilarating experience' to be educated with boys and to be taught by male teachers. Academic subjects like English, French, Latin, mathematics, science and social science were required for students expected to apply for college, but the school also offered extra-curricular activities, along with fine arts and physical education.

Wilford Aiken, John Burroughs's first headmaster, believed that 'school is not only a preparation for life ... it is life'. A geometry student, for example, would learn his subject while studying the architectural design of a house. Roman fortifications and battering rams were constructed for a Latin class. Social studies classes had students 'studying maps and leaflets about city waterworks'. At one point students were even enlisted in planning an industrial arts shop and later helped to dig its foundations.

On 12 October 1923, dedication day for the John Burroughs School, speakers such as the president of the University of Missouri lauded the experimental nature of the school and its democratic spirit. John Burroughs provided scholarships for students from families who could not afford the tuition; the school set a new standard for other educational institutions, public and private.

In an atmosphere of high hopes, Martha Gellhorn felt herself in the vanguard of change. In the fall and winter of 1923, she actively participated in drafting the school's constitution. A group of elected delegates wrote a document brought to the school assembly, where it was hotly debated. The *John Burroughs Review*, the new school magazine, reported that 'almost every member of the school, at one time or another, had addressed' the assembly on constitutional issues. Students and teachers had equal voting rights and jointly ratified the constitution. In the first election under the new constitution, held on 27 March 1924, Martha Gellhorn was elected speaker of the Assembly and president of the Girls' Athletic Association.

In three years at Burroughs, Gellhorn assisted the stage manager of the school's first play, *The Pot Boiler,* and became president of the drama club; she served on committees to pick the school colours and to plan dances; she played on the hockey team as its senior member; she edited the *John Burroughs Review* and supervised the solicitation of advertising. Like her mother, she knew how to bestow compliments laced with good humour, and how to make the simplest tasks seem heroic, calling upon Allah to safeguard her energetic and resourceful sales force in their encounters with tough St Louis shopkeepers.

Gellhorn, a founder of the *John Burroughs Review*, was also a frequent contributor. 'We had a perfectly fantastic English teacher, Francis Seely. He had us *writing – pouring* out literature: poems, stories, everything. We adored writing', Emily Lewis Norcross recalls. Seely, the faculty adviser to the *John Burroughs Review* and a poet himself, inspired his pupils to think not in terms of journalism but of more enduring work.

Much of Gellhorn's high school writing has a mocking, theatrical tone. Even a trivial incident – such as the difficulties of placing a call from a public phone – is transformed into a play with the grandiose title *A Soul in Torment.* A silly prose sketch extols her cherished old hat. 'Ye Exame' presents a bickering dialogue between little brother, big brother, sister and mother on the eve of a school exam. A sketch entitled 'The Sky' has a Stephen Crane-like focus on the hardness and the immensity of the urban environment, which seems to render individual lives meaningless. 'Jemima Smyth, Super-Shopper' briefly experiments with dialect writing.

Gellhorn's poetry in this period deals with the poor, slum housing, travel, her kewpie doll and sunsets in verse that is serious, yet whimsical and gay. She favours simple rhyme schemes and refrains –

although she occasionally sounds pompous and stilted when she reaches for the poetical. In her most interesting poem, 'Hester, Defiant', the speaker identifies with Hawthorne's scarlet heroine, who rejects the ice-cold men who judge her, emphasizing her femininity and courage. Gellhorn puts her most passionate expression into Hester's attachment to her strange, unruly and taunting love child, Pearl.

Gellhorn herself had a rebellious and irreverent streak. Appreciated as a 'character' and satirized in the *Review*, she appealed to her classmates by virtue of her sensible and warm-hearted temperament, which prompted a tribute to the 'magnificent Martie'. While most students idolized the headmaster, Wilford Aikin, she called him 'Wilf' and sat on his desk and smoked. In her senior year she was 'perfectly cast' as 'the courageous Vigdis Goddi' in John Masefield's play, *The Locked Chest*, about a woman who leaves her cowardly husband for refusing to shelter a relative falsely accused of murder.

From February 1925 to June 1926, Gellhorn published in the *John Burroughs Review* forty-two poems (enough for a slim volume of verse). This work meant a good deal to her, but she remained doubtful about its quality. She had met Carl Sandburg at Washington University, where he had spoken to a throng of admirers. She asked his opinion about her poetry, relying on this tough-minded poet to tell her the truth. In a letter full of exclamation marks and parentheses, she confessed her self-doubt and self-assertion. She suspected she was setting herself up for failure. She even speculated the poet would send the poems back to her without reading them. To ensure a reply, she had included a stamped, self-addressed envelope.

Sandburg's reaction is not recorded in his papers. Several years later Gellhorn told a Ph.D. student writing about her work that the poet kindly returned her fledgling poetry with the comment that if writing is a necessity, nothing can stop a person from doing it – sage advice, Gellhorn thought, that cannot be improved upon.

Apparently, in the summer of 1926, just after Gellhorn graduated from John Burroughs, she had her first great romantic involvement, which seems to have continued, sporadically, during visits home from Byrn Mawr College, where Martha enrolled in the fall. Joseph Stanley Pennell had come to St Louis in the mid-1920s from

Junction City, Kansas. In St Louis, he had worked for radio station KMOX and the *Post-Dispatch*, and taken roles in several amateur theatricals. He was a poet. The same age as Gellhorn, he knew many of her friends, especially Erna Rice, a John Burroughs classmate. Rice's family had an Ozark lodge that Gellhorn and Pennell liked to visit. He appealed to her, since she favoured artists and journalists – anyone who might have a fresh outlook. She became the subject of a sonnet sequence he deeply cherished and continually revised, memorializing her beauty. Visions of her haunted his nights as he remembered the way she turned her 'golden head', the way she slept, her voice and the transience of their time together.

When Martha Gellhorn arrived at Bryn Mawr she had no intention of behaving like her mother. To Martha the school seemed stodgy and genteel, especially after her intensive involvement in the progressive curriculum of the John Burroughs School. Too many of Bryn Mawr's students thought only of 'coming out' and how they would be presented to 'society'.

Content Peckham remembered meeting Gellhorn during freshman week:

> We were all sitting on the floor (sort of in a circle) and getting ready to elect temporary class officers. There were several groups that came from large girls' schools, so they were all sort of ganging up. And this dame was marching around in the centre of the circle saying, 'Don't you think so and so (one of the St Louis girls) would be good?' And I thought, *who in the name of heaven does she think she is?* She was electioneering and grandstanding at the same time. I also got the feeling that she thought she would be much better than so and so.

Martha could often be found in the 'smoker', a residence hall room that functioned as a source for all kinds of news. Smoking itself had become a big topic on campus. Articles in college papers called it a rebellion against authority, a sign of intellectuality, a 'gesture of the brothel'. At any rate, the 'very beautiful' and 'advanced' Martha Gellhorn liked to talk as though she already 'knew all about life' and presented an attractive alternative to Bryn Mawr's pieties. Compared with Martha, most of her friends were 'quiet little middle westerners [who] blinked with admiration and envy'. A 'middle westerner' herself, she had, nevertheless, a 'sophistication' that set her apart. She served her fellow students as a kind of 'window on the world'.

Emily Lewis Norcross, a year behind Martha at Bryn Mawr, remembers that her childhood companion's 'wings had begun to spread a bit. She had a perfect horror of being regimented in any way. She would sometimes try to defy the rules by smoking where she wasn't supposed to.' But Martha's minor transgressions drew little attention. She just 'started having a freer life much sooner than the rest of us did', Emily remembered.

Self-government – *the issue* during Martha's years at Bryn Mawr – had always meant an elaborate system of control over student life. To students in the 1920s it had almost nothing to do with independence and everything to do with policing themselves. In their view self-government had become a Byzantine code regulating their lives in the minutest particulars: they needed special permission to attend dances further away than Philadelphia or Haverford and they had to return to campus by 10.30 p.m.; they could not smoke in public off campus; they had to register all departures and returns to campus; men could only visit between the hours of four to six on Sunday afternoons; trousers could not be worn on campus. Students bridled at four years of compulsory physical education and railed at their subjection to the 'humiliation of paternal supervision' that did not give them the opportunity to behave as adults.

Bryn Mawr's policies were not unusual for an era in which colleges did act like students' parents. In fact, the restrictions that progressive and rebellious students such as Gellhorn scorned were not abolished at most colleges until the 1960s.

Gellhorn would later vent her anger at these restrictions in *What Mad Pursuit*, her first novel, and show how they prevented the young from governing themselves. Unlike her classmates, however, she wrote no protest letters to the school paper. Compared with her many pursuits at John Burroughs, her absence from most Bryn Mawr activities – especially in her first two years – is conspicuous. She did not work on the school newspaper; she ran for no important office in college; she did not participate in team sports. On a few occasions an aspect of Bryn Mawr life engaged her – especially if it had to do with politics or with the theatre – and she made herself count.

Gellhorn was writing introspective and personal poetry – publishing it in *The Lantern*, Bryn Mawr's literary magazine. Her work is fairly conventional, except for its austerity and clarity. She uses no baroque metaphors and indulges in no romantic longings. She is, however, disappointed in the mundanity of existence and scrupulously observes futile gestures in a 1920s attitude reminiscent of F. Scott Fitzgerald. Conversation seems full of false brightness and brittleness. In 'Plea', the mocking quality of modern life is effectively conveyed in her evocation of a couple smiling and chatting, and making fun of things that are attractive but bound to disintegrate.

Gellhorn wrote in free verse and in rhyme. She experimented with different verse forms and with line lengths, varying anywhere from two to as many as ten or eleven syllables. Speakers are not identified, except in 'Yseult', in which a young woman is dishonest with herself in order to suppress her suffering. She cannot have the man she wants and must persuade herself to be content with the man at hand, even though she knows she will grow to hate him.

This early poetry is about human integrity: people have trouble facing the reality of their rather sad choices. A more affirmative sequence of three short poems expresses Gellhorn's delight in the sensuality of nature. She vows to enjoy simple, rather delicate pleasures: a bit of sunshine, a rain-drenched leaf and a small wind. She imagines herself to be an enchanting geisha girl; the leaf holds within it a kind of jewel box of colours and the wind is pictured 'somersaulting in the grass'. Solitariness becomes a part of her poetic persona – she sings alone not in sorrow but as the rain sings, beautiful and forlorn.

By the end of Gellhorn's sophomore year *College News* (2 May 1928) listed her as cum laude. She was elected as a 'speaker' for the undergraduate association. As an English major she had outraged her teachers by writing dismissively about Wordsworth. To deflect her instructors' disapproval, 'Dutchy' (a nickname she had picked up) happily changed to French, which she had always found a pleasure. In April 1928 she proudly wrote to Edna about the twenty-four pages of French on Voltaire and his modern disciples that she had painstakingly produced. She had received the highest grade and the professor's warm praise.

In her junior year Martha had a featured role in the French Club production of *Le Professeur*, a one-act comedy. *College News* (12 December 1928) gave her a rave review. The setting was a butcher shop 'with realistic carcasses'. The characters were a 'gruff, ruddy butcher; his very French and very efficient wife; their altogether charming daughter; and an ambitious and starving young professor'. Gellhorn stole the show:

> M. Gellhorn, '30, was the wife. She alone of the cast managed to hit exactly the right note. Her accent, her gestures, and most difficult of all, her intonation, were completely and miraculously French. Hearing her telephone was, alone, worth paddling through the snow to Wyndham [Hall]. ... Her acting was splendid ... and she brought out to the full the comic possibilities of the part.

In early January 1929 Gellhorn attended the Fourth Annual Congress of the National Students' Federation of America, an organization founded in 1925 by 245 colleges and universities. *College News* featured her 11 January report to the undergraduates in the Bryn Mawr chapel. The Congress had been called to reach an agreement among students about a World Court. Instead, it established a continuing association dedicated to developing informed positions on national and international issues and to fostering 'understanding among the students of the world in the furtherance of an enduring peace'.

Gellhorn's fellow students would have little conception of the convention she had attended, so she compared it with one of their huge events, the annual May Day celebration involving nearly the whole student body. Knowing the energy and enthusiasm students put into May Day, Gellhorn conveyed the excitement of an altogether different activity in words the others would immediately understand.

This poised performance for a woman not yet twenty emphasized in very brief compass how the Congress had been organized and accomplished its work. Then she concentrated on a point of particular interest to her audience. Mount Holyoke (in South Hadley, Massachusetts) had a system of governance better than anything she had observed elsewhere. Both faculty and students took part in all aspects of government. Why not? Faculty resided at the college, making it ridiculous strictly to divide students from instructors. Committee work, extra-curricular activities – everything that made up campus life – was determined by democratically elected bodies of faculty and students. Obviously this made for a stronger degree of collaboration and harmony in the college community.

Gellhorn's observations struck hard at just what had been bothering Bryn Mawr for some time. *College News* had editorialized about bringing more democracy to student government, and implicit in the editorials, student debates and chapel talks by Bryn Mawr's dean had been a concern over the increasing lack of co-operation among undergraduates. But most of these expressions of concern had been couched in rather unappealing moralistic language. Students were aggrieved; administrators and faculty members were disappointed. Gellhorn's refreshingly direct presentation cleared the air.

The Congress had been one of the most impressive experiences of her life, Gellhorn concluded: 186 male and female students had met to consider important public issues, with some of the most dedicated students working late into the night. This exciting experience made her feel proud of her generation; they had more promise than some writers had supposed. Addressing the sceptics she asked their question: what was the point of it all? She replied: what was the point of anything? In a modest, almost self-effacing conclusion, she claimed only to have attended an interesting meeting, absorbed certain ideas and hopes, and sincerely sought for a path towards progress. Gellhorn knew her audience well: they would not be swayed by large claims or moved by exhortations to social action. Judging by the accounts in *College News*, no student delivered anything so fine as this speech during Gellhorn's years at Bryn Mawr.

About a month later, on 27 February 1929, *College News* listed Gellhorn as a Bryn Mawr delegate to the Model Assembly of the League of Nations. On 13 March 1929 J. S. McDonald, Chairman of the Foreign Policy Association, published a letter in the *College News*: 'Miss Gellhorn made a brilliant attack on John Rockefeller's report on the Secretariat and was ably supported by her colleagues.'

In her third year at Bryn Mawr Gellhorn moved off campus to a settlement that cared for the poor. She decided not to finish college but completed her junior year. She did not want to be the typical Bryn Mawr graduate: settling down, marrying and pursuing 'the vapoury phantom of general culture', as a *College News* editorial put it. She wanted a self-supporting career.

Gellhorn read Ernest Hemingway and tried to write like him. The popular press treated the influence of *The Sun Also Rises,* published in 1926, like an epidemic. In the spring of 1928 the journalist Richmond Barrett remarked in *Harper's* that young people had adopted *The Sun Also Rises* as their Bible. They had 'learned it by heart and [were] deserting their families and running away from college'. They headed to the sidewalk cafés of Paris, escaping American provincialism, searching for a degree of sophistication and sexual freedom unavailable in Calvin Coolidge's country. To Gellhorn, the world of the novel represented escape from the mundane and mediocre life she had lamented in her poetry. According to Malcolm Cowley, girls modelled themselves on Lady Brett, Hemingway's version of European elegance and charm, a beautiful young woman already on her way to a divorce who must forsake her love for Jake Barnes, a stoical newspaper correspondent emasculated by a wartime wound. As Kenneth Lynn suggests:

> In the twenties, the disequilibrium of life gave rise to a romantic sensibility, especially among pace-setting young people. It was their sense of themselves as historical victims that led them to interpret *The Sun Also Rises* in the light of its modern epigraph [You are all a lost generation] and to identify with Jake and Brett as fellow lost souls.

During Gellhorn's freshman year at Bryn Mawr a review of *The Sun Also Rises* appeared in *College News* (8 December 1926). Entitled 'Pessimism Triumphs', its reviewer noted the source of the novel's title – a passage from Ecclesiastes about the 'vanity of vanities' – and bemoaned the attention given to 'degraded characters leading a vagabond life who magnify its futility by their perverse views and increase the causes of their self-humiliation by prolonging their unpraiseworthy habits'. There was no hope for change, no prospect of 'regeneration'. The American and English characters simply roamed France and Spain 'in the pursuit of pleasure' and of 'excitement of a low order'. Cabaret touring, fishing, fiestas and bullfights could not cover up the 'drab weariness of life'. In short, this was 'sordid subject matter'. With no hint of Christian or democratic values, the novel stood for 'the darker side of life with no note of optimism to brighten it'. The reviewer implied that this attitude prevented the author's work from becoming a 'classic'.

The Bryn Mawr reviewer had failed to engage with the experiences of the novel's characters. Martha had come to feel that Bryn Mawr, on too many counts, had failed to engage with life itself. She wanted to meet more boys. 'I want to see quantities of them this summer', she wrote to her mother. She had had enough of 'convent life'.

That summer (1929) George Gellhorn took Martha and her brother Alfred to Germany. Martha never mentioned this visit in any of her writing, so it is not clear whether or not she sensed that Germany, momentarily stable, was on the verge of collapse, caught in a worldwide depression that would bring massive business failures, staggering unemployment, and mounting political and social tensions.

George Gellhorn took Martha and Alfred to Würzburg, one of his old haunts. There they met Heinz Richard Landmann, a member of George Gellhorn's student fraternity. Gellhorn wanted to show his children German student life. Over sixty years later Landmann could still recall 'a self-assured, searching young lady from across the big ocean, not as deferential as European women. I never told her she embarrassed me as a "good German student" by lighting a cigarette on the street, something taboo in Germany in those days. "A lady didn't smoke in public." '

3

LIBERATION

1929–1930

W HEN GELLHORN abandoned Bryn Mawr in 1929 she found an apartment in New York City and refused her parents' financial support. Subsisting on doughnuts and pawning her typewriter to sustain her over weekends, Martha determined to make her own 'shoestring living' as a journalist.

An angry George Gellhorn, a traditionalist at heart, could not condone the liberated life Martha proposed to follow. He called it immoral. 'You don't get something for nothing, and I paid,' Martha later confessed to biographer Victoria Glendinning. Edna worried about Martha, but she also defended her daughter's right to go her own way. Martha's grandmother, the redoubtable Martha Ellis Fischel, expressed her disappointment in George Gellhorn. He did not realize that Martha's desire for independence did not differ that much from her grandmother's and mother's feelings. Martha Ellis spoke elliptically and with great delicacy, but she did not have to spell things out for Edna. There had been tensions in their roles as mother, daughter, housewife and social activist, but they had chosen not to make those tensions an issue. Knowing how much they had sacrificed, they could not ask Martha to conform.

Martha's letters to Edna are as loving as any mother could hope to have from her daughter. Yet Martha kept her distance because in St Louis she could not escape identification as Edna Gellhorn's daughter. Staying at home meant risking submersion in Edna's enterprises.

Gellhorn's first job in June 1929, just after leaving Bryn Mawr, was at the *New Republic*, an influential journal of political and literary opinion founded in 1912. To her surprise, work there seemed like a continuation of her college education. Stuck in a building on East 23rd Street with prominent commentators and critics such as Walter Lippmann and Edmund Wilson – as well as a bright young book reviewer, T. S. Matthews – she was not impressed. She was supposed to read galleys of the magazine's articles, which she found 'very dull'. So she tended to skip over them. 'They had more typos than they had ever had in all the years of their history, which they also did not find very pleasing', Gellhorn later claimed. She seems to have been on the staff for no more than a month.

One of her pals working on the *Albany Times Union*, a Hearst publication in Albany, New York, suggested she join him. 'You must come; it is unbelievably funny,' he wrote to her. Listening to Gellhorn talk about this period (July 1929), Bertrand de Jouvenel later portrayed her as *'une gamine'*, a wanderer, blindly running away from the lofty Gothic precincts of the Bryn Mawr campus, weary of learning to speak the language of Chaucer and avid to cover the lurid criminal activities of a smoky, stinking town like Albany. She walked into a newspaper office, a blonde in dungarees, and announced, 'My name is Martha Gellhorn. I want to work.'

Gellhorn remembered a newspaper exactly like the frenetic press room in *The Front Page*, Ben Hecht's classic play about newspaper life. Gellhorn was hired as a cub reporter. Her editor, responding to this young, fair-haired woman, did not assign her to important events. With Prohibition still in force her editor was 'always drunk' and apt to fire his staff nearly every day. She said she 'adored' the pandemonium: 'Typewriters and people screaming on telephones, rushing in and out, and, really, everybody was drunk. My job was the morgue and women's clubs and also, as a sort of bonus, streetcar accidents.' She would join her colleagues in a speakeasy awaiting the customary summons back to work. She remembered her six months in Albany fondly, as a lark.

Of course, the *Albany Times Union* could offer Gellhorn few outlets for her ambitions. The newspaper took most of the major national and international stories verbatim from the wire services.

Local news – even of the melodramatic variety – did not engage her. Squalid murders and gruesome accidents – predictable and repetitive – were reported in sensationalistic and formulaic prose. DEATH ENDS ROMANCE, a front-page story with a picture of the slain female lover, features on 'Appetizing Menus for the Week', serialized novels ('The Story of a Hell-Cat Wife Who Couldn't Be Good'), sections on 'News and Gossip of the Stage, Screen and Studio', 'The Woman in the Home' and several columns of society news appeared with boring regularity. In *What Mad Pursuit* (1934), Gellhorn's first novel, her fictional counterpart, Charis Day, works on revisions of news from the competing newspaper: meetings of parents about child psychology, a local dramatic group and the 'Mad Hatter Club Sewing Bee'.

Gellhorn began to establish her journalistic credentials by contributing short, unsigned book reviews to her former employer, the *New Republic*, reviews which led to the publication of a signed article. By express train she could get from Albany to New York City in three hours. On one of her trips she visited the Brooklyn Paramount Theater at Flatbush and DeKalb Avenues, and reported on a sold-out Rudy Vallee performance (the *New Republic*, 7 August 1929). In the spirit of her ironic subtitle, 'God's Gift to Us Girls', Gellhorn conveys both the excitement and the silliness of the Vallee phenomenon. He is the American woman's craving for a 'beau'. American men are too busy working for the money that sends their women to entertainments like the movies to coo 'I Kiss Your Hand, Madame'. Vallee's tender, caressing tones attract all the silly romantic women in the country – which seems to be the only point worth making, she concludes.

Martha's Albany escapade worried Edna, who wrote to Eleanor Roosevelt – already a friend as a result of their participation together in social causes and programmes. Franklin Roosevelt had been elected governor of New York in 1928 and would be re-elected in 1930 on the strength of programmes that established government support for farmers, the regulation of public utilities and old age pensions. Later, after FDR was elected President of the United States in 1932, he and Eleanor would come to represent an idealistic vision of the country that would galvanize Martha Gellhorn.

But in the later summer of 1929 – just before the stock market crash and the onset of the Depression – the Roosevelts appeared quite differently to Gellhorn. Invited to dinner at the Governor's Mansion in Albany, she was furious at being treated like a straying child, she turned sullen and thought Eleanor's tiger's teeth necklace decidedly ugly. She did not appreciate presenting herself for the older woman's inspection or becoming the subject, no doubt, of a report to her mother.

Then Martha's brother visited her and sent word to her family that she was in a 'very unsuitable environment'. She did not identify the brother, but it was surely her older sibling, Walter, who never enjoyed the same affection she lavished on her younger brother Alfred. Told by her brother that Edna was ill, Martha rushed home, only to find that the story had been a ruse to get her away from Albany.

Gellhorn did not explain why she did not return to the newspaper and judging by *What Mad Pursuit* she was lonely in Albany. Only in retrospect did it seem like so much fun. To be sure, Charis Day, a cub reporter, is called a 'lady' and soon earns a new title, 'The Blonde Peril', because she is so aggressive, giving orders to the city editor on her first work day. But Charis's isolated, impecunious existence reflected Martha's own plight. She could not have had much more than Charis: a salary of $20 a week, a 'cell' in a rooming house, 'papered in diseased poppies and furnished with a bed, a dresser, a table and one rocking-chair', and with a 'stygian bathroom' two floors below.

In St Louis, Gellhorn failed to get a job on the *St Louis Post-Dispatch*, although she made contacts that later resulted in her placing several articles with the newspaper. She did not foresee the trouble ahead. The stock market had crashed on 29 October, but it would be more than two years before Gellhorn and the rest of the country would realize that the Depression was not just another cyclical downturn in the economy and turn to a new president with ambitious programmes of social, political and economic reform.

By the end of 1929 Gellhorn was making plans for a trip to Europe and a future as a foreign correspondent. She borrowed money from her family's cook and boarded a bus for New York City, where she arrived early in 1930. By February she had contacted the Holland America Line's trade magazine. 'I told them I would write a brilliant article about how wonderful "student third" was if they'd give me a free passage. That is how I got to Paris', she later told an interviewer.

By February 1930 twenty-one-year-old Martha Gellhorn, possessing not much more than $75 and her suitcase, and knowing no one in this foreign capital, cheerfully expected to obtain a job as a correspondent. If she had a 'passion for France', where she had spent three summer holidays, she understood virtually nothing about actually living there. She enjoyed the ambience of the Place de la Madeleine; its stands of flowers appealed to her craving for a pleasant milieu and the price of a room did little to dent her purse. But her shabby accommodation puzzled her. Why did her room have a mirror on the ceiling? Why so much uproar in the hallways? Why did the clerk seem ruder each time the gregarious Gellhorn passed his desk?

A kind Englishman, the head of the *New York Times* office in Paris, soon dispelled Gellhorn's mystification. Laughing so hard that he cried, he told the earnest job applicant that her residence was a '*maison de passe*', an establishment that let out rooms to the amorous at hourly rates. On his advice, Gellhorn settled on the Left Bank in a student community. In retrospect, she pictures herself as the complete naïf – living on the rue de L'Université in a windowless room with a bath four floors below, bothered by her neighbours' crying, bickering and screaming at each other, charmed by the Chopin played on the hotel's grand piano and shocked to learn about homosexuality when her male companion, an 'ex-Princetonian', was accosted by another male. She pined in unrequited passion for a magnificent 'White Russian balalaika player'.

Gellhorn never revealed very much about these very early days in Paris. Although she emphasized her naïveté, she already had a mature, graceful air, wore clothes well, and paid close attention to every detail of her dress and make-up. She did not associate with the snug coterie of American expatriate writers, but somehow found her way into the company of wealthy patrons, even as she lectured them about their duty to those less fortunate than themselves. She was always good at making professional contacts as well and found a position for a short time on the Paris staff of *Vogue*, which she used as a segue into the fashion world of the city – as a newspaper article later reported:

> Tall, slim, blonde, with a gracefully poised head set off with the
> smartest of haircuts, it was the delight of Paris dressmakers to dress
> her up in their newest models and have her parade them, not as the
> usual mannequin at the race tracks, but as a personality among per-
> sonages. She wore the first halter neck backless evening gown at the
> World Economic Congress in London and the Parisian dressmaker's
> confidence in her ability to show it off was not misplaced. It
> became a hit that swept the fashion world.

Gellhorn did not become a fashion model as such, yet she managed
to be the height of fashion.

In the fall of 1930 Gellhorn capitalized on contacts in her home
town to secure two assignments from the *St Louis Post-Dispatch*. She
reported on the women delegates to meetings of the League of
Nations in Geneva. She presented an appealing portrait of Mary
Agnes Hamilton, a stylish, energetic woman, a Labour member of
the House of Commons and, like Gellhorn, a militant pacifist. Gellhorn delighted in describing Hamilton's smart black dress and her
old-fashioned black beret. She moved briskly and nervously. Gellhorn could tell her hair was closely clipped beneath her tight hat.
She epitomized a slim, tall, athletic and attractive woman. Gellhorn
thought it likely that Hamilton was good golfer and horsewoman.
She strode with an uplifted head, leaving a swirling current of air in
her trail wherever she went. The way a woman could alter the climate intrigued Gellhorn – as did Hamilton's career as a journalist,
novelist, biographer and intimate of political figures who then
became the subjects of her books. Hamilton told Gellhorn that she
much admired young American women but faulted them for relish-
ing their place on the 'pedestal'. Hamilton did not care much for
separate women's organizations. In Britain, female Labour Party
MPs like herself worked beside men and earned their appointments
on merit.

Gellhorn relished her brief stay in Geneva. Her second article on
the League of Nations meeting began with a description of the
Hôtel des Bergues, headquarters for most of the League delegates.
She reported on the congregation of different nationalities, the
women's colourful clothes as against the men's sombre, conventional

dress. She relished the display of Europe's profound political intellects in meetings filled to capacity.

Mademoiselle Hanni Forchhammer, the first woman delegate to the League, became Gellhorn's heroine in this second article. A small woman with white hair, she remained reserved about her personal life and positive about questions of public policy. Growing up in an austere, scholarly environment, she became a teacher, one of the leaders of adult education programmes in Denmark. After 20,000 women marched in Copenhagen for women's suffrage, she was selected to speak for them before the King and Parliament. A champion of human rights, she had travelled the world, investigating the white slave traffic in Asia Minor and working for the protection of women and children in the Near East

Forchhammer had nothing but praise for the speaking and organizational talent of American women, although she conceded that a significant number did little and were 'perfectly parasitical'. She referred to the European myth of the pampered American woman, but on her visit to the country she had seen only the grand ones. Gellhorn took Forchhammer's unassuming, quiet competence as the model of an agreeable feminism. Some feminists denied their femininity and others traded on it, but Forchhammer was indifferent to the entire matter. In Gellhorn's view this seemed the most effective position. Not surprisingly, it was her own.

Gellhorn noticed that Forchhammer lacked elegance. She wore a watch in a rather grand and quaint fashion attached to the front of her dress with a safety pin. The hem of her dress drooped. Forchhammer seemed unconscious of her appearance. For her, work was everything, so Gellhorn judged her not as a woman but as a 'worker'.

Two articles in the *St Louis Post-Dispatch* were the high point of Gellhorn's early journalistic efforts. Returning to Paris from Geneva, she wrote a letter on *Vogue* stationery, trying unsuccessfully to interest the *New Yorker* in her European reporting. She went through a succession of jobs, earning barely enough to support herself. She wrote dull copy for an advertising agency.

With so little money and accustomed to working with student groups, Gellhorn immersed herself in French culture and became ardently involved in politics. Questions of 'unemployment, under-

paid and badly treated workers, the cynicism of old politicians'
engaged nearly everyone in her circle regardless of their social class.

'Real life', Gellhorn supposed, meant seeing things for yourself,
getting out and touring the country, witnessing strikes and protest
marches, visiting slums, mill towns and mining areas all over northern France. 'Real life was the Have-nots', she concluded. The emp-
tier her stomach, the more she identified with the poor. She sought
'standing room at ground level to watch history as it happened'.

4

BEAUTIFUL EXILE

1931–1934

I N EARLY 1931 Gellhorn visited striking textile workers in Roubaix-Tourcoing. Bertrand de Jouvenel, the handsome son of a prominent French politician and diplomat, Henri de Jouvenel, accompanied her. Bertrand was just beginning his distinguished career as a journalist and expert on economic affairs dedicated to the cause of world peace. He and Martha had met during one of her backpacking trips through Europe. Engrossed in conversation, what, she asked him, was his life ambition. 'To fill a bookshelf,' he said.

Like his father, Henri de Jouvenel, Bertrand had 'the talent for being loved'. He inherited Henri's princely, slender figure, which women found hard to resist. Henri was the ambassador to Italy, editor of *Le Matin* and parliamentary politician – playing the mediator in all these roles. But his triumphs were short-lived and, in retrospect, seemed ambiguous and indeterminate. There was nobility in his call for 'a broader community', but he was often ineffectual precisely because he would not stoop to the tactics of partisan contests. Like Henri, Bertrand would work tirelessly to stave off a Second World War, yet their belief that peace could be maintained by diplomacy caused both father and son to countenance ideologies that Gellhorn and her generation came to see as irremediably evil.

Bertrand was eight years old in 1911 when his father fell in love with the novelist and actress Colette. They married and Bertrand, living with Henri's first wife, did not encounter Colette until he reached the age of sixteen. Although he had been exposed to such famous figures as Claudel, Bergson, D'Annunzio and Anatole France, his stepmother's worldliness shocked him. A bookish boy who also loved riding and tennis, he had grown up among servants, fashionable society and the Parisian Jewish bourgeoisie. He had few contacts with children of his own age and knew nothing about women. This timid, trembling, awkward boy, who 'hid behind a piano, in the darkest part of the room' clutching a bunch of flowers he had brought for his first visit to Colette, this spoiled and very shy child, 'educated at home by private tutors' and protected 'by an Irish governess in his mother's spacious apartment', provoked Colette's curiosity. He spent his next summer holiday at her house.

Colette, forty-eight, gave Bertrand, seventeen, massages, filled him with food and tanned him in the sun. She taught him how to swim. She stroked his hip as he emerged from the water and he shivered with a 'thrill he [had] never experienced before'. She gave him a copy of her latest novel, *Chéri*, about a young man who falls in love with an older woman. She was firm with him, a source of strength, but also very tender. Before retiring for the evening, she would kiss him on the cheek. On one occasion she kissed him on the lips. Startled, he almost dropped his oil lamp. 'Hold the lamp steady', she said.

Colette and her female companions joked about Bertrand's innocence. Time to be a man, they thought. He found Colette waiting for him in the middle of the night and they became lovers. For the next six years she was his passion, his teacher and his confidante, while his father lived away from her, intensely involved in the politics and diplomacy that bored her, and with the mistresses that made her jealous. Not until Bertrand showed signs of embarking on his own career did she deliberately break off their liaison.

Bertrand's political interests developed early. His Uncle Robert had died in World War One and Bertrand ardently read the anti-war novels of the time. An enthusiastic supporter of the League of Nations, he attended an international conference in Genoa in 1922, taking a leftist and internationalist position that emphasized the economic reconstruction of Europe and opposed the heavy reparations the Allies required Germany to pay. In the mid-1920s he debated questions of disarmament and national security. But his interest in politics gave way to heavy drinking and womanizing. Married in December of 1925 to the aristocratic Marcelle Noilly-Prat, he carried on a frivolous life in an apartment with lily pads in the tub.

By 1928 Jouvenel had turned again to politics, losing his bid for election as a Radical Party deputy, pursuing his career in journalism, attending a World Youth Congress meeting in Holland and writing a novel, *La Fidélité Difficile*, which explored the agony of a young man, René, divided in feeling between his mistress and his wife. Jouvenel had not been faithful to Noilly-Prat any more than he would be to Gellhorn. The novel represents the epitome of his hedonistic period and is his only work that does not address social or political issues.

In 1930, when Jouvenel met Gellhorn, he was engaged in rejuvenating the non-Marxist left. Editor of a daily newspaper, *La Voix*, an organ of the Radical Party, he argued that France should follow America's example: only an enterprising, innovative culture heavily involved in the development of financial markets could make France once again a great nation. Similarly, Europe as a great entity could progress only if it united – at least in economic terms. He had rejected his earlier enthusiasm for the League of Nations. It had proved powerless in the face of national sovereignty and Jouvenel had to abandon his naïve belief that personal contacts between League leaders would help to ensure peace.

Bertrand was still married when he fell in love with Martha. 'He simply walked out of his home and followed me, and we had a hell of a hard time due to being a scandal … and being penniless and neither used to that condition', Gellhorn told Jouvenel's biographer. She called him the 'least practical man alive; he can hardly tie his shoelaces'.

According to Gellhorn, Bertrand adored her and worried when he had to leave her in the company of his friend, Robert Lange, who was given clear instructions not to lay a hand on her. Lange recalled that they went to a hotel in southern France and kept to the instructions, though only Robert's room had a shower and he was astonished to see Martha come in to use it dressed only in a towel. She subsequently thought of this period as still part of her girlhood.

Bertrand and Martha travelled in Europe for four months, working with pacifists dedicated to a rapprochement between France and Germany. Both fervently wished to overthrow an older generation, which, they believed, was leading them into a second world war. They were a transatlantic couple devoted to the dream of an international community.

Exactly when they became lovers is not known. Like so much about their relationship, this fact remains elusive because Gellhorn obscured such transitions in her life and her part in wooing Jouvenel. In her rather disparaging accounts he resembles a character out of *Of Human Bondage*, playing the obsessed lover Philip Casey to her cool Mildred.

In 1930-1, the first year that Jouvenel and Gellhorn spent together, Colette remained a strong influence on him. Gellhorn claimed that Colette 'hated me at first sight, that was obvious'. Stretched out on a chaise longue 'like an odalisque, with green shadow on her cat's eyes and a mean, bitter mouth', Colette gave Gellhorn a malicious look. 'She insisted that I pencil in my eyebrows – which were so blond as to be non-existent, like the White Rabbit's – using a black crayon, so that the lines almost met in the middle.' Gellhorn did it, if for no better reason than that Colette told her to. Three days later a friend of Gellhorn's said to her: 'My dear, what dreadful thing have you done to your face?' Colette was jealous of her, Gellhorn thought, and Bertrand could not see it. 'Bertrand just adored her all his life. He never understood when he was in the presence of evil.' Colette would not be the last powerful woman whom Gellhorn would call 'a terrible woman. Absolute, utter hell.'

Bertrand and Martha shared the same cosmopolitan tastes. He had grown up in a household supervised by an Irish governess and she had been cared for by a German housekeeper. They felt at home in a multicultural world and craved contact with other societies as a way of informing their own. The narrowness of nationalism disturbed them. They felt they were combating deep forms of prejudice that divided the world. They rejected everything that seemed provincial about personal and public life.

Inspired by his friend, H. G. Wells, whose grand world vision he termed '*la marche future de la famille humaine*', Jouvenel would later become a pioneer in the field of 'future studies'. Informing all his work would be a principle he and Gellhorn pursued in their peace efforts: 'Politics cannot be reduced to institutions ... power lies

above all in the initiative of men moving other men.' And Wells was
the supreme man, their role model, although Gellhorn did not meet
him until 1935. With his youthful laugh, his jokes, his energetic, eru-
dite manner and his floundering in a French virtually impossible to
understand, he embodied a touchingly human and powerful example of the international man. Wells contended that intellectuals had
to articulate the political, social and moral ideas that already existed
in a vague form among the people. He opposed violence as a means
of achieving social justice and rejected the dangerous doctrine that
the end justifies the means. In a few years he would be championing
Gellhorn's great book, *The Trouble I've Seen*, because she used her talent as a writer to provide witness to the suffering and aspirations of
the people.

Wells exemplified generosity of spirit – the very thing lacking in
'*le drame de l'entre-deux-guerres*', as Jouvenel characterized it in his
memoirs. He believed that the victors of World War One should
extend the hand of friendship to the vanquished Germans. This did
not happen and the defeat of his hopes for a united Europe also
doomed his union with Gellhorn. For their love was political as
much as it was sexual. It is significant that Jouvenel should entitle his
memoirs *Un Voyageur dans le Siècle*. Jouvenel scholar Pierre Hassner
points out that Jouvenel selected 'the metaphor of the traveller
exploring uncharted roads, announcing opportunities and dangers
ahead' as the central theme of his life and work. No more than Gellhorn could he stand still. As an internationalist, it is difficult to commit yourself to only one alliance or to one point of origin.

In early 1931 Gellhorn left Jouvenel for a trip home. He would
follow shortly. By the spring she had started on a cross-continental
tour of the United States. She adored travelling. Nothing else could
give her the same lift as the prospect of a journey. Yet she was often
in a foul mood – upset with the Americans she encountered and
disappointed in herself. 'Humanity is a stench in the nostrils of the
knowing,' she declared.

Part of Gellhorn's problem was writing. She had not found the
right subject and herself as a subject soured her. Her feelings were
summed up in a poem, 'Spleen, 1931'. She wrote about going
through Bismarck, North Dakota, the oilfields of Texas and the
prairie. She saw a greyish-brown world from the windows of her

train. She lamented the mediocrity of the people and the towns she visited. She longed for something more than tired-looking roads, crummy stores and heavily made-up girls flirting with train conductors. The banality of the conversation bored her. Who wanted to listen to a stuffy youth in a bow tie piously praising the Deity as the creator of nature? She longed for some kind of robust emotion or deed that would wear away this insipid world.

All this she wrote down, then sent her poem to Joseph Stanley Pennell. At the time he was desperately trying to write a novel, disappointed that his work had not been published, worried about making a living, hostile towards the insularity of his Midwestern upbringing and itching to travel to more stimulating places. He was Martha Gellhorn's male counterpart. Fond of both her parents, he wrote them letters echoing Martha's unquenchable urge to get somewhere. On Santa Fe Railroad Observation Car stationery, he placed three question marks after the letterhead's words 'En Route'. In San Bernadino, California, he felt stranded by the rain in the normally arid climate. Much like Martha, 'Stan' (as she called him) wanted to make literature out of his predicaments. In his diary, as in her letters, a young and aggressive personality pushes against environment and argues with the grounds of existence that others take for granted.

By 1931 they seemed less intimate, but the affinity remained. She wrote to him from California in the middle of April, fed up with people praising their climate, their land, their big buildings, their clubs and their salaries. She had been to Los Angeles, Santa Barbara, Palm Springs and Death Valley. It all seemed so arid. Why keep travelling? Well, she had to admit she liked observing the hills rising from the ground and feeling the wind blowing.

From Reno (27 April) Gellhorn reported to Pennell on the lotus-eating natives. Women in their department-store, mail-order clothes disgusted her, but the magnificent land charmed her. Amorous males had harried her; she actually looked forward to coming home. She consoled herself with a copy of Pennell's verse, which he had just sent her, and luxuriated in lines that sounded like Thomas Wolfe, paeans to the fertile, dark land.

By early May she limped into St Louis on a badly bruised foot that needed treatment in St Luke's Hospital. It was an old injury, the result of a fall on the side of a mountain. She wanted to write to Pennell about her feelings, but she distrusted words. Nevertheless, she began to formulate the themes of her first novel, alluding to the lines from Hemingway and Wolfe that would become its epigraphs:

A Farewell to Arms: Nothing ever happens to the brave.
Look Homeward, Angel: The hunger that haunts and hurts Americans and makes them exiles at home and strangers wherever they go.

On 14 May Gellhorn, back on the road, wrote to Pennell from Indianapolis while changing trains for Pittsburgh. She thought of him holding her as a male gave her a look-over. Yet she did not want him with her. From Dayton she groused about the abominable food, which looked as though it had been put to torture. How could people put up with such crap? If she had not grown up to appreciate the comforts of the middle class, she wondered what kind of criminal she might have become in such sorry circumstances. She was looking none too good herself – kind of wrinkled and flattened. Pennell would not find her very appetizing if he could get a whiff of her right now. She prided herself on roughing it, but when the going got really rough she yearned for comfort in a rather ruthless mood: 'I should have been a female Al Capone – seeking for myself luxury, for all others destruction.'

Finally she took refuge among the rich. On 19 May she wrote to Pennell describing the bucolic setting of a country estate in Bryn Mawr, the home of Kitty McVitty, Bryn Mawr, 1928. Gellhorn enjoyed the garden, the yacht and the dinners – everything that made this kind of life comfortable, if not useful. She revelled in luxury, yet she doubted she deserved it. It was so pleasant to linger among the cherry trees, the magnolia blooms and the wind sweeping the Bryn Mawr campus. Even as she craved Pennell, Gellhorn confessed a compulsion to escape his embrace. She had trouble comprehending this form of self-torture.

In late July Pennell accepted a teaching position at the John Burroughs School. Now in Mexico, Gellhorn imagined him making his peace with St Louis and absorbing its life. She presented an enticing picture of herself, without clothes, lying about in the sun. She got no work done – a problem only because she had to have sufficient funds to finance her trips.

Luxuriating in the Mexican climate, Gellhorn thought about herself. She had a wonderful gift for friendship, she believed, yet she felt 'very faithless to everyone and everything, very anarchistic, and most uproariously bacchanalian'. She confessed to being 'prepossessed with my own body'. Did this make her a superficial person? she wondered. 'Those Grecian Urn people really have the drop on all the rest of us. There's a splendor, a calm, an undesiring desire about staticness which I want.' She would use a phrase from the poem, 'what mad pursuit', as the title of her first novel.

Mexico was lovely and old. It reminded Gellhorn of Europe. It did not cost much to live there, to buy things like flowers or lovely hand-crafted objects for pennies. The art and architecture delighted her. She worked on an article on Eisenstein, who was then filming in Mexico, publishing it in the *St Louis Post-Dispatch* (9 August, 1931).

In 'Mexico's History in a Film Epic' Gellhorn admired Eisenstein's shot of Mayans alongside ancient statues, establishing the continuity between past and present. His attention to details – to dress, to setting and to many other indigenous elements – impressed her. She lauded Eisenstein's focus on the Spanish invasion that oppressed the people and exploited the country's resources. Hardly a Marxist, Gellhorn nonetheless endorsed a film portraying a strong people becoming aware of their power and inevitably pressing forward into revolutionary action.

Some time in mid-August Gellhorn told Pennell that she would marry Bertrand de Jouvenel. Pennell did not accuse her of betraying him, but she interpreted his rather mean tone as implying her perfidy. But she had heard about the marriage announcement in a St Louis newspaper just a week before he did – a curious way to refer to her own wedding plans, but not unlike a woman who would always seem at some remove from her own marriages. In fact, the couple did not marry until almost two years later.

In late September Gellhorn stayed in New York City at the home of Mrs Frederick Vanderbilt Field, who had become a friend of Martha's brother, Walter, during his law school days and subsequently formed a close friendship with Martha. Frederick Vanderbilt Field found Martha an interesting, attractive and entertaining house guest. He liked to talk politics and learned that she was reading Communist writers. But he could discern little about her leftist sympathies, except to say that she was a 'very liberal and observant person'.

At the end of September Bertrand de Jouvenel arrived in America on the *Ile de France* at a moment of grave economic crisis and he had come to observe it first-hand. Gellhorn met him at the dock in New York, dressed in a blue, sleeveless linen shirt, the outfit she would favour during their travels from October to April. To Europeans suffering the deprivations of the post-World War One period, America was Eldorado, a land of the rich, Jouvenel explained in his memoirs. Shortly he would be writing for French readers about men sleeping on park benches, about beggars in the streets and about unemployed auto workers in Detroit. Struck with the spectacle of men, women and children sitting on sidewalks, waiting, he asked: waiting for what? They were in soup lines, out of work, miserable and hungry. Nine million people were looking for jobs.

Gellhorn wanted to show Jouvenel poverty even worse than the urban distress he witnessed. Much to his delight, she proposed they tour the South. They bought an old Dodge touring car that leaned to one side. To Jouvenel the South resembled a 'palette' arranged with every tint from chrome to vermillion. The rivers and ponds were the colour of iodine, with their banks a paler shade underneath a copper sky. Gellhorn remembered the heat and dust. A powder-like coating stuck to their faces and hair. Both remarked on the contrast between the beauty of nature and the poverty of the people, the ramshackle buildings made of planking and the thin people standing in the fields, as if immobilized by 'semi-starvation'.

Like Gellhorn, Jouvenel, besotted with reading Thomas Wolfe, imagined his trip across America as a great epic, with the railroad serving as the symbol of the traveller's quest to cover the whole of the enormous American expanse. He even had his share of adventures in Hollywood, where he met Gellhorn's friends, Martha Love Symington and Emily Lewis Norcross. Much to his amusement, he was hired as an extra. A handsome man with a long face faintly reminiscent of Valentino's, he was picked to play figures in society, even though his body still bore the marks of his failed efforts to become a boxer. He learned how to act the Hollywood version of a French gentleman. He was directed to enter a scene quickly, flapping his elbows as if they were the wings of a penguin, then to seize a lady's hand in order to kiss the inside of her wrist. He raised objections to this practice and was told it did not matter what he had done in France: 'Here you must have the bearing of a Frenchman.' Jouvenel enjoyed acting, which mostly meant waiting around for the star to appear. He found the company agreeable and he earned seven dollars a day. Martha may also have worked as an 'extra', for Joseph Pennell noted in his diary (23 September 1932) that she was supposed to have a part in *Movie Crazy*, Harold Lloyd's latest picture. But when he saw the film he could not spot her. Jouvenel had many entertaining memories of California, including the time he and Martha were recruited by a local sheriff who spent his free time looking for gold.

When not travelling with Jouvenel, Gellhorn returned to her writing. To Pennell, on 28 December, she announced that she had reached the halfway point in writing the 'most gaseous novel' in the world. Preparing to set off for Yucatan, having found a place for herself in steerage, she reaffirmed that travel and writing were her two tonics. She ended her letter to him with a typical jab at St Louis. Was it still the hub of the universe?

Gellhorn completed *What Mad Pursuit* near the end of 1932 and returned to Europe with Jouvenel. They were married in the summer of 1933 in Spain at the home of Colette's old friend, the portrait painter José Maria Sert, whose wife, a sculptress, had just completed a bust of Gellhorn.

Edna, more worried than she would admit about her roving daughter's fate, appeared to welcome the connection with a distinguished Frenchman. At a Bryn Mawr Club meeting in Emily Lewis Norcross's home Edna, called to the telephone, ended the conversation with her head held very high. The *St Louis Post-Dispatch* had called to confirm that Martha had just married Bertrand de Jouvenel. Everyone looked up and said, 'What!' 'Yes', Edna announced, obviously pleased with her news, 'Martha was married two weeks ago in Spain.'

On 8 October 1933 Joseph Pennell received a letter from Gellhorn then staying in Capri. In his diary for the next day he recorded her announcement that she had become Madame Bertrand de

Jouvenel and that she planned to stay in Paris to bring up her husband's young son. She was deeply in love, she confided to Pennell – who could not resist observing that her pleasant note had the lofty tone she used to take with him.

Then the couple separated in the spring of 1934, with Martha going to the Midi to work on a second novel she was never to publish, the story of 'the Franco-American clash, or temperamental differences between the two nationalities'. Although Gellhorn said little about this second effort, it seemed to reflect her ambivalence about Jouvenel and her life with him in Europe. It also seemed to extend the theme of restlessness that had marked *What Mad Pursuit*.

Taking her title from 'Ode on a Grecian Urn', Gellhorn's first novel reflects her 'struggle to escape' the clutches of her time and place. Charis Day, Gellhorn's heroine, quits college in protest over the 'double standard': a coed is expelled for having slept in a male student's dormitory room while he is allowed to remain in school. Whether the cause is a strike or the defence of a radical who has been framed, Charis is prepared to seek justice – notwithstanding the trouble she makes for herself.

Gellhorn presents her heroine as a naïf. Unlike Gellhorn, Charis has no family background or experience abroad that might ease her initiation period. When she is confronted with a corpse in the morgue during her brief career as a cub reporter, she rebels against the sight of a grotesque and destitute-looking body stinking of chemicals. Life must amount to more than this, she exclaims. And when Charis tries, as Gellhorn periodically did, to enjoy the dances, parties and other social activities of her generation and class, she chafes against the utterly prosaic expectations of her contemporaries and bemoans the perpetual emptiness of merely social life. When Charis gets involved in defending a labour leader modelled after Tom Mooney (convicted of bombing and killing people in the 1916 San Francisco Preparedness Day parade), she is disillusioned by his plodding, shabby, ordinary supporters who turn his catastrophe into a boring propaganda campaign, writing drab, shoddy tracts about his case. Charis sees herself, as Gellhorn did, in quest of a higher calling, to achieve, in Charis's words, 'a triumph of living'.

Possessed of Gellhorn's high spirits and of a romantic belief in the idea of 'one grand person'. Charis is a Hemingwayesque heroine who can take tragedy stoically. This is a conviction Gellhorn would invest in various figures from Hemingway to John F. Kennedy and which saves Charis from utter despair when she finds she has contracted syphilis from her first sexual encounter in Paris. Michael, Charis's somewhat older mentor and lover, carefully manages the scene in which her disease is revealed to her so that she does not entirely lose the 'shine' that has distinguished her idealistic persona. The ending of *What Mad Pursuit*, which gives a brief glimpse of a chastened but still determined Charis, suggests the psychic toll Gellhorn's own hectic travels took on her, although there is no evidence to suggest that her sexual adventures gave her syphilis.

Gellhorn had trouble placing the novel with a publisher. Three chapters, in particular, offended contemporary taste. She wanted to write a sexually explicit novel and go into the consequences of Charis's disease, but in the end accepted a friend's advice to revise the offending passages. Better to have one's first novel published – even if it meant making 'concessions'. The Frederick R. Stokes Company finally accepted the novel for publication in 1934.

Gellhorn later disowned *What Mad Pursuit*. She admitted that her father disliked the book with good reason. He once complained of it to Emily Lewis Norcross, who tried to console him, calling it a book his daughter had to get out of her system. Gellhorn never listed it among her published works. The reviewer in the *New York Times* (18 November 1934) judged the novel 'palpably juvenalia'. It remains readable because of the author's great vitality. Gellhorn is very close to her heroine but contemptuous of nearly everything in the heroine's environment. The college Charis attends has almost no distinguishing features; and the same is true of the newspaper that employs her and of most of the other American and European settings. The best parts of the book concentrate on Charis – mountain climbing, for example – and there the rhythm of the scene actually evokes her fitful, reckless nature. Otherwise, episodes are introduced only to dismiss other characters and places as unworthy of Charis's noble aspirations. Although she is criticized for her heedless pursuit of the ideal, in the end she is honoured as a seeker after truth. The novel lacks the tension and self-criticism of mature work, and Gellhorn was not perceptive enough about the very things she rejected to make them come alive in fiction.

Bertrand de Jouvenel, interviewed by Olga Clark in July 1934 for the *St Louis Globe-Democrat*, professed to be 'proud of his wife's first book'. He was visiting Edna and some of Martha's friends, and satisfied his curiosity about her birthplace. Martha Love Symington, who showed him around the city, recalls that he was madly in love with Martha and that she gave every sign of feeling the same about him. At an intersection he saw four churches and wanted to know about them. She explained to him about Methodists, Jews and the other religions that were represented there and in other parts of the city. To Martha Love, he seemed thunderstruck by the great variety of Christians, as if he had never heard of the Reformation: 'Here was this sophisticated Frenchman and he did not seem to have any idea of these splits in the Church.' Soon she was talking about Lutherans and Presbyterians. '"Oh," he said, "how confusing!"' There were as many churches as filling stations.

Given the grim news coming from Germany in 1934, Edna was astonished at Jouvenel's friendly attitude towards Germans. He had already been branded as a fascist in France but defended himself by suggesting, 'the best way not to fight with the Germans is to be friends with them'. Martha's attitude had changed after a visit to Nazi Germany in January 1934. They were travelling with a group of French pacifists of various political persuasions on the left and the right. An outraged Gellhorn watched German police enter her third-class train compartment and seize her group's newspapers. At the station they were met by clean-cut, light-haired, regimented Nazi youths parroting the latest fascist cant. Gellhorn left the home of von Schirach, the leader of these young Nazis, when she witnessed his assault on a servant for spilling coffee. Martha Love Symington, who spent part of the early 1930s in Germany, remembers Gellhorn's letters pestering her for information about the Nazis and about their persecution of the Jews.

Jouvenel worried about anti-Semitism as well, but he remained fascinated with Nazism as a youth movement. Most of his contacts had been with young Nazis who impressed him with their physicality and 'relative absence of class distinctions'. He admired their vitality. He did not want to isolate Hitler and his followers. In power, a demystified Hitler would have to temper his more outrageous proposals, Jouvenel argued, and behave like a normal politician.

Many years later Gellhorn noted the unreality of Jouvenel's politics; he roamed among different political camps and she doubted that his positions were treated with much respect. She abandoned the faith he had in a 'generational' analysis of history. He believed that French and German youth shared a solidarity that marked them off from past generations. The war and modern technology – the speed-up in communications accomplished by the telephone, the radio and the automobile – meant that a new generation, impatient with tradition, mandated that changes occur more rapidly than before. Jouvenel contended that the Nazi youth remained part of a European generation that believed in the welfare state.

This pan-European programme now seemed defunct to Gellhorn. In '*La Plume et l'Epée*', an article she published in Jouvenel's journal, *La Lutte des jeunes*, on 10 June 1934, she asked why revolutionary writers and painters had been unable to endow pacifism with a sense of glory and myth that would animate the multitudes the way Hitler and Mussolini were doing with their propaganda. She knew that artists should not propagandize, yet she longed for someone to compose a marching song that would galvanize a humane revolution in human affairs. She pointed to the powerful scenes in Diego Rivera's murals evoking the suffering and the struggle of the masses for expression, and to Roosevelt's employment of artists who were transforming American life with pictures of labourers in strong colours, in simple designs and in a muscular, virtually photographic style that amounted to a hymn to work.

Struck by the terrible extent of the Depression, she realized that America was no longer secure and wealthy, and isolated from the rest of the world. So she reversed direction – in search of an America that now needed her energies as much as Europe, which, she had thought, specialized in trouble. Gellhorn had also tired of Jouvenel. Near the end of her life she commented: 'It was assumed that we had the hottest thing in bed since Antony and Cleopatra. In fact, it was the opposite. But I felt sorry for Bertrand. He'd followed me all round Europe on my trips with a knapsack, a corkscrew and a bottle-opener and I felt sorry for him.' The marriage foundered, for she no longer believed in him or the vision of the world he championed. She would look for another cause, another hero.

5

A DANGEROUS
COMMUNIST
1934–1936

O N 16 OCTOBER 1934, a sunny day, Martha Gellhorn arrived in New York to see Harry L. Hopkins, Director of the Federal Emergency Relief Administration (FERA). She had come from Paris six days earlier on a pathetic little ship, costing $85 for the passage – all she could afford.

For a young woman with admittedly limited journalistic experience and no record of government service, Gellhorn's access to Harry Hopkins was astonishing. She did explain in *The View from the Ground* that she had the backing of Marquis Childs, a prominent journalist and friend who had secured the appointment with Hopkins, whom Franklin Roosevelt would entrust with many sensitive and controversial assignments, and Hopkins was probably aware of Edna Gellhorn's friendship with Eleanor Roosevelt. But Martha said nothing about her extraordinary ability to cultivate her own contacts and to draw on her family's connections. She never acknowledged, for example, that Eleanor's close friend, Lorena Hickok, also played a vital role in Martha's swift employment in the Roosevelt administration. One of Gellhorn's letters to Hickok (7 January 1935) addresses her as 'Darling' and proceeds to praise Hickok's writing. Gellhorn said it had been worth returning to America and working for the New Deal because she had found Hickok in the thick of it.

Hopkins wanted rugged field investigators to report on the health, nutrition, housing, likelihood of employment and mood of people on relief. The blonde, slender Gellhorn did not appear to be a credible candidate for the job. She had the polish of a 'young society matron' and 'distracting' long legs.

Gellhorn briefed Hopkins on her experience with the unemployed in France. She exaggerated her journalistic experience. He was impressed and offered her employment probably lasting less than two months at $35 a week plus travelling expenses. She detected a glint in Hopkins's eyes that made her suspect he was having a little fun when he offered her the job.

Gellhorn was probably right. Anything but a stuffy government bureaucrat, Hopkins had spent his boyhood in small Midwestern towns, brought up by a wandering father with a 'weakness for poker and bowling' and a Methodist missionary mother. This combination produced in Hopkins 'a militant social conscience' and an 'easygoing gaiety'. Like Gellhorn, he had spent some time working in settlement houses; and like her grandmother, his social work with children made him particularly sensitive to the plight of the poor. Gellhorn could not have picked a better boss. The 'lean, loose-limbed, dishevelled' Hopkins, with 'sharp features and dark, sardonic eyes', had a penchant for profanity and 'concise, pungent' language. His assistants called him Harry. Informal and direct, he embodied the very model of a brash man she could admire. Like her, he contended that 'all walls would fall before the man of resources and decision'.

Gellhorn's first trip as a FERA field investigator took her to a textile town in North Carolina. The conditions she found were appalling and shocked her deeply. A typical case involved a woman with five children. She received a relief check of $3.40 a week. The family had no shoes. Nearly all their furniture had been sold. Food prices had doubled. The poor diet produced pellagra. With no money for medicine or proper food, people succumbed to syphilis and infectious diseases, becoming cripples and imbeciles out of deprivation and plain ignorance.

Latrines fed right into a community's drinking water. Why everyone did not have typhoid puzzled Gellhorn. Homes were no more than shacks with shattered windows, no plumbing and rats. Nowhere in Europe had she seen such shoddy tenements. Tenants had to pay high rents and to purchase food at exorbitant rates from the company stores.

Striking union workers were not rehired. They had no clothes for the winter and were evicted from their homes. Those still employed had to work 'stretch-outs' (heavily increased work loads and schedules) and after long hours operating machinery they could not stop their hands from shaking. Workers fainted and died beside their looms. The conditions reminded Gellhorn of a Dickens novel, she wrote to Hopkins on 11 November. Women ate their lunch standing up next to their machines. She found them lying in exhaustion on cement floors in bathrooms.

Gellhorn cited statistics and gave Hopkins precise descriptions of what she had seen. These people were not complainers. Indeed, they were good-humoured and tremendously loyal to the President, relying on his promise to relieve their suffering. They felt a deep kinship with Roosevelt and put his picture in a place of honour. Although a year earlier Lorena Hickok, Eleanor Roosevelt's confidante, observed Communists organizing 'farmers and working like beavers', Gellhorn thought the feudal conditions made an insurrection preposterous. What she saw shamed a country with lofty democratic ideals.

On 26 November, in Boston, she reported to Hopkins that she saw as many as 'five families a day'. More examples of malnutrition, tuberculosis, rickets, retardation, anaemia, and a multitude of other diseases and maladies disgusted her – especially when she discovered corrupt and inept local relief administrators. She quoted verbatim the desperate expressions of families who could not live on the average half-dollar a day in government relief payment. In early December, after a trip to Rhode Island, she wrote to Hopkins to support mill owners' accusations that only Catholics who were Democrats could become federal administrators. In New Hampshire she saw further signs of graft in the way men were hired to work on certain projects.

In the first two gruelling months in the field Gellhorn lost weight but not energy, raging against politicians and employers who perpetuated a brutal economic system. She stormed back to Washington full of 'blood and thunder'. Hopkins tried to calm her and talk her out of resigning. Gellhorn did not feel the government was doing nearly enough; the government, on the other hand, had to contend with criticism that providing relief and other welfare programmes would deprive the poor of the incentive to work. Hopkins commiserated with Gellhorn, acknowledging that FERA was doing, at best, a 'minimal job'. State welfare budgets and private charitable funds were depleted, and the federal allocation was only $500 million for the whole country. He suggested she speak with Mrs Roosevelt, always a sympathetic listener and deeply concerned about the poor. The letters she wrote to Edna Gellhorn, and the letters from Mrs Roosevelt to many poor people in distress, reveal the first lady's remarkable involvement both in individual cases and in welfare programmes. When Gellhorn conveyed her outrage to Mrs Roosevelt, she convinced Gellhorn she should tell her story directly to the President.

Gellhorn arrived at her first White House dinner in a 'black sweater and skirt'. The fine dishes, the splendid meal and the complacent guests in their formal clothing irritated her. She thought of the Depression-deprived millions lacking the basic decencies of food, shelter and work. Hard of hearing and in the habit of shouting, Mrs Roosevelt stood up at the far end of the table and urged the President to 'talk to that child at your left. She says that all the people in the South have pellagra or syphilis.' This announcement brought conversation to a halt and provoked considerable laughter. A furious Gellhorn wanted to leave, but Eleanor Roosevelt had captured her husband's attention. Indeed, he seemed delighted with Gellhorn and listened to her stories, inviting her to visit him again.

The Roosevelts talked Gellhorn out of quitting her FERA job. They wanted her to gather more reports, maintaining that her work would result in corrective action. She kept at it for nearly a year, travelling across the country, investigating every region and writing to Hopkins at lightning speed.

By the fall of 1935 Gellhorn's attitude towards her relief work had turned rebellious. In a small Idaho town she encountered an all too familiar situation: unemployed men exploited by a dishonest contractor. The men had lost their farms and ranches, and were now digging dirt for an employer who tossed their shovels in the lake to benefit from a commission for the order of new ones. The men had to wait for the next shipment of shovels with no means of support unless they were willing to submit to a humiliating means test. Gellhorn bought them beer and taunted them: 'Are you men or mice?

I'll just tell you this: *somebody* will come and pay attention to you, but you've got to protest; there isn't anybody in that rotten office, so just throw bricks in there.'

The FBI caught up with Gellhorn in Seattle. The Idaho men had broken FERA office windows – incited by her, they said. She had stopped the contractor's scam, but Harry Hopkins called her: 'It's perfectly terrible; I can't tell you how badly we feel about it, but you've got to be fired because of the FBI.' He gave her a month's salary. 'I should be delighted to leave. I've had enough', she told him. To her parents she wrote exuberantly about her new reputation as a 'dangerous Communist'. Gellhorn then set about writing an exposé of the relief programme.

In the midst of cleaning out her office, Gellhorn got a call from the President's secretary who put him on the line: 'Mrs Roosevelt and I have heard that you've been fired because of the FBI, and I don't know if we can do anything about it, but we're both worried about you because we know you haven't got any money, the best thing is for you to come and live at the White House.' She did. Mrs Roosevelt wrote to Lorena Hickok that Gellhorn 'must learn patience & not have a critical attitude towards what others do for she must remember that to them it is just as important as her dreams are to her'. The Roosevelts worried that Gellhorn might seriously run awry by alienating the very people who could help her. After enjoying the comforts of the White House Gellhorn returned home to St Louis.

In December 1935, at the end of an arduous year, Gellhorn nearly collapsed with anaemia. In January her father died before getting to see her first major work, which she dedicated to him, in print. From St Louis she wrote to Eleanor Roosevelt that she would remain with her mother as long as she was needed; none of her family had yet come to an understanding of how to cope with their terrible loss.

In early February 1936 Martha wrote to Eleanor about her need to look for another job. She would probably go to New York, since St Louis seemed to specialize in women who sold dresses in fashionable stores. The Roosevelts thought Martha needed time to consider her next step and they were sure her finances were shaky. They sensed that she did not like the White House that much, but Mrs

Roosevelt assured her she only had to show up for meals whenever it suited her. Otherwise, food in her room would be fine and so were visits from friends or anything else that would make her comfortable.

The Roosevelts' hospitality and relaxed attitudes did not seem unusual to Gellhorn at the time. They joined her in making fun of the FBI. The White House was not then a 'palace' or 'fortress', Gellhorn later pointed out. The Roosevelts simply treated it as another of their residences, with 'just one Secret Service man on duty at night'. Gellhorn remembered the faded but comfortable furniture, reflecting the Roosevelts' plain but pleasant tastes. The old-fashioned bathrooms with brass fixtures and huge claw-footed tubs befitted their unpretentious, homey style. Gellhorn found Mrs Roosevelt's own room austere and unattractive; its 'ugly wall of brown wood closet doors' looked cheap. Besides the bed, she had a few chairs and a 'small desk with glass-fronted bookshelves above it'. Mrs Roosevelt cared little for her own comfort. The White House lacked the pomp and splendour initiated by later presidents. 'It wasn't the citadel of everything', Gellhorn concluded.

The more Gellhorn saw of Mrs Roosevelt, the more she grew to love her as a second mother. Nothing pleased Mrs Roosevelt more than to help other people; caring for others was something she *needed*, Gellhorn emphasized. She did not like to be waited on and would fetch things for herself. Gellhorn would stay up with her some nights to read the mail. Roosevelt answered these letters, many of which addressed her as a friend to whom people could confess their cares and expect help. This 'pathologically modest' woman never claimed the privilege of another's love. While her husband mixed 'lethal martinis' and entertained his cronies after dinner, she retired to her room to work. To Gellhorn, 'he was a charmer, but she was the moral true north'. She did not find him especially 'cozy or comforting' with his wife, but he acknowledged her as the conscience of his administration. He treated Gellhorn like 'a sort of mascot or pet or poodle or something in this *galère*', she later suggested in an interview. Although he was 'nice' to her, she never developed a fondness for him. She acknowledged this great and powerful politician, but Eleanor 'was love'.

The White House was also a quiet setting in which she could

work on the first draft of *The Trouble I've Seen* (1936). When a friend made available his vacant, isolated Connecticut home she left the Roosevelts, full of gratitude for their sensible and loving support but bent on finishing, in complete solitude, a fictionalized version of her relief work. The book put an end to a chapter in Gellhorn's life. It was like getting 'trouble out of her system', she explained to Jacqueline Orsagh, a later student of her work: 'something sick' had grown inside her as she witnessed 'cruelty' and 'misery'. Only by disgorging the experience in an article or book could she return to health and 'throw her energies into her next project'. Her job with the FERA would turn out to be her most sustained period of commitment to working beside her countrymen. She would never feel quite this close to Americans again – and certainly not to the Presidency. In her words, the Roosevelts were unique in their 'private and public fearlessness'.

By early June 1936, Gellhorn was in England, the guest of H. G. Wells, whom she had met at the White House. It would be difficult to exaggerate Wells's fame and what it meant to secure his approval and support. He was the author of classics such as *The Time Machine* (1896), *The Invisible Man* (1897) and *The War of the Worlds* (1898), which Orson Welles would soon adapt for radio so effectively that it aroused genuine fear of a Martian invasion in his American listeners, many of whom took to the roads in panic. After his best-selling and influential *An Outline of History* (1920), Wells had been hailed as a modern sage and prophet. Educated as a scientist, he trained his powerful intellect on society in a series of realistic and comic novels, most notably *The History of Mr Polly* (1910). In 1934 he had published his candid and controversial *Experiment in Autobiography*. He had also produced hundreds of articles on politics, history, science and society, interviewing many world leaders, including Lenin and Stalin.

But Wells, a married man with two sons, was just as well known for his scandalous sexual affairs and his advocacy of free love. He carried on with woman half his age. One of them, the Pre-Raphaelite beauty Amber Reeves, had borne him a child after a year of chasing him. Amber's father, gun in hand, sought out Wells at his club. Wells had avoided gunfire, but he had been punched in the nose by another outraged father who snatched his daughter away from Wells just as she and Wells were embarking on an amour. He had conducted a three-year affair with novelist Dorothy Richardson, who had miscarried his child. There had been a liaison with novelist Elizabeth von Arnim, a tempestuous ten-year relationship with Rebecca West, who gave birth to his illegitimate son (the writer Anthony West), and countless other flings.

For a young woman of Gellhorn's attractiveness to be associated with Wells, then, provoked considerable gossip. After the very public and sensational affair with Amber Reeves, Wells had vowed to be more discreet. But he could not resist intriguing young women or offering his 'free and open hospitality' and his eagerness to share his views with 'nearly anyone'. To Sinclair Lewis, he wrote that Gellhorn had not 'seduced him'. He took a 'purely friendly' interest in her, 'although she is 27 and quite attractive'.

But in a suppressed section in the third volume of his autobiography Wells told quite a different story. 'We liked each other, mind and person', he wrote. He admired Gellhorn's 'adventurous honesty' and they became devoted correspondents. 'I have never had more amusing love letters.' She had even inspired in Wells, nearing seventy in 1935,

> my last flounderings towards the wife idea. ... I love and admire Martha Gellhorn; I shall do what I can to help her in her ambitions and perplexities, but her vigorous young life is not for me. She is extremely incidental. I'll have, as people say, a time with her when next I go to America, and that will be all. We may give very much to each other but finally we shall go our several ways.

In January 1936 Gellhorn and Wells resumed their lovemaking in a Connecticut house a friend had lent her. 'We too had a very happy time together for a week, making love, talking, reading over her second book'. Wells wrote. Clearly energized, Wells even enjoyed digging his car out of a snowdrift, watching Gellhorn in action in her 'ski-ing trousers with her shock of ruddy golden hair in disorder, her brown eyes alight and her face rosy with frost'. His memoir is a vivid portrait of a woman who adapted to all environments with extraordinary style. In New York, for example, he saw and admired her as a 'well-dressed young lady, staying with a wealthy friend on

Park Avenue'. He escorted Gellhorn to the theatre, and he gave a party for her in his sitting room at the Ambassador Hotel. He found her ravishing as she 'flitted in and out of my apartment at all hours'.

Wells secured a British publisher for *The Trouble I've Seen*. Indeed, Gellhorn's British contract is in his papers at the University of Illinois, and it shows that he negotiated on her behalf and even asked the publisher, Hamish Hamilton, to remove standard clauses – such as the stipulation that the author must pay the cost of corrections over and above ten per cent of the cost of typesetting, and the right to remainder copies. Hamilton did not grant these requests, but he did modify other clauses at Wells's suggesting, pointing out that he had to overcome his concern about the 'prejudice in the trade against books of American short stories by unknown authors'. It was Wells's Foreword that would make a 'great difference to the reception of the book both by the booksellers and the critics', Hamilton wrote to Wells.

Gellhorn never acknowledged the intimate role that Wells played in her life and work. In the early 1980s, when his son Gip decided to publish the third volume of his father's autobiography, which would deal with his love life, he contacted Gellhorn, mentioning the 'love letters' she had sent to Wells. She replied that they were not love letters and that Wells's 'silly and vain' story of their affair took 'the cookie'. She was sure that Gip would agree that his father was not exactly 'physically dazzling'. In short, there had been no love affair. Wells had invited himself to stay with her in Connecticut and he had irritated her with his incessant chatter. She claimed that he had a 'vague crush' on her and had 'once suggested marriage'. But regarding anything beyond friendship, she would rather swim the Pacific, she wrote to Gip. She could only manage a half-compliment to Wells's memory: 'He was fun unless he was bullying me intellectually.' In other letters to Gip an angry Gellhorn remarked, 'I wonder that Rebecca didn't kill him.' By 18 September 1984 she warned Gip that if he included her in his father's autobiography she would 'sue everyone in sight'.

To her friend, biographer Victoria Glendinning, Gellhorn wrote that 'Wells needed to add my scalp'. She called him a 'bore' – surely one of the few times that word has been applied to Wells – and deflected further inquiry with the question: 'Why the hell would I sleep with a little old man when I could have any number of tall beautiful young men?' But Gellhorn's friends liked to tell another story – of a young aspiring novelist determined to seduce the great writer. She sent him a case of what she thought was his favourite drink, which on delivery turned out to be something like HP sauce. Even at seventy, H. G. Wells had not lost his zest for pursuing women, or for having women pursue him. Given his sexual prowess and experience, it is difficult to see why he would need to make up any stories about Martha Gellhorn.

The Gellhorn letters to Wells at the University of Illinois are not particularly passionate, it is true, but the small number of them suggests that the collection is not complete. Most of the letters date from the 1940s when Gellhorn was married to Hemingway and when the relationship with Wells had settled into a rather sedate occasional correspondence. Gellhorn and Wells were closest during 1935 and 1936, when he was in the best position to help her, and then she moved on – irked but also stimulated by Wells's constant admonitions to write every day and produce another great work.

Gellhorn did resume the writing of a novel set in Europe and based partly on her work with Jouvenel and their experiences in Germany. In July 1936 she travelled to Stuttgart to do research at the Weltkriegsbibliothek, which documented the Great War of 1914–18. The 'thin grey-faced' librarian whispered to Gellhorn that she did not know how long the library would remain open. The record of a defeated Germany offended the Nazis. Gellhorn watched the library's new director, 'young, blond and handsome in his brownshirt uniform', gallop 'through the trees and untended high grass' and swing from his horse into an open french window. This noisy man who terrorized the librarian and then rode off laughing belonged to the same brownshirts Gellhorn had observed taunting an old couple scrubbing the pavement. She read the 'coarse and belligerent' newspapers describing the Spanish Civil War as a 'revolt of a rabble of "Red Swine Dogs"'. She did not finish her novel, but 'those few weeks turned me into a devout anti-Fascist', Gellhorn wrote fifty-six years later.

By mid-August Eleanor Roosevelt had received an advance copy of *The Trouble I've Seen* and was writing about the book in her syndicated newspaper column. She explained she had been reading it to friends on the USS *Potomac* and at Hyde Park. She described Gellhorn as a 'young, pretty, college graduate, good home, more or less Junior League background, with a touch of exquisite Paris clothes and "*esprit*" thrown in'. Of course, Gellhorn had not graduated from college, but she had the demeanour of a privileged member of society speaking for the hungry and the unemployed:'She has an understanding of many people and many situations and she can make them live for us. Let us be thankful she can, for we badly need her interpretation to help us understand each other.'

With a laudatory preface by H. G. Wells, *The Trouble I've Seen* received rave reviews. Gellhorn became a national figure, with a glamorous photograph of her on the cover of the *Saturday Review*. In his syndicated column Lewis Gannett compared Gellhorn's dust jacket photo with the pose of a Hollywood actress starring in a film that was to be titled *The Virgin's Prayer*. Other reviews referred to Gellhorn's 'young and wistful' expression. Even better, Gannett said Gellhorn was as good as Hemingway in her use of authentic American speech and in achieving 'economy of language'.

In his preface to *The Trouble I've Seen*, H. G. Wells comments on how 'plucky' Gellhorn's characters are. She had travelled in every region of the country and everywhere she saw both the degradation of a people and their determination to reclaim their dignity. North, south, east and west, children, young people, the middle-aged and the elderly – all receive equal treatment in the four parts of her book. In the *New York Times* (27 September 1936), Edith H. Walton expressed astonishment at how well Gellhorn identified with all of her characters. Having read *What Mad Pursuit*, the reviewer expected to find a sensibility that patronized and remained aloof from them. The author was now willing to live with her characters and not just to view them as literary material. Gellhorn put her style in the service of her characters, using their words and expressions. As Mabel Ulrich put it in the *Saturday Review* (26 September 1936), *The Trouble I've Seen* had been fashioned 'out of the very tissues of human beings'.

Perhaps the best single page of *The Trouble I've Seen* is the first. Mrs Maddison stands before her mirror trying on her hat, tilting it towards her right eye, then towards her left. Her face appears confused in the cracked mirror. It is a cheap, thirty-cent, white straw hat shaped like a pot, but it has been lovingly trimmed by Mrs Maddison herself with a 'noisily pink starchy gardenia, in the centre front, like a miner's lamp'. When she walks outside, the flower (safety-pinned to her hat) nods as she walks, bows before she does and sometimes blows 'from side to side petulantly'. This is her best hat, the one she wears when she goes to pick up her relief cheque. It is important to Mrs Maddison that no one should suppose that she needs things. She will take what she is entitled to, but no one must be allowed to think she should be pitied.

Nothing approaching this sort of intimate, involved writing appears in Gellhorn's earlier work. Without commentary, the author conveys her character's integrity, her effort to achieve balance in her life by setting her hat on her head just so. Mrs Maddison has a sense of style. Accepting relief is a blow to her pride, but she will find an honourable way to deal with it. Only a writer who had lived with someone like Mrs Maddison could describe her most characteristic features in such precise and evocative prose, or would think to include the detail about the safety pin in the hat that rubs against her forehead. The enormous care the character takes with her own person is paralleled by the author's concern to find just the right words to describe her.

H. G. Wells commended Gellhorn for her lack of sentimentality and there is indeed a 'salt of the earth' quality to the book. As Edith H. Walton notes: 'Few of Miss Gellhorn's characters belong among the naturally idle and supine. Most of them have been, all their lives, self-respecting and hard-working; they are bewildered by what has happened to them; they look back, pathetically and nostalgically, to the day when they were "real folks".' Mrs Maddison is hardier than most. She agrees to take over an abandoned Negro shack and begin farming with her son and daughter-in-law. But the back-breaking, enervating effort of working the land and rebuilding the flimsy shack is too much for the young couple and they blame Mrs Maddison for bringing them there. Deprived of any continuity or commitment to work, the male characters in this book dream idly of prosperity, and condemn the dole and other institutions of society for providing so little support. As Gellhorn noted earlier in her reports to Harry Hopkins, the very bonds of community were being destroyed in the uprooting and displacement of millions of people. In *The Trouble I've Seen* Mrs Maddison fears that the wind will carry everything away even as she waits for her relief cheque.

In Part Two, 'Joe and Pete', Gellhorn dramatizes the efforts of workers to organize their own unions and to help themselves rather than accept relief. At first there is sheer exhilaration in acting for oneself. Pete welcomes the feeling of being a strong, independent man, striking out for himself and his buddies. Joe is the idolized leader who will fight for workers' rights and a decent wage. Working men feel they cannot lose because they are supported by Roosevelt, who understands their plight. When Joe is compelled to settle for a token wage increase and workers like Pete are let go and blackballed, Pete's vision of a society where he can always find a job and support himself is annihilated. Too ashamed to accept relief, to answer the prying questions of the relief official who visits his home, he runs away from his nagging wife and his responsibilities.

In Part Three, 'Jim', Gellhorn concentrates on the romantic illusions of young people. Jim dreams of becoming a great doctor or a musician and ends up driving a delivery truck. He desperately wants to attain some kind of distinction in his life and resorts to stealing clothes for his marriage to Lou, already pregnant and anxious not to put off their life together for better times that may never come. His idle fantasies about fame and fortune are not merely pathetic because they arise out of a hard-working, fiercely moral spirit.

'Ruby', the last section of *The Trouble I've Seen*, horrified and impressed many reviewers, for it is about an innocent eleven-year-old girl who turns to prostitution as the only means of gratifying her simple desire for roller skates and other things that delight her still childish imagination. The first page of 'Ruby' sets her in motion as a perfect portrait of youth, an exact counterweight to the opening of 'Mrs Maddison'. Ruby enjoys the wind snapping her head back. Her coat, fashioned from her father's cast-off, waves in back of her as her coaster skips over the bumpy pavement and she shouts 'hoo-wee', with one stocking crumpled down around her ankle. Ruby rides her coaster as if she is flying. She borrows it from a boy who worries she will break it. And indeed, there is a reckless, high-spirited quality in the girl that is predictive of her fate. She will do almost anything to attain these emotional highs, these feelings of absolute freedom.

'Lookit me,' she says, 'I'm flying.' When she flies, she imagines 'the wind yelling' at her.

Poorer than most children from families on relief, Ruby has few friends. Most of the kids make fun of her unkempt and unwashed appearance, and she pretends that she wears rags because she prefers them and does not want to soil her dresses. Her father has abandoned the family, ashamed that it has to accept relief. Ruby is out most of the time on her own, inventing games and pastimes until she is taken up by a group of young girls who have set up a part-time whorehouse. Although her first sexual experience is painful and bewildering, she steels herself to the 'work' in order to earn the money that makes her existence a little more pleasant. Eventually she is caught and taken away from her mother.

Gellhorn tells Ruby's story without pathos. It is what Ruby feels she has to do and Gellhorn has to respect the fact of Ruby's adaptability. Bernice Kert reports that Ruby 'was based on a waif Martha had encountered in a Hooverville, Illinois shanty'. Ruby was probably a composite of many children Gellhorn observed, including some in St Louis. 'I knew the river front pretty well and the tragic lives of penniless people camping there', Mary Taussig Hall recalls. One of the sights she shared with Martha was of a little girl going 'clickety-clack' down the street on her scooter. 'Now here's Martha, she comes home for a few days. She goes down to the river front for two hours where I've lived and still she's able to write that story ["Ruby"]. She can do more for those people than all the social workers in the world.' Martha had her impractical side, wanting to 'change all that and get a house for that man who didn't have a house, but she soon found she couldn't do all those good things. Then she left and we went on dealing with all those people', said Mrs Hall.

Finding all the 'promotional hoopla that went along with the publication' of her book distasteful, Gellhorn returned to St Louis to spend Christmas 1936 with her family, the first without her father. She suggested they take a vacation in Florida. The trip would change her life.

6

HEMINGWAY HELL OR HIGH WATER

1936–1937

IN DECEMBER 1936, during their vacation in Florida, Martha, Edna and her brother Alfred were bored with Miami and decided to explore Key West, where Martha wrote to Eleanor Roosevelt: 'It's hot and falling to pieces and people seem happy.' The relaxed, sunny atmosphere seemed 'very fine indeed'. They walked into Sloppy Joe's, the bar that Ernest Hemingway made famous. There he sat, his body darkened by the sun, lounging in a 'grubby T-shirt', 'odoriferous Basque shorts' held up by a bit of rope and barefooted, a bulky figure weighing about 200 pounds. He struck Martha as nothing more than a 'large, dirty man'. She remembered him speaking to the Gellhorns first.

Gellhorn's later account of meeting Hemingway seems suspect on several counts. She said she had never heard of Key West before coming to Miami. Her brother Alfred had the idea to go there. Her mother spotted Sloppy Joe's. None of them knew it as Hemingway's hangout. Hemingway approached them. One or all of these details could be true, but taken together they seem too earnestly designed to deflect attention from Gellhorn's desire to pursue one of her literary idols. After all, the alternative title for her first novel had been *Nothing Ever Happens*, part of a line from *A Farewell to Arms* that had served, she told Joseph Pennell, as her motto.

Martha wore a 'one-piece black dress and high heels', one of her favourite travelling outfits. 'Marty went through a phase in her late twenties when she wore nothing but the little black dress. With her golden hair she looked very effective in her black-and-white' ensembles, one of her friends remembered. Her 'shoulder-length hair, high cheekbones, and full-lipped mouth' gave her an elegant and sensuous look. Another friend noted that 'Martha was a very beautiful woman. When she walked into a room with her carriage and bearing, everyone knew she was beautiful and they were in awe of her'. 'Very blonde, beautiful skin, tall, thin – very dramatic and very amusing in her speech' with a 'low, husky, eastern-seaboard-accented voice', it is not surprising that a shy Hemingway mumbled by way of an introduction that he had 'known St Louis in the days of his youth. Both his wives had gone to school there, and so had [his friends] Bill and Katy Smith.' Skinner (Sloppy Joe's black bartender) watched Martha take a seat beside Hemingway. It reminded him of 'beauty and the beast'.

Legend has it that Gellhorn and Hemingway drank his famous concoction, 'Papa Dobles', made out of 'two and a half jiggers of white Ron Bacardi rum, the juice of two fresh limes, the juice of a grapefruit half, capped off with six drops of maraschino' mixed in a 'rusty electric blender near Ernest's end of the bar'. She talked about a novel she was trying to finish. The thirty-eight-year-old Hemingway seemed a little old to her. She impressed Hemingway's friends as looking a very youthful twenty-eight. In contrast to her fiery, still almost teenage temperament, he 'talked older. He acted older.'

Gellhorn's looks, her talk and her background brought out the protective/seductive Papa Hemingway. Martha, like Hadley, his first wife, had attended but did not graduate from Bryn Mawr. He had met Hadley just after her mother's death; he was meeting Martha just after her father's. Although younger than Hadley, he tried to compensate for the loss of her mother by adopting a parental attitude. Like Martha, Pauline, his second wife, had been educated in a St Louis private school. Trained as a journalist, she was an alluring, stylishly dressed woman when he met her. She had cleverly 'insinuated herself into [his] household' and 'courted' him while Hadley remained in the role of dutiful housewife. Martha, more talented, bolder and better looking than his previous women, resembled the stunningly attractive Jane Mason, with whom he had just ended a four-year affair. Jane had been a problem – too unstable and prone to self-destructive acts, married and close to Pauline in a way that 'inhibited her intimacy with Ernest'. Pauline, relegated to the domestic routine that had done in Hadley, now had to contend with Martha, thirteen years younger and very much at home with herself. If Pauline, as Hemingway wrote in *Green Hills of Africa*, was like a little terrier, then Martha could be compared to a wolfhound: 'lean, racy, long-legged and ornamental', suggests Hemingway biographer Jeffrey Meyers.

That Hemingway met Gellhorn in the company of her mother also gave Martha an advantage. Shrewd, gay, affectionate and open, Edna delighted him and would become one of his favourite correspondents. She was nothing like his own mother (also a doctor's wife), whom he found bigoted and dictatorial.

Hemingway eagerly escorted the Gellhorns around Key West. When he spotted Pauline on the street, he invited her to join them. 'She was very grumpy,' Martha told Bernice Kert several years later and 'he was very sharp. … It never occurred to me that she could be jealous, and who knows if she was; [she] may have had other reasons for being cross.' But Pauline's friends suspected Martha's intentions. As Lorine Thompson observed:

> Martha was a very charming girl and if I had known her under other circumstances I would have liked her very much. She said she came to see Ernest, she wanted him to read a book she had written, she wanted to know him. There was no question about it; you could see she was making a play for him. … Pauline tried to ignore it. What she felt underneath nobody knew.

Leicester Hemingway, Ernest's younger brother, also called Martha the aggressor, talking up the opportunities and the hazards of a trip to report on the Civil War in Spain, which had begun on 18 July 1936, when General Francisco Franco took command of the army insurrection against the Republican government. Later, poet Archibald MacLeish, who knew Ernest and Pauline well, would report: 'I watched Miss Gellhorn conduct her amazing and quite shameless attack on their marriage.'

Gellhorn, on the other hand, told biographer Bernice Kert that 'she never saw him in the evening and remembers only one visit to the Key West house. Neither by word nor gesture did Ernest show anything beyond friendly interest.' Yet Martha later wrote to thank

Pauline for her hospitality and admitted she became a 'fixture' there, 'like a kudu head'. Miriam Williams, Hemingway's cook, saw Ernest and Martha 'outside … kissing and carrying on'.

Edna and Alfred left Key West after New Year's Day; Martha checked into the Colonial Hotel for another week of 'sunshine and swimming'. Ernest accompanied his 'mermaid' on her jaunts while Pauline plaintively remarked, 'I suppose Ernest is busy again helping Miss Gellhorn with her writing.' Gellhorn confided her enthusiasm for Hemingway to Eleanor Roosevelt, writing on 5 January 1937 that he liked to exaggerate; his stories were marvellous and clearly a product of his genius. In another letter she called him 'very lovable and full of fire'. She praised his precision and craftsmanship. Clearly, she looked to him for inspiration. Still struggling with her European novel, she felt her new work was static. He suggested she had fretted too much and that she should simply write and have the courage to throw away inferior material. She was going on doggedly at the rate of ten pages a day but felt she was missing everything. (Eventually she would abandon the novel.) Spain was the place to be: she was certain it marked the start of a world war just as surely as the Balkan conflicts in 1912 had presaged the assassination of Franz Ferdinand in 1914 and the start of World War One. She was not alone, of course, since many young American men volunteered to fight for the Republican government in Spain, serving in what came to be known as the Lincoln Battalion.

On 10 January Gellhorn left Key West by car en route to St Louis. Hemingway caught up with her in Miami and accompanied her by train as far as Jacksonville. In New York, Hemingway signed a contract with the North American Newspaper Alliance (NANA) to cover the Spanish Civil War. He also convinced his editor, Maxwell Perkins, to buy for *Scribner's Magazine* Gellhorn's story, 'Exile', which appeared in the September 1937 issue.

'Exile' is as much about Gellhorn as it is about a German refugee who flees the Nazis because they have ruined his country. Heinrich is not a Jew or a Communist or a pacifist – just a quiet man who has spent his life in libraries researching the history of the postal system. In his view the Nazis are barbarians, noisily marching in the street and mixing up 'history and truth'. Newspapers are unintelligible. The libraries have no new books. The final blow is the Nazi assertion that his beloved Heine, a Jew, can no longer be considered a poet. But Heinrich is no happier living with his cousin in America. His presence crowds her home and he has no means of support. She thinks of the Nazis only as persecutors and cannot grasp Heinrich's point that his leaving had more to do with their pollution of an entire culture.

Gellhorn had a feel for day-to-day existence in Germany and she realized Americans did not have the faintest notion of what the Nazi takeover meant, not just for politics and international affairs, but for learning and art. Heinrich is no hero – in fact he merits his cousin's accusation that he is a 'dirty, messy old German' – but his rather mundane personality is an effective way of exposing how the Nazis infected the very core of civilization. It often frustrated Gellhorn that Americans did not grasp how easily groups like the Nazis were able to destroy democratic values. Most of her life would be spent in a kind of 'exile' from America. It is no surprise that she has Heinrich wonder how a man can establish a sense of home. It was a question she constantly put to herself. The story had its effect on Hemingway, who would eventually write *For Whom the Bell Tolls*, with its famous epigraph from John Donne: 'No man is an *Island* … '. 'Exile' bore witness to the consequences of an aggressively expanding fascism; the story played its part in spurring Hemingway on to Spain.

On the phone to Gellhorn, Hemingway encouraged her to come to New York, where he would arrange her trip to Spain. She demurred, 'flattered and amazed by his attentions', but not ready to rely on his instructions. Yet her letters to him continued. She wrote of her hope that they would be in the same boat when the 'deluge' began. She called them fellow conspirators plotting to get into Spain (obtaining visas had become difficult since the advent of the Franco-British Non-Intervention Pact). He was her 'angel' and she had so much to say to him. He should leave a message for her in Paris if she failed to catch him in New York. Martha sent her 'love' to Pauline, but she urged him not to forget her, for after all they were in the same league and she doted on him. She lapsed into his jargon – referring to him as 'Hemingstein'.

By the end of February 1937 Gellhorn decided to join Hemingway in Spain. She arrived in New York to find that he had sailed for France. Contrary to her expectations, he left no instructions. His silence apparently aroused her. At Fred Field's country home in Connecticut, 'clad in black silk and pearls', she bragged about what an 'extraordinary man' Hemingway was and 'praised his barrel chest, his enormous potency and his skill as a lover'. On 3 March she had a letter in hand from Kyle Crichton of *Collier's* identifying her as its correspondent. She was no such thing – that is, she had no contract to publish in the magazine – but the letter might be good enough to get her into Spain. At about the same time in Paris, Hemingway – just about to enter Spain – met Joris Ivens, who was to become his collaborator in the filming of *The Spanish Earth*, a documentary that would be used to raise funds for the defence of the Republic. 'My beautiful girlfriend is coming. She has legs that begin at her shoulders', he told Ivens. Arriving in Paris a few weeks after Hemingway's departure, Gellhorn is reported to have told P. J. Phillips, a *New York Times* correspondent, that she was 'going to get Hemingway come hell or high water'.

In the middle of March, with a knapsack and fifty dollars, and only the clothes she had on ('grey flannel trousers, sweater, warm windbreaker') Gellhorn got off a train at the Andorran–Spanish border and crossed into Spain. From there she took an antiquated train – full of Republican soldiers – to Barcelona. They offered her food and did not behave as though they were going to war – these young, boisterous, but well-behaved Spaniards whose language she had yet to learn. Barcelona was radiant not only with the sun but with red streamers, the cabbie refused to charge her a fare and the brotherhood of man seemed to reign everywhere.

The war was still in its early stages. Franco's rebel forces had captured Malaga (in southern Spain) on 8 February, but the Republican government's army had checked the attack on Madrid. Gellhorn reached Madrid (via Valencia), where wintry, dark, bomb-cratered streets suddenly shocked her with the reality of war. The city had become a battlefield. Threading her way through the debris called for acute attention. She could sense the entire city expecting another attack, the thrill of living so close to the margins of death.

Hemingway was having his supper in the basement restaurant of the Gran Via Hotel when Gellhorn and his friend Sidney Franklin arrived – having met in Valencia and driven up to Madrid. She remembered that Hemingway lifted his arm and put a hand on her head. She felt as though she had been annexed. Years later she could not recount the incident without smiling. But he overdid it: 'I knew you'd get here, daughter, because I fixed it so you could.' An angry Gellhorn then described how she had made it to Spain by her own efforts.

Gellhorn knew nothing about war, admitted it, then plunged right into battle, determined to learn and to make herself an obliging, useful and entertaining companion. Correspondent Ted Allan, assigned the task of briefing her on the war, 'made a face' expecting a 'dull' meeting. Instead, he 'flipped' for her, remembering her 'wonderful smile, the hair, the great figure' and their splendid time 'giggling and cuddling for warmth' in the back seat of the car that sped her to a rendezvous with Hemingway.

Hemingway took Gellhorn to Arturo Barea and Ilsa Kulcsar, government officials in charge of censorship who also dispensed such necessities as fuel vouchers and safe-conduct passes, and arranged for accommodations. Dumbfounded, these desperately overtaxed officials gaped at Gellhorn, 'a sleek woman with a halo of fair hair, who walked through the dark fusty office with a swaying movement' reminiscent of a movie star. Hemingway told Barea, 'That's Marty. Be nice to her. She writes for *Collier's* – you know, a million circulation.'

Writers Josephine Herbst, Lillian Hellman and other women noted Gellhorn's 'Saks Fifth Avenue slacks, the chiffon scarf and her perpetually scrubbed look'. How she acquired these clothes, given her version of entering Spain with only a knapsack, is not clear. Diana Forbes-Robertson, married to correspondent Vincent Sheean, thought that the usually 'domineering' Hemingway appeared 'weak for allowing himself to be trapped by women'. Martha 'dressed too showily for a war correspondent', Diana suggested, and became 'too assertive in her relationship with Ernest'. Correspondent Virginia Cowles, a Gellhorn confidante, observed that Hemingway 'went around Madrid in a pair of filthy brown trousers and a torn blue shirt. "They're all I brought with me", he would mumble apologetically. "Even the anarchists are getting disdainful".' Poet Stephen Spender recalled that war correspondents in the hotel in Valencia joked that Gellhorn always seemed to be looking for Hemingway. Often he had departed with Joris Ivens for the front.

Gellhorn and Hemingway stayed in the Hotel Florida – a constant target of heavy artillery bombardment and a mere 'seventeen blocks from street battles'. Many of its rooms were destroyed, the elevator rarely worked and hot water was only intermittently available. She had been forewarned about the 'filth and vermin of Spain' and had been sure to pack in her knapsack 'her most prized possession, a new cake of soap'. The food was horrible. Her first meal: 'A tiny portion of chick-peas and odoriferous dried fish', relieved only by the private store of provisions in Hemingway's room brought in from Paris.

On Gellhorn's second night in Madrid, heavy bombardment interrupted her sleep. Not wanting to be alone, she got up and realized she had been locked in her room. No one heard her banging and shouting until the shelling stopped. Then a stranger opened the door. She found Hemingway in a back room playing poker, where he confessed bashfully that he had locked her in 'so that no man could bother her'. His 'possessiveness' annoyed her, but she also took pleasure in his sense of command. She liked the 'big, splashy, funny' side of him. Having sized him up as 'instantly leavable' and 'not a grown-up', she had little doubt she could handle him. He thought the same of her.

Many years later Gellhorn would say of these days with Hemingway, 'in that prehistoric past, we tried steadily though in vain to be discreet'. When the hotel's hot water tank took a direct hit, the escaping steam 'made the place look like a corridor in hell' and 'all kinds of liaisons were revealed', said correspondent Sefton Delmer. '[P]eople poured from their bedrooms to seek shelter in the basement, among them Ernest and Martha.'

Living with Hemingway had its privileges. He did not assume her expenses, but she certainly profited from his easy access to automobiles and fuel, for which other correspondents went begging. She got her quota of his Chesterfields and the whiskey from the 'huge famous silver flask engraved 'TO EH FROM EH''. But she was hardly immune to danger or hardship. She proof-read his dispatches and dashed down bombed streets to deliver them to the government censors. She drove a station wagon for Dr Norman Bethune distributing blood to his transfusion unit. There were times when, just like every other correspondent, she had to scavenge for food. While

Hemingway thrived on figuring out the strategy of the war and scheming to get as close as possible to the front, Gellhorn worked with 'nurses in evil-smelling hospitals', consoling grievously wounded young men. As she subsequently observed, Hemingway never went near the dreadful military hospitals that Gelhorn visited so often.

On the first warm spring day in late March, Gellhorn and Hemingway left Madrid, swerving around vehicles, sounding the horn and shouting as though they were on their way to a fire. Out past the street barricades, they ploughed over 'gutted country roads' on a trip north to the 'red hills of the Guadalajara sector', taking blood to poorly supplied field hospitals. They were exhilarated, swallowing dust and liking the rocking ride, wondering what they would discover when they arrived. In the distance the shelling sounded like a collapsing mountain. Franco's army was digging in against a Loyalist attack. The Loyalists' spirits were high. They smoked and laughed, 'sunbathing and seam-picking' as the correspondents circulated among them. Visiting the American trenches at Morata, Gellhorn joked easily with the soldiers, saying she had arrived in a Ford station wagon 'camouflaged in such a way that you could see it ten miles off; it looked like a moving rainbow'. Milton Wolff, the last commander of the Lincoln Battalion, remembers her as a beauty who had a knack for brightening a soldier's day. She wondered whether the men were homesick. Their trenches prompted her to think of 'flimsy ditches found in empty city blocks, where slum children played'.

At the field hospital, 'a white farmhouse covered with vines and invaded by bees', she watched a doctor applying peroxide to an injured soldier. The foaming liquid in the wound looked like eroded soil, 'ridged and jagged and eaten in'. There was nothing to romanticize in this hospital full of 'desperately tired' men and stinking of 'ether and sweat'. Gellhorn saw a nurse seated on some steps, haphazardly running her fingers through her hair, obviously exhausted. At another hospital she entered a dim room and tripped over two stretchers filled with wounded soldiers. Both armies had spent the day tediously scraping away at each other. But the little town of Morata had become 'the hub of the world struggle against Fascism' – as *New York Times* correspondent Herbert Matthews put it – the thrilling place where Americans and the other soldiers in the International Brigade were stationed to thrust Franco's troops back from their march on Madrid.

Spain was not a depressing experience for Hemingway and Gellhorn. Matthews calls it 'one of the happiest periods of Hemingway's life'. Profoundly convinced of the Spanish Republic's right to defend itself against Franco's fascist rebellion, all three felt, in Matthews's words, 'the joy in man's tragic struggle against the forces of evil'. Before coming to Spain, Hemingway had been much influenced by Matthews's reports and Matthews had quickly befriended Hemingway in the Florida Hotel, writing afterwards that Hemingway 'exemplifies ... much that is brave and good and fine in a somewhat murky world'. He was 'great-hearted and childish, and perhaps a little mad', but he had saved Matthews's life on one occasion and proved many times over his resourcefulness and daring during the war.

Hemingway added spice and colour to everything. When Matthews, Hemingway, Gellhorn, Virginia Cowles and other correspondents watched a Loyalist attack from 'a much-battered apartment house on the Paseo de Rosales', Hemingway dubbed it 'the old Homestead' because it reminded him of his grandfather's house. In the precarious, unpredictable climate of war, he claimed to know the score. Hemingway's assertion of authority had a curious calming affect on people – even when his pretensions were ludicrous. Claud Cockburn, war correspondent for the British Communist paper, the *Daily Worker*, remembered:

> At breakfast one day in his room at the Florida Hotel, Ernest Hemingway was very comforting about the shelling. He had a big map laid out on the table, and he explained to an audience of generals, politicians and correspondents, that for some ballistic reasons the shells could not hit the Florida. He could talk in a very military way and make it sound very convincing. Everyone present was convinced and happy. Then a shell whooshed through the room above Hemingway's – the first actually to hit the Florida – and the ceiling fell down on the breakfast table. To any lesser man than Hemingway the occurrence would have been humiliating. While we were getting the plaster out of our hair, Hemingway looked slowly around at us, one after the other. 'How do you like it now,

gentlemen' he said, and by some astonishing trick of manner conveyed the impression that this episode had actually, in an obscure
way, confirmed instead of upset his theory – that his theory had
been right when he expounded it and this only demonstrated that
the time had come to have a new one.

Every evening, around eleven, reporters would gather at the
Hotel Florida in Sefton Delmer's sitting room. Delmer, a correspondent for the London *Daily Express,* provided a congenial setting to
carry on until the early hours of the morning. Sometimes there was
food that would be 'distributed gingerly' and always there were
enormous quantities of beer and liquor. When it got hot, Delmer
would shut off the lights and open the windows, turn on the
gramophone and play Beethoven's Fifth Symphony, punctuated by
the distant thunder of artillery. This continued until Delmer's rooms
were demolished by an incoming shell. The hotel manager would
not admit the hotel had been hit, fearing he would lose his guests.
But he had little cause for concern. Where could the correspondents
go? In any event, there was Hemingway – cajoling and bullying
everyone to stay put and not give way under 'fascist pressure'.

In such an intimate war no one could expect to stay and come
out unscathed. With no real division between the war and the civilian populace Spain became 'prophetic' of the world conflict to
come, Gellhorn pointed out in *The Face of War.* The correspondents,
the soldiers and their officers were familiar with each other and
could gossip on a first-name basis. In 'Visit to the Wounded' (1937)
she remarked that walking to the front from her hotel was accomplished as simply as strolling from the Metropolitan Museum to the
Empire State Building. She could see all aspects of the war in a single day in her travels from the trenches to the hospital to the hotel.
When she returned to her room one day, she found 'a neat round
bullet-hole in her window ... the maid had forgotten to draw the
curtain' and the police had shot into her room as a reminder of the
blackout restrictions.

Hemingway helped Gellhorn stay out of trouble. When Frederick
Voigt, Berlin correspondent for the *Manchester Guardian,* gave Gellhorn a sealed envelope as she was about to leave Spain, Hemingway
became wary. Voigt had gone around claiming there was a 'terror' in
Madrid: thousands of bodies were being found – although when

pressed by Hemingway, Voigt had to admit he had not seen any himself. Voigt assured Gellhorn that the envelope contained 'only a carbon copy of an already censored dispatch'. He was just making certain his newspaper would have it if the original did not arrive. Hemingway insisted on taking the envelope to the censor's office. The censor opened it to read an article about the terror in Madrid: Voigt had put Gellhorn in the position of smuggling an uncensored dispatch out of the country. Hemingway was so furious that he had to be restrained from punching Voigt.

Gellhorn and Hemingway were so caught up in their defence of the Republican government that they did not report the brutal elimination of various elements of the Left fighting for the Republican government. Soviet agents in Spain practised a systematic extension of the terror that would lead, on 11 June 1937, to the execution in the Soviet Union of eight Russian army chiefs and 35,000 army officers accused of disloyalty. Spain was about more than the fight against fascism; it was also about Stalin's consolidation of power at home and abroad, a power that would not brook any independence or opposition even among its allies. In his letters, Hemingway would later express regret about his failure to expose Soviet terror and in *For Whom the Bell Tolls* he revealed at least a partial recognition of Soviet tyranny. Gellhorn never confronted this ghastly aspect of the Spanish Civil War, preferring to the end of her life to condemn only the Western powers for their failure to intervene on the side of Republican Spain.

On 27 April Franco's fascist allies destroyed Guernica in an air attack and that week Gellhorn joined Hemingway in a tour of what he described as 'ten hard days visiting the four central fronts'. They climbed the 4800-foot Sierra de Guadarrama. From horseback they surveyed the Loyalist armies. It was often impossible to return to Madrid for the night, so they took their sleep in crude encampments or just pulled off the road. At one point they ventured out in an armoured vehicle, 'hunched in the dark interior', hearing the rebel machine-gunning rattling against the sides of the car. This was the trip on which Hemingway taught Gellhorn about different kinds of gunfire and when to hit the ground. If anything, she showed more courage than he did, for he proceeded with a caution born of wounds he had suffered in World War One. Her bravery moved him and his devotion to the Republic touched her. Without the bond of this common cause Gellhorn suspected she could not have become so 'hooked' on him. She remembered feeling: 'We were all in it together, the certainty that we were *right*. ... We knew, we just *knew* ... that Spain was the place to stop fascism. This was it. It was one of those moments in history when there was no doubt.'

7

A WINDOW ON WAR

1937

MARTHA GELLHORN had come to Spain in a spirit of fellowship. She would consider herself fortunate if she escaped with her life. Once there, however, it seemed inadequate just to absorb some Spanish, witness the war and comfort the wounded. She was a writer; she should write, Hemingway told her, Matthews told her. But what were her qualifications to write about war? she asked herself. And who would want to read what she had to say about it? What could she possibly report that would be newsworthy? Surely she would have to focus on some turning point in the war and all she knew about was the daily shelling – a fact of life for everyone who lived in Madrid. Yes, but being bombarded every day would certainly not be what people in other parts of the world were accustomed to, Hemingway pointed out.

All right, Gellhorn would confine herself to what she had seen and heard. She wrote a piece that *Collier's* called 'Only the Shells Whine' and published on 17 July 1937. 'High Explosive for Everyone', the title she gave it in *The Face of War*, her collection of war correspondence, more accurately conveys her feeling that the conflict in Spain excluded no one. This total war presaged a world cataclysm in which not just nations but whole peoples would be destroyed. It is an extraordinary dispatch – better than Hemingway's ego-ridden reports about Spain – because it is direct, concrete and deeply felt. Gellhorn's sympathy for the Republican government is implicit, but there is no editorializing; the writing appears to be transparent – a window on war. In this respect it resembles *The Trouble I've Seen*, for there is no doubt that the author has experienced what she has written.

Constructed like a story, 'High Explosive for Everyone' begins with a 'thud,' the sound of the shells leaving the rebel artillery with a kind of 'groaning cough' until they are heard 'fluttering toward you'. Then there is the quick acceleration of sound and the huge boom of the explosion. Shifting to the second person 'you' – as Hemingway frequently did in his dispatches – Gellhorn brings home the dreadful closeness of war. When the shells land very near you, they seem to whistle and whirl and spin, whining higher and higher like a 'close scream' until they tear up the streets in 'granite thunder'.

Using understatement the way Hemingway or Dashiell Hammett would in a story, Gellhorn alludes to her own hysteria by changing to the first person, describing her descent to the hotel lobby, concentrating on her breathing because the air sticks in her throat. The strict controls she puts on her language are themselves indicators of the discipline she had to maintain during the constant shelling. War is given a face, an intimacy and immediacy: a window shatters 'gently and airily, making a lovely tinkling musical sound'; in doorways people await the next bomb with 'immensely quiet stretched faces' while the 'whistle-whine-scream-roar' of the shells vibrates in Gellhorn's throat; a sliver of coiled steel is sheared off an incoming shell and 'takes' a 'little boy in the throat'. There is a delicacy, a light touch in the prose, that makes the ugliness of death and destruction all the more appalling. It is not just these people, this earth, that has been violated; it is Gellhorn's representative human sensibility that is under attack.

Having plunged her readers into the daily bombing of Madrid, Gellhorn turns to other vignettes of war: Pedro, a janitor, and his family are staunch supporters of the Republic, proud of the fine apartment they will not abandon in spite of the heavy shelling and hopeful about a government that has made it possible for women to have careers; four men in a military hospital – one with a bad chest wound, one with his face shot off, two others with a smashed knee and a head wound. The soldier with the bad chest smiles, but it is too painful for him to speak. The one with the smashed knee sits and props his leg on a chair, talking about his friend with the head wound, who is also out of bed painting a portrait. Jaime has always had a dream of becoming an artist, Gellhorn is told. Now is his opportunity. The irony is that he is encouraged to paint because the damage to his head has dimmed his vision. He must be encouraged to think his eyesight is all right. Without making a point of it, Gellhorn mentions that one of the men is Hungarian and this scene concludes with the entrance of a Pole carrying flowers, for she wants to convey the extraordinary diversity of the men fighting for the Republic and for (as far as she is concerned) the fate of all free human beings.

After the depiction of the military hospital, Gellhorn gives a brief account of her visit to a play put on by soldiers, one of whom has trouble remembering his lines but who steps forward to recite a poem he composed in the trenches. As in most of her pieces about Spain, this first one emphasizes the craving for human expression that waxes even as the bombs obliterate it. Each night she hears the gunfire, the explosions, and imagines what it is like at the front, thinks of the calm, courageous civilian population that carries on. When the city finally quiets from the last artillery exchange she knows it is only reasonable to return to bed.

Gellhorn has never made great claims for her war correspondence. She was not trying to create a style; it simply emerged out of her rapid compositions. She had a problem to solve: how to choose out of the welter of information precisely those details that best told the story. Her superb choices – highly particularized and yet exemplary – speak for both herself and her subjects. Her letters to her editors at *Collier's* give ample evidence of how passionately she cared about the shape of her reports; they were accounts that had to be as vivid as possible.

In some ways, Gellhorn was more fortunate than Hemingway, since he came to the war with a well-known style and an identity as a novelist, war correspondent and man of action. His dispatches show that he had become a prisoner of his public persona. Although he achieves many of the same effects as Gellhorn's – describing the 'heavy coughing grunt' of shelling, 'the high inrushing sound, like the ripping of a bale of silk' – his pieces have a curious jocularity, with references to himself as 'this half-asleep correspondent'. He can be as striking as she in describing the dead, lying 'like so many torn bundles of old clothing in the dust and rubble', and he is more graphic about war's atrocity – the driver of a bombed car lurches out of it, 'his scalp hanging down over his eyes, [sitting down] on the sidewalk with his hand against his face, the blood making a smooth sheen down over his chin'. He is a more comprehensive reporter, explaining the strategy of individual battles and giving close-up pictures of infantry attacks. A brave man putting his heart into the Republican cause, he never quite levels with his readers, never tells them that his side is fighting a defensive war and that its victories slow but cannot stop Franco's envelopment of the entire country. Hemingway presumes an authority, a self-importance that paradoxically makes his dispatches less compelling. He is too confident, for example, in supposing a soldier is lying about the way he was wounded. The correspondent/warrior shows another soldier 'having trouble with his rifle' how to unjam it by knocking 'the bolt open with a rock'. His work in Spain lacks Gellhorn's intensity, focus and unity – in part because he was expected to supply newsworthy articles, whereas she wrote for a weekly magazine that wanted human interest stories. She did not have to key herself around major battles or significant events.

Between them, Gellhorn and Hemingway employed what Phillip Knightley identifies as the 'two distinct techniques' of war correspondents. Hemingway presented himself as a 'battlefield correspondent trying to report the overall scene, to give a contemporary observer's account of how a battle was lost or won'. He opened up this technique by making himself and occasionally a friend like Sidney Franklin into characters with whom readers could identify. Gellhorn, on the other hand, concentrated on war's 'effects on the individual', and followed the intimate destinies of combatants and noncombatants alike. Her range was narrower but more profound. She never approached her material with the great novelist's glibness, conscious of saving his best words for *For Whom the Bell Tolls*, which he hoped would be regarded as the definitive work of fiction on Spain. She put everything she had into her miniatures of war.

According to Leicester Hemingway, some of the writing in Spain was a joint effort: 'Ernest worked on his own material, worked over

Martha's; she in turn copied out his material, and they combined their thinking and sometimes their phrases in magazine pieces under one by-line or the other.' Perhaps so, but these writers went their separate ways and developed distinct areas of interest and expertise.

In May 1937 Gellhorn and Hemingway returned to the States to solicit support for their cause and to promote the distribution of *The Spanish Earth*, a film about the horrors of the fascist onslaught. Film-maker Joris Ivens sent Hemingway telegrams reminding him of the narration he promised to write for the film and of the Writer's Congress in New York he had planned to address. Gellhorn took an important role in seconding Ivens's pleas. She knew Ivens associated with Communists and she distrusted their efforts to insinuate themselves into the Spanish *causa*, but they were on the right side in the battle to save the Republic. As Eleanor Roosevelt remarked in her newspaper column, Gellhorn had returned from Spain with the profound belief that 'the Spanish people are a glorious people and something is happening in Spain which may mean much to the rest of the world'. On 21 May the *St Louis Globe-Democrat* carried a news item quoting Gellhorn's prediction that the Loyalists would win because of their 'unlimited supply of courage'. It had been a 'tough bloody winter', with shortages of food and fuel, but the morale in Madrid was 'so good it [was] almost incredible'.

On 4 June a nervous, flushed, halting Ernest Hemingway prepared to speak to a capacity audience of 3500 people at the Writer's Congress in Carnegie Hall. He 'stood in the wings, muttering he was not a speechmaker'. Archibald MacLeish introduced him to deafening applause. Novelist Dawn Powell watched Hemingway and Gellhorn, wearing a 'silver fox chin-up', take the stage. In the huge, hot, smoky hall, with his glasses fogging over and his face breaking into a sweat, he jumped to his feet, tearing at his tie as if it were gagging him, and launched into a seven-minute oration before the clapping had stopped. The problem for the writer, Hemingway told the Congress, is always the same: how to tell the truth. He opposed fascism because it 'is a lie told by bullies. A writer who will not lie cannot live or work under fascism … It seems a nasty sort of egotism to even consider one's own fate' with the destiny of the world at stake. Rounds and rounds of applause followed him as he 'rushed to the wings'. A thrilled Gellhorn wrote to Eleanor Roosevelt about how he had put his enormous prestige at the service of a crusade greater than himself.

Fascism aimed to reverse the progress made in the past 200 years in democratic and liberal societies. Fascism meant a new inquisition, a reign of irrationality, and nihilism – in the words of a fascist general: death to the intelligentsia. Gellhorn addressed this fear that writers would be silenced when she spoke on 5 June before an 'afternoon closed session' of the Congress at the New School for Social Research. She spoke not as a public figure but as a modest participant in the *causa*. She marvelled at how little attention writers paid to themselves in Spain. They had come as a testament to their belief in freedom and individuality, expecting no recognition. At the front they had created their own newspapers, which had become a vital element in soldiers' lives. The writers were there to witness history as it happened, to give it a shape and an interpretation.

After the Congress Hemingway headed for Bimini to finish revisions of *To Have and Have Not* and Gellhorn stayed in New York, pestering her contacts in government and labour to do something about Spain. She implored the Roosevelts to send wheat, if nothing else, to the Spanish Republic. It seemed to Gellhorn that the President did not dare alienate American Roman Catholics sympathetic to Franco and was shocked by stories of Republican atrocities, including the raping of nuns – a charge Gellhorn vehemently denied. Of course, such atrocities had been committed, but it was not a fact Gellhorn ever acknowledged. Her dispatches concentrated on the suffering of people in those parts of Spain the Republican government still ruled.

Franklin Roosevelt, however, was concerned about more than Republican atrocities in Spain and about the Catholic vote. The strongly isolationist mood in America made it difficult for him – whatever his sympathies – to become involved in foreign wars. Bitter memories of World War One and Woodrow Wilson's inability to persuade the country to join the League of Nations meant that the President had to be cautious. To have made Spain a key issue – when neither Britain nor France was coming to the Republican army's aid – would have been to risk tremendous public disapproval at a

time when he was still attempting to implement his controversial
New Deal social programmes.

At the end of June, Hemingway returned to New York to record the
narration for *The Spanish Earth*. Gellhorn had helped in the creation
of sound effects to simulate the terrifying noise of exploding shells.
She poured out her enthusiasm to Eleanor Roosevelt and wrote her
several letters to set up a showing of *The Spanish Earth* at the White
House. While sympathetic to Gellhorn, Mrs Roosevelt thought
Gellhorn's feelings prevented her from forming an objective analysis
of political and social issues. Gellhorn took the criticism well –
indeed, she seemed to crave Roosevelt's steady, compassionate, but
sober interest in her affairs. At the White House screening of *The
Spanish Earth* the Roosevelts declared themselves impressed with the
Loyalist cause, but the US policy of non-intervention did not
change.

On 17 August Hemingway sailed for Spain on the *Champlain*.
Two days later Gellhorn left on the *Normandie*. They were still pretending to lead separate lives. On board she met Dorothy Parker and
her husband, Alan Campbell, who took an immediate liking to Gellhorn, although they did not share her 'idea of shipboard fun … an
energetic workout in the gymnasium'. Parker admired Gellhorn's
physique and judged her a spirited, courageous and decent human
being. They had a great time together, except for the sulking company of Lillian Hellman, who tagged along with the Campbells.

In early September Gellhorn, Hemingway and Herbert
Matthews convened at the Café de la Paix in Paris to discuss the
grim war news. The Republican government had lost two-thirds of
the country to Franco. The strategic situation looked improved
when Gellhorn, Hemingway and Matthews visited Belchite,
recently taken by Loyalist troops. The first American reporters to
conduct a thorough inspection of the Belchite sector, they scaled
'steep, rocky trails on foot and horseback and followed raw new military roads in trucks and borrowed staff cars'. There was not much to
eat, except for the bread and wine given to them by Spanish peasants. Cooking had to be done over open fires. They slept in open
trucks on mattresses and blankets. It had started to snow, but Gellhorn took it all without complaint. Hemingway was impressed.

For her *Collier's* readers Gellhorn described Belchite before the attack: a walled town, looking like a grey boulder set atop a hill. It had collapsed from bombing and shelling; the streets were impassable and the houses sagged. The smell of decomposing corpses arose from the mounds of wreckage. Household items were scattered everywhere: furniture, kitchen utensils, a sewing machine in the middle of the street. Soldiers had to work with their mouths covered. Gellhorn was full of grit – eyebrows, teeth, hands, clothes – there was no escaping it. She recognized some of the soldiers in the American Brigade, a part of the original 450, some of whom had never handled a gun before they came to Spain. Some had died before ever really becoming experienced soldiers.

In the spring and summer more Americans had arrived, having trekked in small groups across the snow-covered Pyrenees. How odd to hear these American voices from different regions sounding just the way they might at a sporting event or a hamburger stand. Gellhorn wrote about Bob Merriman, the Chief of Staff, who talked like the college professor he was and who became the model for Robert Jordan, the hero of *For Whom the Bell Tolls*. He explained the strategy of the Belchite attack, marking it out on a dirt floor, and he described the house-to-house fighting, the advance backed up with hand grenades and bombing, and how the rebels made a last-ditch stand with their machine-guns in the cathedral tower. He told the story shyly, a little awkwardly, and Gellhorn obviously liked his lack of bravado. He had pressed forward in spite of multiple wounds that were not treated until the battle ended. At this point the correspondent could not resist remarking on her enormous respect for her fellow countrymen. The soldiers enjoyed talking with Gellhorn, who had a gift for engaging them in conversation. It was just chit-chat, but they were pleased that this attractive woman had come to visit them – although they were not particularly impressed with Hemingway's celebrity.

From Belchite the three correspondents drove north towards Brunete, the site of a great battle in July. As they swung west and descended into a plain, Gellhorn felt the cold air that had been blowing over the tailgate of the truck giving way to summery breezes. High up on an observation post she tried to imagine what it had been like in midsummer, the sun and the bombers bearing down on the plain, pursuit planes shelling the roads and the Americans rushing up Mosquito Ridge into machine-gun fire. Now it was 'as quiet and beautiful as wheat country in Idaho'. In camouflaged cars dodging shell craters, Gellhorn, Hemingway and Matthews tried to plot out exactly how the offensive had taken place – on an exposed plain, with houses being blown up even as the Loyalists surrounded the village.

One of the correspondents' cars had British and American flags on its fenders as a sign of neutrality, but evidently fascist artillery men identified it as a Loyalist staff car. As the car bounced down the road, a shell hit the dirt about a hundred yards away. The next one tore up more earth nearer the car. Leaning against a shattered house, the correspondents watched the earth spray upwards, the road churning up into a column of explosives. In July the bombs had burned the fields and afterwards little 'purple flowers like crocuses' had sprung up. The correspondents left as the fascists continued their shelling.

On the way back to Madrid, Gellhorn, Hemingway and Matthews visited the Teruel front. The Loyalists had 'shut tight and strongly barred' what had been called the 'open door' Franco might have entered in a 'drive to the coast'. Soldiers slowly loaded donkeys with blankets for the winter, women in dark clothes walked quickly down the road on 'strong bowed legs, chattering like birds', devouring grapes they had gathered in the fields. They had fled Madrid and gone from Barcelona to Valencia, carrying essential household items.

8 October: Madrid was quiet as fascist attacks shifted to the Aragon front. In the good weather with the bars packed, Gellhorn wrote to her mother, mentioning a wonderful dinner with Dorothy Parker in Herbert Matthews's room. When it rained, Gellhorn and Hemingway diverted themselves gambling at dominoes. At the Sunday flea market one could buy canaries or silver watches that never worked. Gellhorn found Hemingway a jolly, joking companion – although they did quarrel and spent boring days hanging around the press office hoping for something new to report on.

Tired of war, Hemingway and Gellhorn managed to get into the closed Madrid zoo. The keepers could not resist compliments from foreigners who had come so far to enjoy the lovely grounds. Once inside, observing the handsome baby llama, a magnificent yak and the admirable hippopotamus, they began to speak about the war. How would anyone at home ever comprehend or sympathize with this unique event? In one of her *Collier's* articles, 'Men Without Medals', Gellhorn had tried to accustom her American readers – so used to the regularity of life, to the normal sounds of elevated trains and people walking safely on sidewalks, to the acute small sounds of a country night – to the idea of their compatriots who had come to fight for freedom in Spain. How could the people at home visualize a world where such different things got combined: a zoo and gun sites in back of a monument to Alfonso XII; a café occupying part of a smashed building, a shaky divider set up to hide the mess; four women getting permanents who stayed put even after the floors above them were hit by artillery fire. You could follow new traces of blood to the popular bars, but the people of Madrid simply refused to be cowed by these assaults on their existence.

During the breaks in the fighting Hemingway worked on his play, *The Fifth Column*, which is about Philip Rawlings, a Loyalist secret agent in love with Dorothy Bridges, the beautiful woman with whom he lives. Set in the Florida Hotel in a room identical to Hemingway's and Gellhorn's, *The Fifth Column* is a curious exaggeration – sometimes an inversion – of their complicated relationship. Bridges is a Vassar girl who speaks in a cultivated voice. She is obsessed with cleanliness and comfort. She dreams of seaside resorts and luxurious trips. Although she has talent as a writer, she is lazy and freely admits she knows almost nothing about the war. She rarely thinks of how dangerous it is to be in Madrid and, when the danger is pointed out to her, she accepts the imminence of death in matter-of-fact fashion. She is such an enthusiast and romantic that she tends to gush, calling everyone darling. She has very beautiful blonde long hair ('like a wheat field') and loves to brush it. Rawlings remarks that 'she's got the longest, smoothest, straightest legs in the world'. She is vain about her appearance, but that too she pretty much takes for granted. She has her moments – when she is passionately sincere – but on the whole she is a hedonist. Rawlings knows he should not tie himself down to this woman but confesses, 'I want to make an absolutely colossal mistake'. He sums her up this way: 'Granted she's lazy and spoiled, and rather stupid, and enormously on the make. Still she's very beautiful, very friendly, and very charming and rather innocent – and quite brave.' Although she cannot cook, Bridges has a knack for making things cosy and home-like, and Rawlings dreams of making a family with her.

As a Loyalist agent, Rawlings is assigned to investigate fifth columnists within Madrid, traitors actually working for Franco. He has a bad conscience because he has had to kill for the cause and because he has lost a good man through a mistake he could have averted. He has trouble maintaining discipline among the men he is in charge of and comments bitterly, 'I'm a sort of second-rate cop pretending to be a third-rate newspaperman.' He is also a rather big, sloppy man, self-important and condescending, and there is some merit in Bridges's accusation that he is a 'conceited, *conceited* drunk-ard. [A] ridiculous, puffed-up, posing braggart.' Rawlings ends their romance, knowing she represents a soft, humane side of himself he cannot afford to entertain so long as he is 'signed up' not only on the Loyalist side, but on the side of the 'fifty years of undeclared wars' he expects to be fighting. Rawlings realizes, in other words, that Spain is just the beginning of the fascist assault on democracy. Yet there is no question that when this couple parts company they are still deeply in love with each other. Something in their affair, and in the play itself, is unresolved, making *The Fifth Column* one of Hemingway's least satisfying works.

Martha Gellhorn was not stupid and Ernest Hemingway was no Loyalist agent. Otherwise, the portraits he limns in *The Fifth Column* are recognizable caricatures of himself and Martha. She was as fastidious as he was slovenly. While he figured the safe angles in the Hotel Florida – as Rawlings does – Gellhorn calmly accepted their vulnerability to bombing. She had come to Spain not knowing much more than Dorothy Bridges and she had a lazy, luxury-loving streak, a gregarious, ingratiating manner that men found irresistible.

Everyone to whom Hemingway showed the manuscript recognized that he had used Gellhorn for his depiction of Dorothy Bridges. A very confident woman, she did not let the burlesque of their liaison bother her. She considered his 'impish humour ... one of his most enjoyable assets. ... If he needed to portray her in such a light, perhaps it had something to do with his own conflicts', Bernice Kert suggests. At any rate, Gellhorn did not think Bridges a credible character but rather an extension of the divisions in

Rawlings's own psyche; she did not have a full life as a dramatic character.

This troubling focus on Bridges mirrored Hemingway's uncertainty about Gellhorn. Proud of her independence, he also wanted her to be his protégée. Stephen Spender remembered lunching with Hemingway and Gellhorn in Paris during the Spanish Civil War, and Hemingway boasted about taking Gellhorn to the Madrid morgue every day to inure her to the grim realities of death. Gellhorn vehemently denied Spender's account, accusing him of being an 'apocryphiar'.

The Fifth Column reflects a weariness that had set in during this second sojourn in Spain. The dismal November weather – constant rain turned the streets into a yellowish mud – bogged down the mood of hope that a new Loyalist offensive would throw back the fascist incubus. Rumours and paranoia spread. Hemingway, having lunch with the head of the secret police, suddenly left, fearful for Gellhorn's safety. He had to know where she was. Searching through the mud and the debris, he found her. She acknowledged his concern, but it surprised her. Usually her safety did not worry him. After all, every day they walked to the war and joked with the men in the trenches. Her only injury had been the bruising her head received when she clambered out of a dugout. In the dark trenches she had to touch the walls to move forward, ducking tunnel supports and skidding on duckboards in the mud.

In December Gellhorn reluctantly agreed to return to the States to lecture on the war, with her fees designated for medical aid to the Republic. An extraordinary speaker (she had also done broadcasts from Spain), she was certain to do the cause some good, but the hectic trips exhausted her. Hemingway had nagged her not to leave Spain. Jeffrey Meyers is probably right in suggesting that he treated Gellhorn's leaving as an act of betrayal. Meyers has pointed to 'the theme of personal loyalty' in *The Fifth Column*. Philip Rawlings's proposal to Dorothy Bridges parallels the offer Hemingway thought he was making to Gellhorn: 'Would you like to marry me or stay with me all the time or go wherever I go, and be my girl?'

At the end of the year, Hemingway received word that his wife was in Paris awaiting him and an opportunity to save their marriage.

She fashioned her hair in an imitation of Martha's. But when her husband arrived, Pauline could not control her temper. Nothing moved him – not even her threat to throw herself off the balcony of their hotel room. Yet they sailed home together to spend three fitful months in Key West. He had trouble writing. Making a home with Pauline no longer seemed to interest him. Fixated on Spain, he wrote to her parents that in Madrid he had felt free of his family and possessions and obligations. He had been on his own and truly his own man.

Gellhorn was not faring much better. She had left for Paris the day after Christmas dinner with Hemingway. She got sick from the rich French food and disgusted with friends who cared little about the Spanish Republic's plight. She cashed a royalty cheque for *The Trouble I've Seen*, using part of it to pay what she owed Hemingway for her time in Spain. On board the *Normandie*, bound for New York, she wrote him a glum letter. She wished him well in the holiday season but did not say when they would meet again.

8

THE AGONY OF HER
OWN SOUL

1938

O N 7 JANUARY 1938 Martha Gellhorn addressed 3000
people on the University of Minnesota campus. She compared Spain to a 'single cell where the body's illness could
be fought and arrested'. Dan Brennan, in the audience, watched as
she 'leaped, spread her legs, threw up her arms like a cheer leader'
and shouted, 'VIVE LA REPUBLIQUE!'

On 23 January Edna Gellhorn wrote to Eleanor Roosevelt
describing Martha's arduous lecture tour. Edna had heard her
daughter speak in Minneapolis and Milwaukee, and assured Mrs
Roosevelt that the accounts of Martha's superb speeches were accu-
rate. Eleanor would shortly hear from Martha herself, who would be
home soon for a brief break feeling depleted. On 28 January she
spoke to an audience estimated at about a thousand at the Sheldon
Memorial in St Louis.

Gellhorn lectured to a Chicago audience, including an enthusiastic Grace Hemingway, who promptly wrote to her son about what a
pleasure it had been to meet Martha. One newspaper account
observed: 'With a short black dress setting off her taffy-colored hair
hanging childishly about her face in a long bob, Miss Gellhorn
looked sixteen but spoke in a luscious, deep, free flowing voice with
words of maturity and an emphasis of authority.'

Gellhorn lectured in twenty-two cities in a two-month span and
hated it. She called her audiences 'idiotic lazy cowardly half baked
flabby folk'. They crowded round and called her an 'inspiration'. The

celebrity treatment bothered her, she wrote to Wells. She marvelled at the memory of him, 'collected and amused', signing autographs. She detested irrelevant questions about how she got her start and why she did not wear a hat and whether women should marry. 'Now which ones are the Loyalists, Miss Gellhorn, I just can't keep them all straight', she was asked. 'Oh Christ. War and floods and the unemployed never did to me what those audiences did', she told Wells. It was like trying to 'save the damned in one hour'. Feeling like evangelist Billy Sunday and Moses, she would awaken in the morning weeping 'bitterly and hysterically'.

Gellhorn caught a bad case of the flu. A doctor urged her to quit the tour before she broke down completely. So she forfeited the fees for the rest of the lecture circuit, returned home for a short stay and left on 13 February to recuperate in the Bahamas.

When Gellhorn arrived in Paris at the end of March, she found Hemingway in the company of correspondent Vincent Sheean and his wife, Diana Forbes-Robertson. The fortunes of the Loyalists seemed very grim. They had lost Belchite, over which they had fought so bravely, and were in retreat. Sheean and Hemingway went off without the women to discuss their entry into Spain. When they returned, they withdrew their invitation to Diana to come along. She accused Martha of engineering this sudden volte-face – although Martha was also excluded from their plans. Both Martha and Diana complained. Sheean left it to Hemingway, who remarked, 'Spain's no place for women.' To this Gellhorn rejoined, 'If Diana puts a foot on that train, so will I.' To Diana, Martha seemed like a 'boy-woman' who allowed Hemingway the upper hand in this instance. Hemingway and Sheean decided to take the train to Barcelona and then 'phone to say whether "the women" might come'. They did.

Gellhorn, now a seasoned war correspondent, sized up Hemingway's 'military pretensions', teasing him in the company of Robert Capa, the photographer, who befriended the couple. In Hemingway's room in Barcelona's Hotel Majestic Gellhorn challenged Hemingway even as she aped his gestures – flinging herself backwards as she sat down, stretching 'her legs in the elegant black slacks', running a hand through her hair and announcing 'Jeez, I'm pooped.' Sheean and his wife 'smiled. Martha sounded like Ernest's echo'.

Gellhorn acquitted herself well in the six weeks of dangerous reporting on changing battle lines and travelling along narrow roads and bridges lined with dynamite. Roads were congested with refugees, carts, lumbering animals and tired soldiers. Pink almond blossoms signalled spring as 'Martha and her companions dove from their small, open car into a ditch to avoid being strafed by a Rebel monoplane'. In one bombing raid alone she had seen more than thirty silver Italian planes in wedge formation dropping bombs over Tortosa. The civilian population seemed remarkably calm. She had heard a man walking down the street, singing to himself after the bombers left. The good humour and steadiness of the soldiers heartened her. The outgunned and bombed Loyalists retreated in good order.

On Good Friday, 15 April, at 4 a.m. Gellhorn, Hemingway and Sefton Delmer left Barcelona under a bright full moon. Overhead they spotted Italian bombers and leaped into the ditches once again. There were stories about the torture Franco's Moors inflicted on male and female captives, but Gellhorn never wavered and Hemingway was proud to have this poised woman beside him. Returning to Barcelona only for a bath and some sleep, she emerged at dawn to accompany him on the approach to the Ebro river, now in Franco's possession. They had to make a run for it through an irrigation ditch as machine-gun fire came closer and closer.

Gellhorn's grace under pressure seems to have stimulated Hemingway to broach, for the first time, the idea of marriage. A reluctant Gellhorn suspected his ardour would slacken if she became a wife, not just a lover. She could tell that making love to her gave him intense pleasure. But the physical side of it seemed 'the least important part of their relationship' to her. She had the best times with men who were her chums, 'chaps' who had no special claim on her. In a discarded draft of *The Fifth Column* Hemingway suggested that Dorothy (Martha) was distressed to think that she was 'fated' to marry Philip (Ernest). But now she wanted him in spite of her misgivings, not realizing that she and he could only be happy so long as she remained his mistress. Although Gellhorn would later concur that it would have been better to continue only as Hemingway's lover, at the time such a decision would simply have given in to his fantasy of having a wife, a comfortable home, children and a woman on the side. The paradox for Gellhorn was that only by marrying Hemingway could she assert her independence. She was not, after all, a kept woman or any man's plaything.

Gellhorn and Hemingway bided their time in Barcelona, then in Paris, before he returned home to Key West. In May and early June she prepared for *Collier's* assignments in Czechoslovakia, Britain and France, writing to her editor about her premonitions of war. It could break out at any time, probably in Prague, and she would take a quick look at conditions there before the shooting started. In October 1937 riots had broken out in the Sudeten German part of Czechoslovakia, where the population agitated for absorption into Hitler's Third Reich. On 11 March 1938 Hitler's troops entered Austria and the next day he declared the country part of Germany. During the first week of May the two fascist dictators, Hitler and Mussolini, conferred in Rome.

In a letter to Eleanor Roosevelt Gellhorn mentioned her need to earn money (she had given some of her earnings away to needy soldiers), but she vowed to return to Spain to see the war to its end. Although the Loyalists suffered severe equipment shortages, she assured Roosevelt that the Republic would fight on – if only American aid were forthcoming. A dispirited Hemingway doubted his future with Gellhorn. As Bernice Kert observes, 'He was sinking into the same state of helplessness that had overwhelmed him in 1926, when he was tied to one woman, in love with another and wishing for something wholly unpredictable to rescue him.' In Key West he began writing again – short stories and political articles that primed him for writing his next big novel. At first Pauline was polite, but after a few of his tantrums she turned sour. In the damp August heat the couple quarrelled continuously. He declared his loyalties, writing a dedication for *The Fifth Column* – 'To Marty and Herbert [Matthews] with love' – which he later dropped.

In the first week of June Gellhorn and Virginia Cowles travelled Britain, surveying sentiment about the prospects for war. London appeared to be a bustling, fashionable, thriving peacetime city. Unemployment had dropped dramatically as soon as the government began to rearm. Workers had enough extra money to enjoy themselves on a Saturday night with a few drinks. Housing was decent and not too expensive. There were the usual entertainments – like a Sunday cricket match. It seemed unreal to Gellhorn. She accused the great London newspapers of downplaying the troubles abroad. So did the radio. And newsreels were edited so that the public seemed scarcely aware of the bombing of China and Spain. Britain appeared to be a 'fine green island' unconnected to the ugly affairs of foreigners. Gellhorn went to a workers' meeting said to be about the imminence of war, but nobody mentioned Spain, Austria, or China; nobody wondered what Britain meant to do with all its new weapons.

Gellhorn formed her judgements rather hastily and without understanding the context of what she did see. Certainly the Spanish Civil War was much discussed, as was Hitler. But less than twenty years since the end of World War One and still recovering from the Depression, people tried to enjoy themselves. And a Conservative government referred warily to rearmament, given the Labour Party's violent opposition to it.

The ARP (Air Raid Precautions) had plans to train more than half a million people as wardens to manage the population when the bombs began to fall, yet Gellhorn insisted that the British public did not have the wit to see the preparations for war. The poor were indifferent and the rich were smug, thinking the proper response to bombing was simply to organize evacuations and supply everyone with cheap, ineffective gas masks. Gellhorn wrote to Wells, 'Why don't you shoot Chamberlain like a good citizen? What a man. With a face like a nut-cracker and a soul like a weasel.' How long would the British people tolerate the 'bastards' who ruled Britain? Gelhorn wondered.

After a week in Britain, Gellhorn spent less than a week touring France, finding the population not nearly so sanguine about their fate. But the country had no firm foreign policy. The government appeared prepared only for appeasement – as long as that would maintain the peace, no matter how dishonourable. Even worse, it had neglected to ally itself with Russia, a powerful military force. The slowly growing fascist party within France thrived on the government's cowardice.

France was mechanizing its army, concentrating on mobility and speed, and building up its navy. It had a weak air force, although new planes were in production. Gellhorn did not seem impressed with the Maginot Line. France could not go it alone. It depended heavily on its allies, especially Britain. Unlike the workers in Britain, the French were well informed. They understood the grim precedents set in China, Spain and Czechoslovakia. They impressed Gellhorn as conscientious citizens who realized that someone had to put an end to aggression.

Gellhorn did not have to penetrate very deeply into the French countryside to find monuments to the Great War. There were still dangerous areas of explosives marked off with barbed wire. Northern France had buried within it the bodies of thousands of soldiers from Britain, France and Poland. The French lived every day with the tragedy of war.

On a Sunday morning in August Gellhorn watched a parade of Social Democrats go down the main street of Prague, one of the world's most enchanting, story-book cities. From Castle Hill she looked over the dark roofs of the city and the soaring church spires. In the street stood President Beneš, his head uncovered and exposed to the bright light, reviewing for nearly half a day the floats and bands of his people, marching twelve abreast in impeccable harmony. To Gellhorn it all seemed extremely elegant and merry. The word of the day was 'Democracy', emblazoned on every banner and sign. The Bakers' Union advanced down the street with breakfast rolls atop their heads; Slovak peasants danced past with colourful, embellished costumes; Boy Scouts busily fixed food and ducked in and out of the smoke of a campfire on a truck that served as a mock forest. They sang and cheered, and saluted the president and the people. They talked about freedom and of the need to fight for it. War was less than a hundred miles away at the closest border.

It was not as far from Prague to Peoria as Americans might think. Sooner or later they would have to recognize the threat to their own freedom. On a sightseeing tour a guide had stopped the bus at City Hall and pointed out an ancient baroque clock. It dated from 1490, before the discovery of America, when Czechoslovakia was free. The country had its liberty now; it would preserve its freedom for the future, he vowed. This land reminded Gellhorn of

America: in back of the town of Troppau small hills reminiscent of the Ozarks bent around the countryside. The parade in Prague, Gellhorn implied, represented all free people. As in Spain, the citizenry were taking their stand against fascism. If only she could open American eyes.

In March 1938 Hitler annexed Austria. In May the Czechs partially mobilized their army. Gellhorn remained there to see it: Czechoslovakia stood as the only European country ready to halt Hitler's advance. In August, in Prague, she admired the high spirits of a people prepared to fight for their independence.

Germany surrounded half of Czechoslovakia, including its capital, Prague. A hostile Hungary on the southern frontier and an unsympathetic Poland to the north hemmed in the Czechs, whose allies, France and Britain, appeased Hitler with signs that they would not go to war. Even worse, Konrad Henlein, leader of a German nationalist minority, excited by Hitler's call for *Lebensraum* – more living space for the superior German state – violently agitated for unification with Germany. Other minorities, chiefly the Magyars and the Slovaks, demanded territorial settlements and autonomy. The fragile, ethnically diverse Czech republic, created in 1918 out of the break-up of the Austro-Hungarian monarchy, felt the full pressure of Hitlerian nationalism.

Which way would the world turn? Gellhorn observed the Czechs preparing for an invasion, for air raids, for gas attacks. There were plans to evacuate children, to conserve the food supply, to conceal munitions factories from aerial bombardment – in short, to do everything possible to protect the civilian population and to strengthen the army. But the Henlein Nazis – perhaps slightly over half of the 3½ million Germans in Czechoslovakia – spoke of the country's doom: the Czechs were starving their German minority; the Czechs had wilfully taken jobs that should have gone to Germans; the Czechs had thus caused the Depression. Nazi radio broadcasts provoked the Sudeten Germans (Hitler's name for the German minority) by claiming the Czechs had humiliated them. Germany was a major power and a 'great race'. Czechoslovakia was a minor power and 'a small Slavic race', complained the Henleinists, who saw no reason to be ruled by an inferior people – especially after Hitler's annexation of Austria.

In spite of these enormous external and internal tensions, Gellhorn saw a struggling democracy worth preserving. President Beneš had triumphed over divisiveness and helped to found a liberal democratic government. A treaty of friendship with France, Yugoslavia and Romania, the redistribution of lands once held by the Church and the nobility, and the improvement of living conditions for the peasantry proved the country's leaders had done well. Surely the display of the people's high regard for Beneš and their military mobilization would – if nothing else – give Hitler pause and shame Czechoslovakia's allies into finally opposing German aggression.

September: Hemingway joined Gellhorn in Paris in late summer during a cool and quiet period when the empty city resembled a village with friendly people. Describing this period in her novel, *A Stricken Field* (1940), Gellhorn's heroine Mary expresses thoughts about her lover John that paralleled Martha's own about Ernest. In Madrid and in Paris they had done wonderfully. Why risk a marriage? It meant becoming tied down and getting trapped in routine. The very nature of their relationship depended on absence, on their being apart some of the time. Perhaps marriage could be for the periods when they were separated, when she could refer to her husband and his opinions. Ernest became the wonderful John of *A Stricken Field* with whom she laughed and ate five times a day. She would smile at the picture of him drinking coffee on a café terrace in Paris, pausing to 'hold hands' with her on a sunny day, then resuming his reading about a boxing match.

Reuniting with Hemingway in the Parisian fall (after a brief vacation in Corsica) was a guilty pleasure. Gellhorn had left Czechoslovakia to its fate, not knowing how she could be of help, but still ashamed that she had the freedom to leave while her Czech friends were trapped, and sending Eleanor Roosevelt a 2000-word report on anti-Nazi refugees, some of which would later be incorporated in her novel. She took some comfort in supposing that Hemingway would somehow have handled it better. In *A Stricken Field*, Mary imagines turning to John to confide just how miserable she feels. If Hemingway with his knowing air often took an irritating, proprietary hold on Gellhorn's life, he also represented the one person to whom she could turn for strength. His enormously powerful ego had its positive role to play in her life. To Bernice Kert, Martha insisted that 'real life in Paris with Ernest was in no way as lovely as the fiction'. To be sure – yet he inspired her fiction.

In September 1938 Hitler demanded autonomy for the Sudetenland. Civil unrest, followed by martial law, put even more strain on the Czech state. Meetings between Hitler and Neville Chamberlain in Germany did nothing to resolve the crisis, but after appeals from Franklin Roosevelt and Benito Mussolini, an agreement was reached in Munich on 29 September 1938. Neither Czechoslovakia nor the Soviet Union (which had offered itself to Czechoslovakia as an ally) was invited to Munich. Germany occupied the Sudetenland immediately, with plebiscites to follow to determine the status of minorities in Czechoslovakia. The plebiscites were never held. Although France and Britain promised to defend Czechoslovakia's new borders, the country had been effectively split apart and its economy ruined. Beneš, under Hitler's fierce attacks, resigned in October, realizing he had no nation left, especially after Poland and Hungary took over parts of northern and southern Czechoslovakia. A democracy that on 3 September had been able to mobilize 800,000 men for war no longer existed by 8 October, the day Martha Gellhorn flew into Prague for her last visit.

From Paris, on 22 October, Gellhorn wrote to her *Collier's* editor, Charles Colebaugh, about her efforts to contact Beneš through his protégé, Jan Masaryk. Beneš was avoiding comment on the agonizing truth that Czechoslovakia had become a Nazi satellite. Police stopped her at the gate of Beneš's house. Although she got a message through to him, he refused to speak to members of the press. After other futile efforts Gellhorn quit, realizing that most of Beneš's officials in the Foreign Office were fleeing Czechoslovakia and the concentration camps to which she was sure they would have been sent. Having obtained translations of Czech state department documents, she concluded that the British government had behaved duplicitously, withholding information from Czech officials until the very last minute as part of a carefully planned strategy of forsaking the country.

'Obituary of a Democracy', Gellhorn's article about the dismemberment of Czechoslovakia, appeared in the 10 December 1938 issue of *Collier's*. She wrote of a people who had been stunned and betrayed, of Czech soldiers returning home with rapid but awkward strides. With dejected and confused expressions they joined their humiliated civilian counterparts in quietly watching the Czech artillery pass by. One soldier, like many others, was trying to find out what happened to his village. Was it Czech or German now? To Gellhorn he emphasized how isolated the Czechs felt. He was sure the French and British would find themselves in the same predicament once Hitler demanded Alsace-Lorraine and other territories. Poland would also find itself alone when the Führer moved to use it as a corridor to Central Europe. All of a sudden Czechoslovakia had been turned into a poor country. Its people, including the Sudetens, would suffer. Yet what could the Czechs do when their allies had refused to help them?

There was talk of labour camps for the unemployed. Many Czechs were trying to leave the country, scared by reports of friends who had been intimidated or who had already vanished. The Henlein police had begun to terrorize towns, to point in the streets to the 'dirty Czechs' who had opposed them before the Munich pact. Gellhorn heard from one woman who had been struck across the face by a Henleinist and warned that all Czechs would be sent to concentration camps. Indeed, there were already reports of new camps on Czech soil at Carlsbad, Eich and Elbogen. Czech women had been forced to scrub public buildings and military outposts while Henlein's female followers threatened and vilified them.

Gellhorn heard story after story of a people dishonoured and tortured, of Czechs forced to kneel before the statue of their founding father, Thomas Masaryk, and defame him while swearing allegiance to Hitler; of a people so ashamed they committed suicide by poisoning themselves or throwing themselves beneath trains returning them to the Sudetenland. She had seen an old man with his teeth and ribs kicked in, his limbs blackened and swollen from beating. He stood in her mind for the unbearable vision of a people degraded by fascist terror.

Gellhorn knew journalism could not convey the tragedy of Czechoslovakia. She wrote against deadlines and within the confines of journalistic conventions that put the focus on what she could immediately see and hear. She could absorb only so much at the speed required for filing her reports. Although her writing for *Collier's* bore the unmistakable stamp of her personality, it could not render the full force of her conviction that events in Czechoslovakia would shortly shake the whole world.

In *A Stricken Field* Mary Douglas, a war correspondent, arrives in Czechoslovakia more than a week after Munich. The big news has already been reported, but Mary believes she is recording historic events. Like Gellhorn, she is not interested in journalism per se or in getting exclusive news items into the press. Her writing is more than a trade or a profession; it is a commitment to fighting for a better world. It has grown right out of her anger over injustice and inhumanity, and it represents a crystallization of her deepest feelings about democracy and self-determination.

The war correspondents in *A Stricken Field* are a disorderly group of heavy drinkers, faded-looking and sloppily dressed, striking poses that will eventually appear on the jackets of books advertising their memoirs. Mary's familiarity with these reporters is the result of their frequent meetings over the years on journeys to great cities and to out-of-the-way places. In these circumstances she has developed much affection for them and has enjoyed their warm intimacy and banter. They are sometimes a pompous lot, but they have been honest with her and willing to share their experience and advice. If she has no special regard for their reporting, it is because they write less than they know and care less than they should about their subjects.

The kind of solidarity Gellhorn felt with her fellow reporters is best expressed in the scene where Mary, newly arrived in Prague, forgoes the questions she would like to ask her bored and tired colleagues. She knows they rely on her to divert them. After all, in their view she is a woman, not as well informed as they are. She does not count in the way they do. They already have the information she needs, Mary thinks, or they have little interest in the material she wants. By assuming a casual and engaging pose she puts the men at ease.

Like Mary, Gellhorn tolerated the male prejudices of correspondents. She could be very good-humoured about their chauvinism and held her own in a man's world with no hint of defensiveness or touchiness. She enjoyed male attention, relished her femininity and was not particularly bothered by the special category men might try to put her in. She would do her job, and enjoy herself as a woman and as a correspondent.

Gellhorn gives Mary many of her own characteristics: fine legs, a taste for beautiful clothes, high spirits and a sharp tongue. Gellhorn had always been careful about her appearance, for it had often created a sensation, put her at the centre of things and given her the edge over colleagues without her flair. When Mary arrives well-dressed and made-up for a gathering of correspondents, her entrance is taken by one of them as a provocation. He treats her like a model aiming for a certain impression, that of a woman who walks into the room like a heart-breaking beauty. Rather than taking offence, she welcomes the idea of a party and suggests they go out dancing.

When Mary first greets her colleagues, one of them asks if she has been with 'old John' recently. Mary replies proudly that she has just left John, who is still in Spain and still committed to reporting the Republican side while these reporters have gone on to their next story. Indeed, to a correspondent's remark that things have settled down in Spain she replies matter-of-factly that there is an impending battle at Ebro — the very battle in which Hemingway and *New York Times* reporter Herbert Matthews would distinguish themselves.

Although Gellhorn had scorn for the facile skills of her trade, she used them well. Her articles had the clarity and colour that Mary Douglas puts into her work. Like Douglas, Gellhorn collected statistics, interviewed important businessmen, politicians, professionals and celebrities, and gave a panoramic view of the places she visited. Gellhorn was not immune to the romance of her career, but it seemed superficial to her. The glamour of her role should be the least of it, especially when she reflected on how little she and her fellow correspondents really understood about the events they were covering.

The question Gellhorn put to herself in Czechoslovakia is the same question that troubles Mary in *A Stricken Field*. Given the enormity of the evil about to be perpetrated on the Czechs, what was one to do? With the Germans grabbing more territory, coal mines, industries, railroads and people nearly every day, how could one individual make a difference? After Munich, the Czechs were a beaten people. It was impossible for them to be individuals any more. They advanced sluggishly, unsure of their direction, waiting, feeling isolated and in despair. They had swiftly retreated into the security of silence. Prague was now a prison. The correspondents in Prague did not dare imagine what they might do to change the course of events. Government censorship often made it impossible to file honest stories; some reporters worked for newspapers that supported the Munich pact; others were burned out and unable to cope with the human tragedy they had witnessed. Czech police were directed to return all refugees (many of them anti-Nazis) within two days to the Sudetenland or to other parts of Germany from which they had fled. Rita, a refugee, asks Mary to help these homeless people; as a writer, perhaps she can rouse an international outcry. At the very least her words can put pressure on Britain and France, which in turn might force the Czechs to withstand Hitler's orders for a few weeks and permit the refugees enough time to find asylum in other countries.

Although Mary agrees to Rita's proposal, she is dubious that public opinion can be a force for good, since it is a lot simpler to incite anger than it is to ask for assistance. The Nazis had already proven as much. But Mary consents to visit the refugee houses in order to inform herself of the facts she will use to awaken public outrage. Like Gellhorn, who would send a report on the refugees to Eleanor Roosevelt, Mary is enraged and heartbroken over their plight, and determined to reach people in power and to press her case.

Under League of Nations auspices, a High Commissioner for Refugees, Sir Neill Malcolm, visited Prague for two days in early October 1938. Gellhorn was incensed to discover he had not seen any of the refugees. She accosted him at his hotel and carried on in her customary way. She banged on the table, raised her voice and made her plea. To her amazement, he asked for her advice on a plan of action.

Gellhorn described this encounter with Malcolm in a letter written some time in November 1938 and fictionalized the incident in *A Stricken Field*. In her letter, she gave only the barest details in a hammer-blow style that summed up the vigour with which she pursued her mission on behalf of the refugees. She suggested he see General Syrový, a World War One hero to the Czechs and now Prime Minister. Malcolm should make every effort to persuade Syrový to suspend the expulsion order. Malcolm agreed to meet

Syrový if Gellhorn got the American minister in Prague to arrange
the appointment. When the first secretary of the American Legation
rebuffed her, she telephoned Syrový, identifying herself as Sir Neill's
interpreter, and secured the appointment. Then she contacted General Faucher, who had resigned his position as head of the French
Military Mission because of his disgust over his country's betrayal of
Czechoslovakia. She primed Faucher to attend the meeting with
Syrový, telling Faucher about the refugees and asking him to praise
Malcolm to Syrový beforehand. In effect, Gellhorn manoeuvred
Faucher and Malcolm into acting as stand-ins for the very imperial
powers that should have stopped Hitler's drive to rule Europe. Her
hopes, however, were set too high. Syrový could not be budged. She
did not blame him, for she realized the Czechs dared not oppose
Hitler without much stronger backing from France and Britain.

Nothing could ever be the same for Gellhorn after Czechoslovakia. She had been brought up to see her fate reflected in the destiny
of others. Like Mary, she would always respond positively to pleas
for help because she did not feel she was entitled by birth to 'passport, job, love'. Gellhorn had grown up with this feeling: good fortune had to be somehow repaid. What you had was not yours alone;
it was meant to be shared with others. The thought of living at
someone else's expense, of enjoying liberties and luxuries others
could only dream about, discomfited her. In the world she had come
from private pleasure and public service were both essential to a fulfilled person. Happiness itself was not due to oneself unless it was
due to others. A world in crisis had to be reflected in the agony of
her own soul.

On 3 November 1938 Gellhorn and Hemingway made their final
trip to Spain. They knew the Loyalists would lose. In the third winter of war, Gellhorn's last dispatch from Spain reflected her own
ebbing hopes. The International Brigades had been disbanded. German and Italian pilots and soldiers continued to bombard Barcelona.
In an elegiac mood, Gellhorn praised the Republican army, which
had matured during the war and had maintained its good spirits.

Gellhorn, Capa and Matthews were among the 'last ditchers',
staying on after Hemingway left for New York in late November,
after thousands were fleeing to the safety of France. Naturally there

was an 'intense camaraderie and *esprit de corps*' among this small band. The constant hammering of air raids – sometimes spaced no more than fifteen minutes apart – destroyed the composure of even the most experienced correspondents. In such chaos and terror no one managed more than a few hours of fitful sleep. One night Capa stayed with Gellhorn in her hotel room and they huddled together in the dark, quivering in the cold.

Gellhorn tried one more plea to Franklin Roosevelt. Eleanor showed him Martha's letter: no other president in the world could lead the democratic forces. She spoke to him almost as if he were her father. Surely in this cowardly, terrified and directionless world there was one honourable and courageous man who could unite people by the example of his own bravery and force them to realize their responsibility to human beings less fortunate than themselves? Franklin Roosevelt did agonize over Spain, but – as Eleanor explained in a letter to Martha – people did not have a clear position on Spain and were not so sure as Martha about what should be done.

On 20 December Gellhorn arrived in New York. She had come home believing that Britain, France, and America had failed Spain and, as a consequence, had failed the cause of democracy itself. She doubted whether democracy could surmount this blow it had struck at its own values. A few months later she wrote to Eleanor Roosevelt: 'I am opposed to this oncoming war. I do not give a hoot what happens to either England or France. In a truly belligerent mood, I wish they could all be wiped out at once, and leave Europe clean for a new sowing.'

9

TRAPPED

1938–1940

GELLHORN SPENT THE Christmas of 1938 in St Louis
with her family. For the first time in ten years she celebrated the holiday in this traditional way. Eleanor Roosevelt sent flowers and Martha felt her spirits lift. She could not
ignore her sorrow over Spain and Czechoslovakia, but it comforted
her to be among contented people protected in their splendid geo-
graphical isolation from European wars. Then Martha Ellis Fischel,
her eighty-eight-year-old grandmother, died of a heart attack in the
early morning hours of Sunday 8 January, and Martha remained in
St Louis to be with a grieving Edna and then took her for a vacation to Naples, Florida.

In early March 1939 Gellhorn joined Hemingway in Cuba. At
work on *For Whom the Bell Tolls*, it made him depressed to recall the
good friends he had left in Spain. Hardship and danger there had
been stimulating and strangely soothing. He had never slept better
or felt more secure. He had bad dreams now; he had never had any
in Spain. He had departed from Key West, from Pauline and the
constant visitors who interrupted his concentration, and settled into
the Hotel Ambos Mundos in Havana, which had no phone. By 8.30
a.m. he was writing and he usually worked without interruption
until 2 p.m. every day. After that he kept fit by playing tennis and
swimming. At just under 200 pounds – a very good weight for him
– he felt 'happy and healthy'. Gellhorn admired his discipline: 'I owe
him the painstakingness of writing', she later admitted.

Hemingway had always relied on Pauline to critique drafts of his work and to bolster him. Now he turned to Martha. She called the new novel dedicated to her 'funny, wonderful, alive and exciting'. She also had reservations. Years later she remembered severely criticizing it, and that Hemingway nursed his injured pride by reading the novel to his ignorant hunting and fishing cronies, who gave him the unqualified approval she withheld. She had quarrelled with him about his work in Spain and she had a low opinion of the articles he had written there. Gellhorn, in retrospect, may have exaggerated her differences with Hemingway, although a comparison of their dispatches from Spain show hers to be much more crisp and without the attitudinizing and self-referentiality that began to creep into Hemingway's prose and that would become even more noticeable in his reporting during World War Two.

The hero of *For Whom the Bell Tolls*, Robert Jordan, is equal parts Ernest Hemingway, Robert Merriman (leader of the Lincoln Battalion) and the author's imagination. Like Hemingway, Jordan is obsessed with his father's suicide, thinking it a shameless, selfish act. Jordan's greatness is that he dedicates himself to others. His work for the Spanish Republic, his mission to blow up a bridge so that the fascist advance can be halted, are signs of his total involvement in humanity: 'That bridge can be the point on which the future of the human race can turn', he tells himself.

Hemingway gives Robert Jordan's beloved, Maria, some of Gellhorn's physical characteristics, but he scrupulously deprives Maria of Martha's argumentativeness, her independence and her sharp-edged humour. In Cuba, Gellhorn shared Hemingway's regimen of writing in the morning and early afternoon. Then they would swim and play tennis. Except for splendid meals in Havana's French and Spanish restaurants, they stayed away from the city's nightlife. The hotel bothered her. He had promised to find a house for them. Instead, she had to endure a 'small second-floor room' full of 'fishing gear' and his 'beat-up typewriter'. Always a fastidious person, Gellhorn could not tolerate the mess Hemingway seemed habitually to thrive in. She had real estate agents show her rental properties and she found a place with interesting possibilities only a twenty-minute drive from Havana. It had one storey, a sixty-foot living room, a filthy swimming pool, a tennis court overgrown with weeds and fifteen acres of rich farmland. Called La Finca Vigia, the site of an old watch tower, it offered a magnificent view of Havana. Hemingway took one look, said the rent ($100 a month) was too much, called the dilapidated place hopeless and went off on a fishing trip.

Using her own money, Gellhorn went ahead, hiring painters, a carpenter, two gardeners and a cook. Much like the narrator in her story 'Luigi's House', she imagined herself making a home for her man. It was a sensuous feeling, just standing on the doorstep, looking at the garden full of 'stringy dahlias', roses and the 'candelabra vines'. How restful to hear the humming flies, fat and sluggish, expiring at the end of the season. The sea breezes brushing past the eucalyptus trees, the fresh looking rock mountains arrayed against the sky, the 'three mimosa trees and the old well and the rusty gate' suggested a sense of permanence absent during her hectic pursuit of war. For the moment it seemed enough just to sit on the doorstep and enjoy a cigarette.

'Luigi's House' idealized the real thing. To Jane Armstrong, a State Department employee in Havana, Gellhorn complained about her new domestic role and the danger of succumbing to the fate of women who kept house and did not write. Jane, who had typed the manuscript of *Green Hills of Africa*, and her husband, Richard, a journalist with the International News Service in Cuba, were old friends of Hemingway's to whom Gellhorn quickly warmed.

Home from his fishing trip, Hemingway appreciated Gellhorn's work on the Finca and immediately moved in. His wealthy Cuban friends witnessed Martha's concern and admiration for him, but they wondered why he had to end his marriage to Pauline. Why not have a wife and a mistress?

Gellhorn put no pressure on Hemingway to marry. Pauline was no obstacle for Martha. 'Jealousy of other women was not one of her problems', notes Bernice Kert. Indeed, as Hemingway became more ardent on the subject of marriage, she seemed to withdraw. She confided to Eleanor Roosevelt, 'There are a lot of tricky angles to trying to do your work and still be a good woman for a man.' Hemingway wrote her in-house notes, reminding her of how much help he had been in editing her stories and how much 'Mr Scrooby' (his penis) needed her. A psychiatrist friend of the couple observed a Hemingway desperate in his fear that he would lose Gellhorn. 'The problem was not that Martha loved him too little but he loved her too much', Michael Reynolds concludes.

Hemingway promised 'I will never interfere with your career, your friends, nor whatever the other things are that one interferes with.' He did not share Charles Colebaugh's fear that 'marriage would interfere in any way with your career'. On the contrary, he romanticized their coupling, dreaming that 'we have been pursued by and fought gangsters, the gestapo, Nazi troops etc the type where you hold them and I squash their head in with a rock. Last night we did in Capt Fritz Weidman. You brought me the Lowell in the nick of time and I shot him in the stomach and we left him lay.' Hemingway's letters to Gellhorn often have this schoolboyish grammar and gusto. He liked to nickname her Mook, Ticklie, Chickie, Pickly, Bonglie and he tried out other monikers: 'Dearest Pocklechock (Alaskan for sweetheart)'. Sometimes she was Marty, one of the boys; sometimes Marta, his heroine of the Spanish Civil War. Without her he remained in 'suspended animation'.

From April to August Gellhorn wrote many of the stories in *The Heart of Another* and completed *A Stricken Field*. She slowed up in mid-June, complaining about fatigue and about the grind of turning out chapters, and took time off to explore the junk shops of Havana with Jane Armstrong.

Near the end of August Gellhorn came to New York to deliver her completed novel. *Collier's* wanted to send her to Russia and she began preparations to sail in mid-September. She also managed to meet with Eleanor Roosevelt and obtain a letter of recommendation:

> To All American Foreign Service Officers:
>
> The bearer of this note, Miss Martha Gellhorn, is an old friend of Mrs Roosevelt's and mine. For a period of five months or so Miss Gellhorn will visit Russia and various other countries. Her purpose is to secure material for publication by one of our weekly magazines.
> I will appreciate it if you will kindly give her every assistance.
>
> Very sincerely yours
> [signed] Franklin Roosevelt

Gellhorn was pleased – as she made clear in a telegram to Eleanor Roosevelt and in a note to the President.

On 1 September 1939 Germany invaded Poland, having prepared the way by signing a non-aggression pact with Russia on 23 August, which in effect nullified the declaration of friendship signed by the Soviet Union and Poland on 26 November 1938. On 3 September Britain and France declared war on the Third Reich. Gellhorn, still bitter about Spain and Czechoslovakia, despaired for Europe. 'I did not think it was a phoney war, I thought it would be a hell-on-earth war and a long one', she later wrote in *The View from the Ground*. 'The powers of evil and money rule the war.' But she had no idea of the holocaust awaiting the Jews. When she had last seen Germany in the summer of 1936 it was hosting the Olympic Games and the evidence of persecution seemed to elude her. 'I was obsessed by what Hitler was doing outside his country, not inside Germany', Gelhorn admitted.

On 13 September, during a brief stay with her mother in St Louis, Gellhorn came down with the flu and took the advice of her doctor and of Edna to postpone the Russian trip. She told Edna that she would marry Ernest as soon as he could arrange his divorce. He had driven Martha to St Louis, then left to visit the new Sun Valley Lodge in Idaho, where she would join him shortly. The Lodge's owner, Averell Harriman, appreciated Hemingway's 'publicity value'. The famous author would be photographed enjoying the mountain air, and the hunting and fishing.

Lloyd Arnold, the hotel photographer, had heard about Hemingway's failing marriage. The author seemed hesitant and barely audible when he introduced Gellhorn to the photographer in the dining room. But she made it easy for them, smiling at Arnold and inviting him to join her and Hemingway. Martha and Ernest were an informal couple. He sometimes referred to her as 'the Marty', and they were known to Arnold and other friends as Ernie and Marty.

For six weeks Gellhorn followed the Hemingway regimen: writing in the morning, riding, tennis and shooting in the afternoon. An 'ecstatic' Hemingway praised Gellhorn as a quick study who plunged right into a swamp in hip-waders, even though Arnold and Hemingway had to pull her out of one mud patch. This sporting life meant little to her, but she wanted to please Ernest. She learned how to shoot a shotgun. As Lloyd Arnold recalled, she 'responded to [Hemingway's] wishes with a firm will'. To please Martha, Ernest (who did not like horses) used to accompany her on horseback rides in the mountains. The couple carried wine and sandwiches in saddlebags. One of the lodge's guests, Clara Spiegel, whose husband knew Hemingway from their ambulance-driving days in Italy in 1918, remembers that Martha was 'a barrel of fun and sharp as a tack'.

In mid-October Gellhorn got a call from *Collier's*. Would she go to Finland? It looked as though the Russians might invade, now that Stalin had come to an accommodation with Hitler. This was the period of the 'phoney war', when Great Britain had yet to engage in an attack on Germany and Finland appeared to be the most likely place of action. She discussed the trip with Hemingway. She wrote to her mother that he was selfless in these matters, wanting only the best for her. Perhaps he could join her. If not, they would reunite in Cuba after New Year's. Martha needed the money, she confided to Edna. She was hoping to marry Ernest by the spring and she hated to leave him. Sun Valley seemed like 'paradise', but she contented herself with the idea that once married she could say to *Collier's* that she and Ernest worked together.

Both Gellhorn and Hemingway were reacting to the war that had started in Europe in September. She had always assumed they would get there to cover it. But his letters reveal his uncertainty about the role he would play. When the dates were fixed for the Finnish trip, Hemingway suddenly balked, complaining, 'What old Indian likes to lose his squaw with a hard winter coming on?' Lloyd Arnold's wife, Tillie, thought 'Martha's ambition and restlessness' drove her to leave Hemingway. Did she really have to go, especially when 'things were going well'? Gellhorn did not like making excuses or pleading lack of funds, but no one seemed to realize she had to pay her own way. She also had to admit her lust for adventure had got the best of her. 'Tillie, I suppose you're right – but it's in my blood and I *have* to do it.' To Charles Colebaugh at *Collier's* she could hardly contain her excitement, saying she felt 'husky as a well-pastured horse'.

After indulging his feelings of abandonment, Hemingway dropped the pose and praised Gellhorn's courage to his friends. Yet he could not resist saying that if he could 'just get her out every day of this short week of pheasant season that's left, it might cure that itching in her feet'. Martha asked Tillie to keep her eye on 'this big clown ... see that he's shaved and cleaned up when you go out on the town, and to the little parties – I'm depending on *you*.' He promised to obey Tillie and to be 'a good boy'.

Having signed a non-aggression pact with Stalin, Hitler had been free to attack Poland on 1 September. Two weeks later Russia took Poland from the east, absorbed Estonia, Latvia and Lithuania. Finland alone held out against Russian pressure. To get there Gellhorn had to travel through mined waters and not many ships risked it. But she managed to book passage on a small Dutch ship, the *Westenland*, and sailed on 10 November from Hoboken, New Jersey with a cargo of American wheat destined for Belgium. In 'Slow Boat to War', she describes food that tasted like 'boiled cardboard', dead bodies buoyed up by lifebelts and basketball-shaped mines bobbing on the rough sea off the coast of England. Finally, out of a fog she sighted Belgium, as her boat, awash in the moonlight, slowly entered the Scheldt River.

Gellhorn arrived in Helsinki on 29 November, the day before the first Russian bombing raid on the city. To Hemingway she wrote that the scene reminded her of Spain. The Finns would fight. Hemingway's letters bucked her up. She called herself a survivor, not the heroine he celebrated. Their life and their work were as one, she wrote him in a 'long emotional letter'.

Gellhorn described a war that started at exactly 9 a.m. in Helsinki. Women huddled in doorways saying nothing, showing no sign of hysteria or anguish. People sought refuge in the forest, exhibiting the curious, stoical calm of a nation determined not to be bullied by Russian might, even though they were 3 million against 180 million. Everything seemed frozen solid in the horrid cold, but the Finns knew how to manoeuvre and the trapped Russians were unable to hit their enemy accurately. Gellhorn wanted to push on to the front – ignoring the warnings of military men, as she had done in Spain. She reported on the well-equipped and trained Finnish army, and the high morale of the troops guided by a field headquarters notable for its calm and order. The poorly prepared, ignorant Russians shocked the well-educated Finns.

Seven-year-old Martha with her mother, Edna, and other St Louis suffragettes campaigning for the vote in 1916. (*League of Woman Voters*)

▷Well into her fifties Edna Gellhorn remained a handsome woman with considerable presence and poise. (*St Louis Mercantile Library*)

John Burroughs School while still under construction in 1923. The Spanish-style architecture, white plaster walls and red-tiled roof were intended to evoke St Louis' role as 'the gateway to the Southwest'. (*John Burroughs School*)▽

◁ At John Burroughs Martha was appreciated as a 'character' and her warm-hearted temperament led the school's *Review* to pay tribute to 'magnificent Martie'. (*John Burroughs School*)

In her senior year Gellhorn was 'perfectly cast' as 'the outrageous Vigdis Goddi' in John Masefield's play, *The Locked Chest*, about a woman who leaves her cowardly husband when he refuses to shelter a relative falsely accused of murder. (*John Burroughs School*) ▽

◁ Joseph Pennell, who shared Gellhorn's frustration with the provincial world of the Midwest, as well as her literary ambitions. (*University of Oregon Library*)

Bottom left.
Gellhorn's first husband, French writer and political activist Bertrand de Jouvenel. (*Bertrand de Jouvenel*)

Bottom right
H. G. Wells in his study c1935, the year of his brief but passionate affair with the twenty-six-year-old Gellhorn. (*Rare Books & Special Collections Library, University of Illinois Library*)

◁ A studio portrait taken in 1937 during one of Martha's lecture tours in the US in support of the Spanish Republican cause. (*John F. Kennedy Library*)

▷ Martha in Spain, 1937; she arrived with a knapsack and fifty dollars. (*Franklin Delano Roosevelt Library*)

On holiday in Sun Valley in 1941, Gellhorn adopted the Hemingway regimen: writing in the mornings and vigorous outdoor activities such as duck hunting or canoeing in the afternoons. (*John F. Kennedy Library*)

Gellhorn enjoyed a good relationship with the Hemingway children. Jack, the eldest, seen here (second from left) on a family shooting excursion in Sun Valley, and Martha were, as his younger brother Patrick (on left) noted, both 'handsome young people, blonde and radiant and pleasing everyone with their charm and high spirits'. (*John F. Kennedy Library*)

▷ Nine-year-old Gregory Hemingway (centre) who had had a difficult childhood responded affectionately to Martha's warmth. Patrick (left) was the quiet one who regarded Martha 'more as a friend than a stepmother'. (*John F. Kennedy Library*)

◁ Honolulu, January 1941. Hemingway did not respond warmly to hospitality Hawaian-style. At one point, bedecked with flowers, he threatened to 'cool the next son of a bitch' who touched him. (*John F. Kennedy Library*)

▷ Edna's presence always had a calming influence on tempers during her visits to Cuba. (*John F. Kennedy Library*)

On assignment for *Collier's* in China during 1941. *Above*: Martha and escort in the seventh war zone; as she made clear to her readers, the Chinese suffered severely from lack of equipment and supplies. *Below*: at a Chinese headquarters accompanied by Hemingway who accepted the role of second fiddle with reasonably good grace during Martha's trip to China. (*John F. Kennedy Library*)

One night in December the Russians presented the Finns with an ultimatum: unless the Finns agreed to Russian demands, Helsinki would be bombed off the map. Frank Hayne, an assistant American military attaché to Moscow now reassigned to Helsinki for the war, noticed a lovely blonde sitting quietly at a corner table in the Hotel Kamp restaurant. He thought she might be an American. It was Gellhorn, he found out, after introducing himself. Would she like to be evacuated? 'Christ, yes', she answered. He was a little surprised at her directness but urged her to get her things. Back in five minutes, carrying only her pyjamas and a whisky bottle, she obviously had been through other evacuations.

Gellhorn spent Christmas in Stockholm writing her reports on Finland and observing the Swedes agonize over how much help they should provide for their neighbours. The Swedes sympathized with Finland, for they realized their own precarious position: they were vulnerable to both German and Russian invasion. Which great power would move against them first? In 'Fear Comes to Sweden', Gellhorn advised her *Collier's* readers that the Swedes believed they would eventually have to go to war and reported on the country's campaign for military preparedness.

Gellhorn planned to be home shortly after New Year's, but she delayed her return long enough to travel to Paris, where she hoped to secure the release of Gustav Regler, whom she had befriended during the Spanish Civil War. In 'Good Will to Men', an autobiographical story, she wrote in detail about this disheartening period, which summed up for her the demoralized state of European civilization. The story begins with Elizabeth (a correspondent much like Gellhorn) at the Dutch–Belgian frontier. It is 4 a.m., she is in transit to Paris. Elizabeth and her fellow train passengers have to lug their baggage across the tracks to customs. None of the inspectors lends a hand – not even to open the heavy door for elderly people and families straining under the burden of their bundles. As the inspectors examine the baggage with filthy hands, Elizabeth realizes these are people who do not care about the destiny of others and who cannot be bothered to show the most common courtesy. The prospects for interesting the French in the fate of a German refugee are not promising.

It is a fatiguing trip. Elizabeth arrives in Paris feeling ground up and filthy. She has been done in by the foul air of the train, and by an angry and despondent dullness. But Paris is enchanting: the Champs-Elysées looking so expansive and calm and attractive, the Arc de Triomphe appearing like a magnificent 'dark ruin'. Everything is quiet and snow-padded, utterly different from the ominous silence of Helsinki or Madrid. Perhaps her influential friends in government will help free Max (Regler's name in the story). They want to know about Elizabeth's assignment in Finland and about her life in America as she searches for a way to tell them about Max. They reminisce about their days in the Midi when they were young. But her French friends are preoccupied with their war and have no interest in German Communists like Max – even if he is a fine writer and an anti-Nazi. The French are interested in the French, not 'foreigners'. Not very 'human' of them as far as Elizabeth is concerned. She is advised to return to America where she can indulge in her humanitarianism. In retrospect, Elizabeth realizes she has not been very tactful in pleading Max's case, but she feels he is a 'hostage' for herself and it is shameful not to work for his release.

After Finland, Gellhorn felt peculiar. For the first time in weeks she was not rushing to catch some boat or plane or train, or on her way to obtain some visa or military safe-conduct pass. This time there was no disaster to hurry to, no reason to observe people with a reporter's note-taking sensibility, making inquiries and writing it all up for *Collier's*. She enjoyed the kind of life that puts Elizabeth into a 'violent expensive hurry', but now Gellhorn had only Regler to think about. He might perish of the cold in a crowded camp with no facilities for medical care or hygiene. Regler remained weak from a near fatal wound in his back. Yet he always praised Paris and French culture, even though the French had put him into a camp only because he was a refugee/exile from Germany, in possession of worthless papers issued to him by the Spanish Republic.

An idealist, Regler fought for the Republic even after witnessing Stalin's terror in Russia. Gellhorn realized he was a romantic with a foolish tendency to wax eloquent about the working-class soldiers in Spain. Like Elizabeth, she saw these 'heroes of the people' for what they were: taxi drivers and shoe salesmen suddenly thrust into the roles of military officers trying to fight a war with inadequate preparation. But Regler was an individual worth saving, and Gellhorn now only believed in individuals. In 'Good Will to Men', Elizabeth is dismayed to learn that Tom, one of her most fervently dedicated colleagues, no longer cares what happens to men like Max. Tom is played out after twenty years of trying to awaken people to the dangers of another European war. Elizabeth's last illusions are lost when she appeals to Karl, one of Max's fellow Communists in Spain. Karl supports the Hitler–Stalin pact. Karl does not say so, but it is clear that he has no interest in freeing Max, who has lately spoken critically of the Communist Party. To Karl, Max is more useful as a martyr in a camp, and people like Max and Elizabeth are unreliable. Rather than following the Party's dictates, they have their own moral code. Suddenly Elizabeth understands that Karl never was her friend. He only played a role in Spain and used her so long as she complied with Party policy.

With Eleanor Roosevelt's help Regler secured his release, but like Elizabeth, Gelhorn no longer could see any principles at stake. Now she looked forward only to a war of survival, she later wrote in *The Face of War*.

After the debacle of France, Gellhorn could not wait to get home. But visa complications, problems with flights and bad weather delayed her. On 2 January 1940 she cabled Hemingway that she was terribly upset and sorry to disappoint him. To Eleanor Roosevelt she wrote in support of the Finnish fight for independence. Mrs Roosevelt agreed with Gellhorn that the United States should aid Finland but stay out of the war. She read Gellhorn's letters to friends in the White House and drew attention to Martha's articles in *Collier's*, calling them in her newspaper column 'among the finest on the war'.

Gellhorn managed to get to Cuba to spend part of January with Hemingway. At his urging, she signed a comic statement: 'Mrs Martha, or Mrs fathouse Pig' pledged that she would never abuse her prospective husband because he was a 'fine and sensitive writer' who should not be deserted. She stipulated that she had signed of her 'own free will and in [her] rightest mind and with love'. The childish prose did not disguise Hemingway's ultimatum. Since she had nicknamed him 'the Pig', becoming Mrs Pig would require a fidelity she had not yet shown him.

Gellhorn enjoyed January and February in Cuba, and wondered

what she had done to be so fortunate. Only Hemingway's heavy drinking bothered her. During one spree he had started with absinthe, consumed an entire bottle of red dinner wine and then switched to vodka when they went into town for a pelota game. Then he had downed whiskey and sodas until three in the morning. Yet he awoke the next day ready to write. This herculean drinking represented a 'counterforce' to the writing that sapped his energy, Hemingway claimed. He tried to make amends by taking Gellhorn to the movies, one of her favourite entertainments.

Leicester Hemingway, Ernest's younger brother, remembered Gellhorn joining them for drinks and a swim. She would dive into the pool and surface, laughing and reaching for a drink. 'That's my mermaid. What a woman that one is', a grinning Ernest told his brother. Leicester found her 'enchanting', a raconteur with 'brains, beauty, and the body of a Circe'.

Although Charles Colebaugh tried to entice Gellhorn with more assignments for *Collier's*, she loathed the idea of leaving Cuba – in part because of an overwhelming disgust with European appease-ment. The Finns had fought bravely but lacked the aid needed from France and England. A furious Gellhorn suggested that leaders like Chamberlain and Daladier should be shot. She was also tired and wanted to get on with book writing.

On 20 March two Hemingway sons, Patrick and Gregory, came to Cuba. Nine-year-old Gregory, not a very happy boy, responded affectionately to Gellhorn's warmth. She was as much a playmate as a surrogate mother. In his memoir he evokes an Edenic setting: 'Mango trees lined the driveway leading up to the house, and tall royal palms grew beside the path leading down to the swimming pool in back. Flowers and bougainvillea vines bloomed all over. Hummingbirds made their tiny neat square nests in the tropical foliage, and I could watch for hours a mother sitting on her eggs, one of the most regally beautiful sights I've ever seen.'

Then, in April, Hemingway's oldest son, sixteen-year-old Jack, completed this new family arrangement. He had first met Martha at the première of *The Spanish Earth*. He recalled that 'a gorgeous blonde lady' had dashed up to him and said, 'You must be Bumby; I'm Marty.' She was a 'marvellous creature' who could say fuck 'so naturally that it didn't sound dirty'. Depending on the occasion, she could 'talk like a trooper or a high-born lady'. The more he got to see of her, the more natural it seemed for his father to be with her.

Jack shared Gregory's admiration of the home Gellhorn had created, but he noted that to get there meant driving through the 'worst slums' he had ever seen 'and the stench when we passed the tannery was not to be believed'. Like Gregory, Jack held vivid memories of the Finca, especially the pool with its 'two Grecian bath houses and the trellis-covered terrace at the western end where the step led into the water'. Beside it, the tennis court, made of 'crushed coral limestone, pale pink', glared in the blazing sun. Beyond the wire fence was a 'stand of bamboo'. A guest house, vine arbours that provided shade, gardens of papayas and assorted vegetables, the ceiba tree and orchid plants completed the picture of this paradise. The house's large, airy rooms and high ceilings made the perfect setting for Hemingway's fine oil paintings, bullfight posters and African trophies.

Jack liked to sleep in. So did Martha. Ernest, on the other hand, was up early even if he did not plan to work. He wrote at a big desk next to a big double bed and bookcases. Martha wrote in a 'beautiful large bedroom off the east end of the living room'. This is where she had her desk and where she and Hemingway slept in a 'giant double bed'. Ernest had the better view. She could see only a courtyard and hear the constant coo-cooing of white pouter pigeons.

Jack called Martha a good sport about the typical Hemingway entertainments – singing 'old favourites' or picking up on the 'current Cuban popular songs'. Sooner or later, however, the boys would hear about Finland and the terrible state of the world. Patrick, the quiet one, observed that Jack and Martha were a lot alike: 'handsome young people, blond and radiant and pleasing everyone with their charm and high spirits'. Locating his feelings somewhere between Gregory's and Jack's, Patrick regarded Martha 'more as a friend than as a stepmother'.

After Jack left, Martha wrote to his mother, telling Hadley that they had had many talks about all sorts of things. She empathized with his anxiety over his college boards, remembered how awful she had found them. They were chums. She had even listened agreeably to all his talk about fishing – although she had to admit she had no experience at it and did not know the first thing about the equipment he described. She complimented Hadley on raising such a handsome son. She now felt like one of the Hemingways.

Hitler's invasion of Denmark and Norway in April, and of the Low Countries in May, outraged Gellhorn. She put up wall maps and purchased a radio, not wanting to miss a single day's news, and became fascinated with the fact that they could hear about the next crisis every fifteen minutes. She wrote to friends, trying to convince herself there was no reason for her to take the world's troubles on her shoulders, but she had an 'itch' to know more. When the rains came her perfect house spouted leaks and the living-room ceiling collapsed, showering everything with plaster dust

As paradise disintegrated, Gellhorn gave way to rage attacks on the deplorable state of the world. She began to get on Hemingway's nerves. Still absorbed in his writing, he made it clear to her he did not give a fuck about current affairs. She left for New York, getting there on 22 June, the day France surrendered. It felt good to be a little nearer the action and then to spend a few days with her mother, where she could feel spoiled and indulged.

By the end of June Gellhorn returned to Cuba. In July Edna visited. Martha believed that Hemingway loved her mother. Edna had great charm – Leicester Hemingway observed. But it was more than that. She saw very deeply into people's characters but never intruded into their lives. She had sized up Ernest Hemingway very carefully and told her daughter she felt sorry for him. Martha was stunned – and irritated. Feel sorry for this hardy man who had been so successful? Edna did not belabour the point, but her daughter 'wondered later if perhaps her mother sensed an emotional instability in Ernest that had not yet surfaced'. At least one Hemingway biographer believes that he began making his first veiled threats of suicide as early as his move to Cuba with Gellhorn.

Edna did not allow Ernest's unreliability to bother her. When he kept her and Martha waiting for two hours while he got engrossed in telling a friend about his new novel, Martha stomped into the bar, obviously beside herself with anger. 'You can stand me up,' she shouted, 'but you can't do that to my mother.' His apology did little to assuage her fury. He got up, paid his bill and dragged himself after her. Edna thought it was funny. Most people marvelled at the way

Martha refused to coddle Ernest, but he would value her spirit only so long as she remained on his island.

In early September Gellhorn and Hemingway arrived in Sun Valley, having travelled separately from St Louis and Key West – which seemed prudent. 'Absolutely lamentable females' from St Louis had spotted her in Hemingway's company and she did not want to embarrass her family. She wrote to Clara Spiegel that she had hoped to marry Hemingway in Cuba, but there had been delays that had put off the ceremony until the autumn. She actually preferred going on as they were. They had had four good years and marriage made her feel trapped. It did not help matters that her mother had advised her not to marry Hemingway.

Just before leaving Cuba on 23 August Hemingway had also written to Spiegel, expressing his realization that with Gellhorn in Sun Valley he would have his hands full preventing her from setting off to cover 'war, pestilence, carnage and adventure'. But he also knew she enjoyed the off season when fewer people spoiled the scenery. The spectacular landscape usually engendered her warmest feelings about America.

At Sun Valley Gellhorn began to assemble and revise her stories for *The Heart of Another* and Hemingway corrected proofs of *For Whom the Bell Tolls*. They were joined by his three sons and got along together well – hunting and fishing and riding. Gregory remembers having to 'be careful when Marty was around'. She tried to 'enforce discipline'. She 'had more primness than natural spontaneity', but he was charmed by this 'beautiful girl. … Her hair was honey blonde then, cut shoulder length, and she had a way of tossing it when she talked, not unlike a filly in a pasture tossing her mane.' Her eyes were 'warm and mischievous … and sparkled when she smiled'. She laughed with such absolute abandon that it could seem 'sinful'. He compared her skin to Ingrid Bergman's. It was 'fresh and clear, with a glow of perpetual health and purity'. He could talk to her about anything or feel just as comfortable saying nothing in her company. He adored the way she talked to him 'like an equal', taking his opinions into account.

Both Gellhorn and Hemingway enjoyed meeting Gary Cooper and his wife, who were also Harriman's guests at Sun Valley.

Hemingway wrote to Max Perkins in praise of Cooper's honesty and friendliness. Gellhorn was so taken with Cooper that (according to Hemingway) she wanted Ernest to dress better and emulate Cooper's clean appearance. Short of contracting some wasting disease liked tuberculosis, Hemingway did not see how he would ever make Cooper's light weight. Even if he did, he would be stuck with the 'same goddam face'. Ernest did not like having his rough edges smoothed. Martha had stopped calling him 'The Pig', but he did not mind arousing her fussiness. She liked him 'well barbered', but he let his hair grow, vowing not to get a haircut until he finished his novel.

Dorothy Parker and her husband Alan Campbell visited Sun Valley in mid-October. She knew Pauline was holding up the divorce and demanding more money from Ernest. Parker had known Hemingway for fifteen years. With women he was 'no cinch'. Gellhorn handled his tough-guy routines gallantly, even when she found rats in her sleeping bag. Parker wrote to Woollcott about Gellhorn: 'I think she is truly fine.' Parker observed Hemingway's children give Gellhorn 'love and friendship and absolute trust I have seen them come to her, with their paper and pencils, and ask her to tell them what to write to Mama. Well, just think what a cruel woman, or a vindictive woman, or even, God help us, an ordinary woman could have done with that. And Martha was just perfect.' Dorothy Parker believed that the marriage, now set for 21 November 1940, would endure.

But Gellhorn, all afire to visit the Far East, pestered Hemingway to come along. He did not expect to get much enjoyment out of going down the Burma Road, but he supposed he would get used to it – perhaps even like it – and then Martha would want to head for Keokuk, Iowa just as he had got used to the Burma Road. Maybe he would grow to like Keokuk, Iowa too, he wrote to Charles Scribner. It seemed that this couple could never quite find the right equilibrium but were hoping marriage itself would provide the solution. He drank less now, and she took this as a sign of a stable future. Although she rejected his suggestion that she write under the name of Martha Hemingway, she took no offence.

Then Edna visited Sun Valley and tried to persuade the couple not to marry. Martha had already listened to her mother's reservations, but Ernest, who had profound respect for Edna, was shocked.

Nevertheless, the couple were married in Cheyenne, Wyoming by a justice of the peace. News accounts referred to the marriage as Hemingway's third and Gellhorn's second. In St Louis Mary Hall, Martha's friend, remembered Edna's reaction to the marriage announcement: 'We were all so excited about it, and Edna said, "Well, we'll see, we'll see. Don't get too happy too soon." '

At their first stop in New York City Martha had to accustom herself to a deluge of reporters. She compared her hectic life now to a 'runaway elevator'. She looked forward to a meeting between Hemingway and H. G. Wells. Gellhorn's former lover 'took an immense liking to him' and seemed satisfied to think her 'a settled and a happy woman'. But a disappointed Gellhorn learned that Hemingway had not enjoyed Wells's witty conversation.

Husband and wife celebrated Christmas in Cuba. *For Whom the Bell Tolls*, an enormous success, became a movie property and Hemingway used his newfound wealth to buy the Finca. He wanted to relax. Martha wanted to visit China – to fulfil a dream of her adolescence. For a short week they honeymooned at home, where a part of her wished to stay – as Ernest confided to Archibald MacLeish in a letter extolling her beauty, their happiness, and her last-minute desire to call off the China trip and break her contract with *Collier's*. Things had gone too far for that, Hemingway had decided, so the trip was on with no more crying and complaining about it.

Martha called Ernest a good sport about the Orient and a darling at home, referring to her as Mrs Hemingway every chance he got. Although he easily managed to get an assignment from Ralph Ingersoll, editor of *PM*, to cover the Orient, Gellhorn knew this was her show, that she was dragging him along against his will. They would also be separated for several weeks while she investigated Singapore and the Dutch Indies for *Collier's*. If he had proposed to leave her for a similar period, she would not have stood for it, she admitted to Eleanor Roosevelt. Meanwhile, Hemingway boosted his ego by telling a reporter she had gone to Finland to help support his writing of *For Whom the Bell Tolls*. 'He interpreted everything in terms of himself', Gellhorn later told Bernice Kert.

Curiously, Pauline Hemingway's thoughts at this time serve as a commentary on the conflicts in Ernest and Martha. She wrote to his mother Grace about the divorce, expressing relief that it was now over. She compared 'The Heart of Another' to a dark forest and thought it a miracle that 'people did anything right in this world, considering what they had to contend with'. 'The heart of another is a dark forest' – the very words Martha used for the epigraph to the short story collection she handed to Maxwell Perkins shortly after the beginning of the new year.

10

HORROR JOURNEY AND HUSBAND

1941–1942

I N FEBRUARY 1941 Gellhorn and Hemingway set off for China via Hawaii. They found Honolulu tiresome. He disliked the excessive politeness, all the alohas and the leis wrapped round his neck. He was going to 'cool' the next son of a bitch who touched him. He liquored up at one literary to do and waved Gellhorn off when she attempted to cut off his supply of refills.

Gellhorn's ostensible assignment was to report on the Japanese army in action and on the Chinese defences. On 19 July 1936 Japanese troops had occupied Peking, initiating a Sino-Japanese War. The aggressors quickly invaded and occupied Tientsin, Shanghai and Nanking (where they killed approximately 350,000 civilians). By 21 October 1938 the Japanese had taken Canton and by early 1940 the occupying forces controlled the north-eastern third of China, including its major seaports.

The Roosevelt White House had asked Gellhorn and Hemingway to gather intelligence on their political ally, Chiang Kai-shek, and his rivals for power, the Communists. This may be why Gellhorn also met with Chou En-lai, an encounter she did not write about until nearly forty years later. At any rate, she could not wait to visit the mysterious Orient, the land she had read about in Fu Manchu and Somerset Maugham. Nothing – it turned out – was as she had imagined it. In her memoir, *Travels with Myself and Another* (1978), she included her trip to China among her 'horror journeys'. Hemingway, on the other hand, came with no expectations and proved remarkably adaptable to an environment that struck Gell-horn as the most appalling she had ever experienced.

The first stop was Hong Kong, surrounded on three sides by the Japanese, home to half a million Chinese refugees, and full of colour and excitement. Still in good spirits – indeed, claiming she had never been more pleased in her life – Gellhorn came down with a bad throat and could not swallow. But she shrugged it off and busily cultivated sources, making arrangements to travel to the front. Hem-ingway collected an entourage wherever he went. It did not matter to him whether they were city cops or crooked Chinese business-men and gangsters. Hemingway was a hunting man, a drinking man. Forget talk about politics or literature. Set him down with a vast liquor supply and he would listen to the stories of the locals or entertain them with anecdotes. Gellhorn had little patience for these marathon bullshit sessions. 'M. is going off to take the pulse of the nation', he would amiably inform his cronies as she crept away.

Gellhorn and Hemingway did their flying in China on the CNAC (China National Aviation Company), the only part of roughing it in China she really liked. The company flew freight and passengers in DC2s and DC3s with steeply sloped floors, canvas chairs encased in metal frames and toilets concealed by green curtains that provided a tiny rounded picture of the land below. With no sophisti-cated instrumentation and unpressurized cabins, pilots like the redoubtable Roy Leonard flew after dark in bad weather to elude the Japanese air force. The amenities in these unheated planes were coarse blankets and paper bags for vomiting. Landing was never easy, since the Japanese bombed airfields. Runways had to be constantly moved and rebuilt. Gellhorn loved this seat-of-the-pants flying.

Hemingway delighted in Chinese novelties: snake wine, other local brews, delicacies and firecrackers. The wine had healing prop-erties and prevented baldness, he claimed, and he collected bottles of it for friends. 'Very disappointed' that Gellhorn demanded he stop lighting firecrackers in their room, he diverted himself with a boxing partner and horse racing. So what if the Chinese cheated by apply-ing dye to the horses? Gellhorn grew more dismayed every day at the sight of pathetic opium dens and slimy brothels. She inspected the legal system and other institutions. People slept on the pave-ment. This hungry and feeble slave culture, hawking and spitting on the street, afflicted with malaria, tuberculosis, leprosy and cholera, roads deluged in mud and the most primitive plumbing she had ever seen, repelled her. People smelled like shit. The overcrowding made her claustrophobic and hysterical. She had to leave at once!

Hemingway told Gellhorn: do not suppose these people take the world as you do. He saw more than the exploited masses. He saw people having children, setting off firecrackers and in some measure enjoying life – even if it did not square with her principles. Why judge China by standards it had not set for itself? In their hotel room in Shaokwan, she noticed they had only one bowl. What should be the washing procedure? Their teeth first, then their faces? Do not wash at all, Hemingway advised her. In retrospect, she deemed his attitude 'heroic'.

Out in the field on a reporting assignment, Gellhorn did not know where to relieve herself. No trees or bushes. Just the mud and the 'bare rice paddies'. A latrine, some kind of bamboo monument, could be got at only by climbing a flimsy ladder. From the top of the tower excrement dropped into a 'five-foot-tall Ali Baba jar'. Gellhorn told Hemingway it was not for her. No one had supposed it was, he replied. Try the duck pond – a favourite of the locals – he suggested. That was worse. She began to edge up the shaky ladder when the air raid alarm sounded. Hemingway called to her: what to do now? She would stay aloft, she told him. The planes quickly flew over and Gellhorn descended to a laughing Hemingway. What an ignominious death it would have been, he pointed out. How would he have explained her demise to a world that knew her as a daunt- less journalist? Or, as she once described herself to her *Collier's* edi- tor, the 'disaster girl'.

Watching a group of lepers in various stages of physical disinte- gration, Gellhorn suddenly remarked she had had enough. 'So far,' Hemingway replied, 'we've still got our noses.' Gellhorn found most government officials insufferable and showed little interest in the military officers. Her interpreter, Mr Ma, spoke both Chinese and English very poorly. He had two American college degrees, loved to eat, knew nothing about military operations and not much about anything else. Gellhorn wanted to know why a certain mountain had been burned. To free it of the tigers who ate the vegetation, Mr Ma replied. Now they would look somewhere else for food, her perceptive guide pointed out. Gellhorn liked that goofy explanation: 'vegetarian tigers'. And the name of that tree, Mr Ma? 'Ordinary tree', the authoritative interpreter replied.

Gellhorn did her duty collecting information for *Collier's*. Her readers learned about the nine war zones, the Japanese drive to divide and conquer China, the Chinese army's lack of equipment and supplies (5 million superbly disciplined men who had no shoes), the gross underpayment of soldiers and the hatred of the Japanese that made it virtually impossible to prevent Chinese soldiers from killing their prisoners. She and Hemingway travelled in the seventh war zone, a territory the size of Belgium held by 150,000 Chinese troops.

Hemingway did the lion's share of public speaking, drinking Chinese officers under the table and in general behaving quite extraordinarily as a patriotic American sincerely concerned with giving comfort to his country's ally. Gellhorn never did learn to tolerate the burping and farting sounds the Chinese made while eating, overflowing toilets and grimy hotel rooms covered with mashed bedbugs. As Gellhorn realized, Hemingway nailed her when he observed: 'M. loves humanity but can't stand people.' Her rather lofty view of the world rejected life in the raw.

The Hemingways had a memorable meeting with the Generalissimo and Madame Chiang. For her *Collier's* readers Gellhorn gave a lavishly attractive picture of the couple, including Madame's Chiang's bewitching smile, movie star figure, luscious skin and smooth features – even the way she applied her make-up (rouge, lipstick and 'a faint dark eye shadow') and the way her 'ink-black hair' swelled 'back from her forehead' and was 'caught in a knot at the nape of her neck'. As in all her *Collier's* reports, Gellhorn avoided expressing her political opinions. Instead, she concentrated on how hard Madame Chiang worked, getting up at six-thirty in the morning and not retiring until about midnight, and on her complete devotion to her husband's rule of China. After spending a quiet hour with him in the morning, she would answer correspondence, later receive important government officials, visit schools, hospitals and other institutions, compare notes with her husband on an afternoon walk, then after dinner receive guests (foreigners) and work at her desk until bedtime. Gellhorn was rather surprised when Madame

Chiang suddenly asked her if she found it difficult to be a wife. It was an 'okay job', Gellhorn replied and quickly changed the subject, not wanting to compare her problems with Madame Chiang's. Gellhorn then quoted Madame Chiang's statement that she always dropped everything when her husband wanted to talk or to go for a walk. It was difficult being on call but her 'duty' was to him. In her devotion she resembled 'all other women', Gellhorn commented, who found their lives interrupted by their husbands' demands, not wanting to disappoint them.

A reader of Gellhorn's *Collier's* article would never have suspected that she was intensely critical of the Generalissimo and his wife. The Chiangs were not prepared to acknowledge their authoritarian government, and Gellhorn as their guest felt constricted by their hospitality and their position as American allies. She made Madame Chiang angry when she asked why the government did not help the lepers. A furious Gellhorn then had to sit through a lecture on Chinese civilization. Not knowing much about China when they arrived, Gellhorn and Hemingway realized only later just how much propaganda the Chiangs had spoken.

In a clandestine meeting with Chou En-lai, Gellhorn was impressed by his simple clothes and his apparent ease with Westerners. She marvelled that they could share the same jokes, since Chinese humour had seemed entirely foreign to her. Although living underground, he appeared to represent the country's future. She did not know enough to judge or to remember what he said. Rather, his demeanour convinced her that the Communists would prevail. Hemingway concurred, reporting to the Office of Naval Intelligence and to Henry Morgenthau, Secretary of the Treasury, that Chou was 'brilliant, charming, and intelligent'.

Towards the end of the trip Gellhorn contracted the 'China rot', a skin disease that made her hands peel. It was not – Hemingway hoped – the first sign that her nose would fall off. The remedy, an application of foul-smelling ointment, required her to wear gloves to prevent the spread of the disease. Hemingway preferred to keep 'upwind' of her. Yet he had been such a good sport all along that she felt immensely grateful to him.

The first stop after leaving China was Rangoon. It had a large Chinese population and was part of the Burma Road that served as

Chiang Kai-shek's army supply line. In the intense heat Hemingway behaved like a 'beached whale' and Gellhorn had trouble breathing. She put out her hand to touch him, to express her gratitude. 'Take your filthy dirty hands off me!' he shouted. They watched each other in 'shocked silence'. Was this the end of their 'horror journey'? They rolled on the cool marble floor, 'laughing in [their] separate pools of sweat'.

Gellhorn's *Collier's* pieces on China had one simple message: the Chinese would endure. It did not matter that the Japanese controlled much of the country. The Chinese could take any amount of suffering and hardship. Exhausted after nine hours of riding horses, with nothing to eat or drink, Gellhorn observed that her Chinese companions seemed as fresh as ever. She and Hemingway visited a thousand-acre airfield the Chinese had built without machinery in a hundred days. Later, in St Louis, Hemingway showed a reporter a picture of 75,000 Chinese working on this airfield, 'mixing concrete by wading in it and tromping the gravel in, like peasants crushing grapes with their bare feet to make wine'. They would outlast foreign conquerors. 'In the long run,' Gellhorn told her Chinese interpreter, 'I'd hate to be Japanese.'

For the most part Gellhorn and Hemingway pursued separate news stories, although she admitted borrowing (with Hemingway's sanction) some of the intelligence he had gathered on the Cheng-Tu airfield. He had turned down several assignments (at a dollar a word) about the front because he did not want to compete with his wife. He was more than a little nettled when one of *Collier's* editors accused him of scooping his wife on the Cheng-Tu airfield piece. He pointed out that the magazine had got a bargain with him along on the trip acting as Gellhorn's 'courier, bedbug sprayer and safari organizer'.

In May of 1941 Hemingway began his journey back to Cuba while Gellhorn finished up with a few more reporting assignments in Java and Singapore. In Honolulu he wrote her one of his most endearing letters, confessing that he had been 'just gnawing sick dumb lonely for you'. He catalogued his desire: 'I love you … like a caribou loves mud … like Mr Roosevelt loves his place in history … like Mrs Chiang Kai-Shek loves being Mrs Chiang Kai-Shek … like the sea loves the beach and rolls on it all the time.'

During the summer of 1941 in Cuba the Hemingways special-ized in improvised late suppers and Sunday pool parties. They invited guests from the American embassy, who observed a disor-ganized if genial host. Martha liked eating late and sleeping in, but keeping the chaos under control amounted to a full-time job. Like his other women, Gellhorn deplored his unhygenic habits, including dirty fingernails and hair. She told one female friend that he thought nothing of greeting her at the front door of the Finca, his drawers down, ready for sexual play. He considered it manly to be dirty. He took his revenge years later when he told A. E. Hotchner:

> She liked everything sanitary. Her father was a doctor so she made our house look as much like a hospital as possible. No animal heads, no matter how beautiful, because they were unsanitary. Her *Time* friends all came down to the 'Finca', dressed in pressed flannels, to play impeccable, pity-pat tennis. My pelota pals also played, but they played rough. They would jump into the pool all sweated and with-out showering because they said only fairies took showers. ... That began the friction between Miss Martha and me – my pelota friends dirtying up her *Time* pals!

Hemingway's vile-smelling tomcats roamed everywhere – including on the dining-room table. Gellhorn had to instruct inept servants about cooking, although she knew virtually nothing about prepar-ing meals.

Hemingway did not exaggerate by very much, for Gellhorn admitted she liked her home to be as 'shiny as my German soul requires'. Instead, she got involved in 'domestic dramas', mentioning an instance in which the maid knifed the cook. Sensitive about how the poor lived since her FERA days, she tried to make her servants' home life a 'thing of beauty'. But Hemingway called her a fool because the servants kept turning their quarters into a 'temporary pigsty'. Gellhorn could see the humour of her efforts, yet 'I keep doing these things', she confessed to friends.

The Heart of Another appeared in the fall when Gellhorn and Hem-ingway were enjoying a healthy holiday in Sun Valley. Good reviews confirmed her belief that it was her best book yet. It had depth and the promise of better work to come. Hemingway had hovered over the production, advising Max Perkins (who edited both husband and wife) on book design and promotion, as well as taking Gellhorn's dust jacket photograph. Reviewers commented on the result: 'Pure Hemingway – romantic under a surface of hardness.' Every writer in America had been influenced by Hemingway, Gellhorn suggested to Eleanor Roosevelt.

The stories set in Cuba, Finland, Germany, Spain and France read like a virtual map of Gellhorn's own itinerary. 'Luigi's House' followed the fanatical desire of a fastidious woman to make her home a special, comfortable place for her husband, returning from the Spanish Civil War. In her efforts to spruce up the place she has to dislodge Luigi, a peasant who has lived a rather decrepit existence taking care of the vines on the property. She cannot understand why he so fiercely resents her improvements and he is incapable of telling her he fears her ultimate aim is to throw him off the land. Her confident manner is so unsettling that the man finally hangs himself. It is as if Gellhorn were writing a cautionary tale for herself, pointing out the consequences of her mania for improving the world.

'November Afternoon' grew out of days Gellhorn and Hemingway had spent in France in 1938, when he was still weighing his commitment to Pauline against his romantic interludes with Martha. The story's couple walk along a river canal. The woman comments on the pleasant, settled life people have on barges. The man asks a workman what he is fishing. The woman soaks in the lovely smell of the water and the leaves. The man concentrates on the fish. He walks quickly away from his companion, alone with his thoughts. Sensing she is snubbed, she follows him without haste, reflecting on her 'unreal problems', the problems the rich have with their relationships – not the genuine problems like catching fish, worrying about cargo on a barge or getting the washing done. She is fed up with the passions of her heart. His steady aloofness turns her frustration into anger over their predicament. Why did they have to make life so complicated? Yet why should she shoulder the blame when he was the one who would not settle down? The man feels torn in many directions, obligated to others and concerned that he should not hurt or disappoint them. The couple eventually return to the city after failing to find a country place for the weekend and the woman fears she has driven him away. The characters in the story are not named and the male character's responsibilities are not identified, but the precarious state of the woman's feelings − her wish to know where she stands in her man's life − are evocative of the ambiguous position Gellhorn found herself in, one that not even marriage to Hemingway could clarify.

Several stories in *The Heart of Another* have a female narrator or centre of consciousness cut off from others by her impregnable self-sufficiency. It is not that Gellhorn or her female alter egos cannot feel for others; rather, her accomplished women lack a certain susceptibility. They do not have the openness to experience that Hemingway recommended. Except in 'Luigi's House' there is, in the words of one reviewer, no 'driving force or emotional centre' in the stories.

There was an air about Gellhorn, a way she had of arrogating the atmosphere to herself, that could be imperious and offputting when it was not comical. During a Sun Valley−Grand Canyon vacation with Ernest in December, she stopped at a Navaho trading post in a dusty little town. Martha, 'blonde and chic, stood at the counter'. In what Ernest remembered as her 'best Bryn Mawr manner' she called out rather haughtily, 'Have you any beads? I want to see some beads.' Bent over a display case near her, an aged Indian extracted from his pocket one bead no bigger than a pinhead. 'Here bead', the ancient one said, gravely offering it to Martha. 'Now you see bead.'

Gellhorn and Hemingway were in a bar outside Tucson, Arizona when they heard the news of Pearl Harbor. Hemingway was angry at the destruction of the American fleet. Gellhorn longed for a European assignment, even though she believed just as strongly that she and Hemingway should retire to Cuba and work on their fiction. In a letter to Charles Scribner, Hemingway reported her contentedness. He was still very much taken with her beauty and reassured by her eagerness to get back to Cuba. On 12 December he wrote to Scribner from San Antonio about a wonderful tour in Indian country. He had never seen Martha look lovelier or more cheerful.

January 1942: Bent over contour maps, Gellhorn studied war. She read about arms and tactics. She rued the fact that women were not allowed into combat zones and would trade in her sex for a shot at reporting the war. She felt more than the journalist's desire to report on great events. To Bill and Emily Davis, friends of Hemingway's who had also become her confidants, Gellhorn signalled her change of mood. She wrote a long letter reflecting on the generation that had gone to Spain and had been 'specially deformed' because of it. The *causa* had represented the 'sum total of the remaining hope of youth, with a reasoning and logical hope of adults'. When 'no one important cared', that hope had been destroyed. Her initial reaction had been to withdraw in bitterness: 'I felt such despair for the human race that I thought truly they were forever bitched'. Her only real gesture towards further protest had been her novel, *A Stricken Field*. 'But if you have no part in the world, no matter how diseased the world is, you are dead', she continued. To be charitable, kind and generous did not suffice. At first this new war had made her 'unable to see or think; the rage over the past making it impossible to function in the present'. She would have to store her memories, control her fury and find 'some way of hoping for the future of mankind', of loving the 'good ones and the good things'. It had become a matter of 'self-preservation'. This rambling, repetitive letter represented her thinking aloud about her unresolved feelings. She had 'no ideas or plans' and could only suppose that 'after squirming around like a stuck fly', she would 'know how to think and then finally how to act'.

In the meantime, Gellhorn remained the devoted wife, joking that Hemingway was her 'liege lord'. They would cool off by going to the movies. She thought Hemingway enjoyed the fighting and shooting, and 'looking at the bodies of those far-off and desirable women'. She would enjoy the pigeon shooting – the only woman who hung around with the old 'shoot-fools'. She rather relished the way they hurried out when she missed her target, shaking her hand and congratulating her on the beauty of her shots when she did strike a bird. It was rather merry – all this bowing and joking and calling each other 'Caballero' and 'Señor'.

In February her fellow correspondent, Virginia Cowles, visited with war news and they reminisced about their days in Spain, prompting Gellhorn to declare everything entirely too lax in this 'Latin, Catholic, tropical, leisurely, unstable, sinful and corrupt country' that her increasingly fitful husband cherished. Anything might happen during his rages. He might throw glasses, shoot out a window, hurt or embarrass his guests. Gellhorn feared for her family crystal and bought cheap glasses for him to hurl during his tantrums. If he seemed a genius, he also appeared to be half mad. She could no longer josh him out of his bad moods. Years later she speculated that Hemingway had more than a foul temper. She noted his 'terrible suspicions of people (mad and ugly) and a sense of persecution – he who was the favorite of the Gods – and total unreliability in emotion; his greatest friend this week, too great a friend, was suddenly denounced as a swine and enemy the next week. I thought it was just a filthy nature – and there is that too – but also clearly clinical madness.'

On a June visit Gregory was shocked to hear his father tell Martha: 'I'll show you, you conceited bitch. They'll be reading my stuff long after the worms have finished with you.' Yet Gellhorn gave Mrs Roosevelt a benign report: Ernest was teaching the children how to shoot and fish. 'I teach them table manners (which is very funny).'

Gregory Hemingway also remembers his father's plan to turn his forty-foot boat, the *Pilar*, into a 'sub-destroyer'. Deploying two men in the bow equipped with sub-machine guns and two in the stern with BARs (Browning Automatic Rifles) and hand grenades, Hemingway would steer his boat next to a sub. Then 'a pair of over-the-hill jai alai players with more guts than brains would heave The Bomb ["a huge explosive device, shaped like a coffin, with handles on each end"] into the open hatch of the conning tower'. 'What if The Bomb misses, Ernest?' Martha wanted to know. A sub's conning tower was higher than the *Pilar*'s bridge and the sub's hatch measured only thirty inches across. The bomb would probably bounce around, blow up, and drive the conning tower into the stranded *Pilar*. Then the sub would pull away and use its six-inch deck gun to 'blow the *Pilar* right out of the water'. Not giving Ernest a moment to reply, Martha said, 'Kitten, you need a vacation'. She suggested he write that article he promised to do on the way the Chinese watered the human faeces they sold to truck farmers. 'Don't you think I know the realities of war?' Ernest countered. He reminded her of the 237 or 238 pieces of shrapnel that had been taken out of his leg in World War One. 'Love, this time, if that bomb misses, they won't find two hundred thirty-eight pieces of *you*', Martha retorted. When Ernest praised a crew member for his loyalty, if not his intelligence, Martha responded: 'Yes, I think his uncle went down on the *Titanic*.'

Hemingway exploded when Gellhorn ridiculed his German submarine hunting. He claimed to be performing important intelligence work (he did file detailed reports with the American ambassador in Cuba who forwarded them to the State Department). After all, German subs had sunk ships off the east coast of the United States, in the Gulf of Mexico and off the coast of South America.

William Walton, a Hemingway friend and later Gellhorn's lover, observed: 'It takes two to tango, you know. Martha was a wicked, wild bitch. Oh, the joint cruelties.' Leicester Hemingway believed that Gellhorn cheated on his brother. Ernest referred to one of her favourites, Felix Areitio, a Basque jai alai player, as 'my rival'. Much later he would write to Bernard Berenson claiming that she had betrayed him. Gellhorn repudiated these stories, but her carefree behaviour provoked them. She liked to play tennis with the handsome Areitio and they were openly affectionate with each other. She thought nothing of jumping into his arms after tennis so he could 'carry her up to the house'. One of Hemingway's friends, Mario Menocal Jr, deemed Gellhorn indiscreet but not unfaithful. Robert Joyce, an American diplomat who frequently visited the Finca, asks: '*Where* in Cuba could she have had a secret affair? They lived in a village twelve miles from Havana. And when either of them came into town they were immediately recognized as distinguished *Americans*.' Hemingway would have killed Areitio if he had really believed in the affair, asserts his son Jack.

As Jeffrey Meyers suggests, Gellhorn's *The Heart of Another* may be the most persuasive evidence of her fidelity to Hemingway – or at least of her unwillingness to abandon it for Areitio. In 'Night Before Easter' she even names the handsome pelota player Felix. The female narrator mentions their tennis games, the bond they share because of the war in Spain, the pleasure she has in talking with him, admiring his mouth, the way he smiles. When she dances with him, however, he senses her reserve. The movements are all there, but they are inhibited. No real intimacy, it is clear, can develop between them.

Cuba corrupted both Gellhorn and Hemingway. He wrote nothing of value after publishing *For Whom the Bell Tolls*. Often he could not summon the energy or the concentration to write. *Liana*, her novel with a Caribbean setting, did not go well. She had to get away – even if only for a few weeks in Miami.

At first, Hemingway took her little side trips in his stride, although his correspondence portrays a lonely and lovesick man. He read the letters and clippings Gellhorn sent him from Florida to his cats, who were 'pleased and promised to do their best'. Dingie missed her terribly and never moved when Ernest spoke Martha's name. After eating a couple of turtle eggs, Mr Scrooby 'kept mistaking simple linen sheets for Ringling brother big top and his responsability to hold all up so that the show might go on'. He encouraged her to press on with her novel, noting that he had often failed but he had carried on, eventually producing good work. 'In proportion to the years we have been writing I have written no more stories than you have and only four novels.' Writers like Wells had set a wonderful standard for her. Few writers could claim to have written more than one good book, he believed. But there was a grandeur and sense of history in the sustained effort: 'All the work you do though is part of the same pyramid when the Mayans come back and run excursions to ruined temples of San Francisco de Paula [engraved on the Finca's stationery] and guys in foot thick lenses dig around for bits of your old pottery ... and thousands write theses on whether you were as good as you were beautiful.' Gellhorn had an 'eye and ear ... better than anybodies', he insisted. 'You are my hero and always will be and I will be good and try to live up to my hero.'

Gellhorn's short hop to Miami was a warm-up for a trip to the Caribbean, a defence area where a woman reporter could work. She made the complicated arrangements through Charles Colebaugh at *Collier's*. Gellhorn wrote to Mrs Roosevelt that she was spinning 'like a top' with joy to be going on a trip. If she did not have the inspiration to write a great novel, at least she could work hard and she loved the kind of life where she could put what she needed in a suitcase. She had grown to detest housekeeping and servants were often a problem. With Gellhorn away in Miami on a short trip, Hemingway fired Mercedes, their cleaning lady. This 'criminally' lazy woman left the house dirty, dropped her cigarettes into wastebaskets, and used Gellhorn's lipstick and Gloria Bristol beauty preparations. 'She was getting mighty attractive with Miss Bristol's aid. But still thought she had to go', Hemingway wrote to his wife.

But Gellhorn felt reassured that Hemingway could do without her. He loved his children: they would be fine with their father teaching them about boating and hunting, and telling them the most marvellous stories and jokes. He was also busy editing a book of war writing. She was leaving, in other words, without a sense of guilt.

Gellhorn wanted to write about the exotic and live like a pirate, she wrote to Colebaugh. On 16 July her credentials from *Collier's* and other documents arrived. One item identified her as Martha Hemingway. That was all right, she informed Colebaugh, but there should be no confusion. Her articles were always signed Martha Gellhorn, 'always', she emphasized. It was too late to cultivate another name for herself. She secretly hoped to spot a German sub; Hemingway was not the only one indulging fantasies in this first summer of America's involvement in the war.

II

THE UNENDING BATTLE
1942–1943

IN PORT-AU-PRINCE, Haiti, on 20 July 1942, Gellhorn began her quest for signs of German subs or agents in the Caribbean. In the suffocating heat – Gellhorn always liked it hot – she preferred 'travelling light' and not knowing what each day would bring. She found pure pleasure in the role of journalist/observer. Anti-colonialist to the core, she watched the Haitians take charge of their land, in the process securing more respect from the whites.

9 August: Puerto Rico's poverty troubled Gellhorn. Men enlisted in the army as a 'health cure'. Her piece on Puerto Rico really masked her main objective – to soak up the Caribbean atmosphere for her novel and to play the explorer of unknown lands. Absorbed in her note-taking, examining but not analysing what she saw made her happy. She liked taking life on the fly, mastering the quick impression and relying on the authority of her own eyewitness testimony. The idea of history, of rethinking initial judgements, rarely engaged her. She had a restless temperament unsuited to prolonged study of a subject. In her letters from this period she confessed that she was no Proust or Jane Austen and that she would never have the patience or genius to write a masterpiece. (She failed in several attempts to read Proust, losing patience and preferring thrillers.) At heart she was a journalist, she insisted, content to travel and to report.

Recognized as the wife of the '*grande escritor*', she disliked benefiting from his name and felt relieved when 'an Austrian refugee waiter' asked her to sign his copy of *A Stricken Field*. Yet Gellhorn missed Hemingway. She grew frantic when his letters and cables did not reach her. She worried that he had rejected her and wrote with relief on 2 August when his mail got through to her and she knew for sure he still loved her. She could only accept herself as his when on the move. His everyday intemperance ground her down. Like some Huck Finn of the sea, an innocent abroad, she dreamed of picking up survivors from torpedoed ships, finding caches of enemy provisions for submarines or clandestine radio transmitters.

Hemingway wrote to his first wife, Hadley, about how much he detested living alone, but he wrote Gellhorn cheerful, supportive letters: 'I'm so proud of the marvellous work you are doing. ... Maybe you can sink a submarine yourself.' He dreamed they were 'on the lam in Wisconsin. You'd been hurt and I was taking care of you and you loved me very much. We didn't have any money and we had an old car and there was a four state pickup order out for us when I woke up.'

To Gellhorn the very names of the Caribbean islands conjured up delicious visions of charting new territory. She became positively 'chirpy' when a motor boat deposited her on Tortola after a four-hour drenching ride in the rain. With not much more than one dusty street and a bunch of weathered shacks, nothing attracted her, and she hired Carlton de Castro, the local ladykiller and owner of a dilapidated thirty-foot sloop, the *Pilot*. It had a hold for potatoes and a single sail that looked like a 'patchwork quilt'. With no equipment – certainly no instrumentation – and a dinghy full of holes attached to the boat, Gellhorn, in her shorts, shirt and sandals, set off with Carlton and his dishevelled crew of two in the hurricane season to see the islands. She scrunched up in the dinghy, lying on her hatch cover mattress, her umbrella stuck out for protection from the sun and ducking every time the boom swung over her. A passing boat full of Carlton's friends inquired as to his cargo. 'De lady', he replied to their amused shrieks.

The boat pitched and rolled in peculiar ways that kept the queasy Gellhorn off balance. The crew's cooking of fish and onions nauseated her. After two full days at sea she prayed for a sub to appear and end her misery. Eventually they made it to Anguilla with

Gellhorn enumerating the extent of their adventures: they had seen 'three hurricane-birds and four flying fish'. She had lost her umbrella and her skin blistered. What could the natives have made out of this shabby figure in soiled clothes and knotted hair, with pimpled, reddened skin?

In St-Martin Gellhorn swam naked in the sea and relived her youthful, unencumbered days. She called St Barts an ugly arid island, but she did meet three interesting figures who became the prototypes for the main characters in *Liana*, the novel that had stalled in Cuba. Jean, a young 'boat bum', used up a modest inheritance and felt stranded and altogether too safe on this serene shore. He yearned to enlist with the Free French but remained fettered by a witch's voodoo charm, especially effective since she was his lover. Although Gellhorn advised against his believing in superstitious nonsense, he seemed genuinely fearful. The witch turned out to be a lovely mulatto with the feline grace of a jungle cat – a cat-woman who distrusted Gellhorn and would not eat with her. Another Frenchman, middle-aged and subdued, regretted his marriage to a black woman, claiming he had succumbed to the stupor of the island: miscegenation had ruined these people and had produced moronic children who were impossible to teach. What was the point, anyway? he wondered. How could they use an education on St Barts? Out of these three characters Gellhorn would produce a triangle that evoked powerful feelings about race, education, politics and sex. All three characters would be magnificently transformed to reflect the tensions and the contradictions of their environment.

The Caribbean trip raised interesting questions about culture. Gellhorn observed that each island took on the customs of its European rulers and the Europeans seemed largely oblivious to this phenomenon, preferring to maintain the fiction that the races were separate, that the mingling of minds and bodies did not result in profound consequences for humanity. Gellhorn found these handsome people of mixed blood enchanting.

Alone on this trip, Gellhorn met many people who seemed alone in their struggle for a sense of belonging and identity. She had her own need to be a wife, to share her interest in humanity with others, yet she enjoyed her isolation. Her only companion had been a cat, which she cared for like a child, feeling guilty when the rough sea voyages sickened it. She even made an impassioned speech for the animal at St Kitts, which prohibited the importation of cats and dogs, and succeeded in bringing it along.

It is not possible to improve upon Gellhorn's hilarious account of her Caribbean adventures in *Travels with Myself and Another*: her encounters with Bush Negroes lubricated with reeking coconut butter, who squeezed and stroked her to the accompaniment of raucous laughter; a bizarre white couple living in a crude cabin praising a life of sin and deploring the craziness of contemporary life; her protest against a village incident in which a woman's screams convinced her some horrible torture had commenced. Hustled out of the village by her guide, whom she preferred to call Mr Slicker – because of his sunglasses, red bow tie, crumpled hat and suit, and oily manner – it took her years to realize (with a friend's help) that she had probably intruded on a childbirth. All in all, the trip was really quite ridiculous. Charles Colebaugh, her editor at *Collier's*, circulated her reports to the staff. They were worth a 'good giggle' and convinced her editors they were right to remain where they were. The absurdity of Gellhorn's adventures did not escape Hemingway, who wrote to his friend, Evan Shipman, that if Gellhorn succeeded in getting sunk along with her sailors, *Collier's* might consider doubling the fee they usually paid for her articles. On second thoughts, perhaps the magazine would ask him to write a piece in homage to her.

Correspondence between husband and wife turned bitter in early September. Mr Scrooby 'probably will be permanently ruined from disuse', he complained. Her acid remarks about the rundown condition of the Finca and his inability to see to the repairs and to supervise the servants provoked him to counterpunch: 'Boy you can hit.' She kept her shots coming and then: 'You're in your corner and mother is handling the towel and she tells you how wonderful you are and how well you are going.' She was giving it to 'who loves you like a fucking dope'. He expected to be out on a cruise one day and return to find a

> loveing note on half sheet of paper saying everything was so horrible and we were all just a phase in your life anyway and you were off to run for Congress and to always remember what fine men we were all, me especially, and how you loved me especially because I was such a good mon and you would maybe, no surely, write some

time after you were in the Cabinet and just address you care of Nelson Rockerfeller.

By late September, Gellhorn had returned home from the Caribbean and the couple apparently were reconciled. Gellhorn told Mrs Roosevelt:

> It's lovely to be home, though. We now have five cats; one small refugee dog; two hunting dogs that spend their time pointing lizards, cats and chickens exclusively; six lovebirds, three tree ducks, and forty-two pigeons. We also have a tiny pretty rooster and his wife, who are far too jolly to bother making eggs. The place is more of a menagerie than a farm, but still very wonderful and someday, somehow, you must come and giggle with me about it.

Ernest wrote to Patrick about Martha and Gregory going out into the 'back country' and running into big coveys of quails. She began a draft of *Liana* and finished three articles for *Collier's*, which she delivered to New York in person in early October.

As always, Hemingway's letters followed her: 'Cook continues very good. Juan has painted all the doors white. Everybody still seems enough under the spell of your presence to be working hard.' He sent detailed instructions about how to lighten her hair: 'They get in hurry and use ammonia with the peroxide which is enemy of hair texture and can only be used with much soap.' Worried that their acrimonious exchanges in early September had alienated her, he emphasized 'I am much better and kinder than I used to be. ... I promise you I won't go around all the time like Samson pulling down the pillars of the temple.'

But a Hemingway at home caused Gellhorn problems in New York. During a lunch in New York with Dorothy Parker and *New Yorker* editor Harold Ross, Parker attacked Gellhorn and Hemingway for sitting out the war. In a letter to Ross, Hemingway admitted that 'Marty had to take it all' – including Parker's accusation that the couple 'took no part in this war because we were used to going to little wars where we could be important'. Hemingway dismissed the indictment as 'Dotty's Goldstarmotherhood' and remarked, 'That's why I never come up to town.'

From New York, Gellhorn flew to Washington DC for several days at the White House, hearing the latest war news from the Roosevelts.

She missed Hemingway and the Finca. She wrote him suggesting that only a divorce would keep them lovers.

Gellhorn returned to Cuba in November, for what Hemingway – again losing his temper – called 'a spot of domesticity'. The more she wanted to retreat into her private, literary world and finish her novel, the more he craved an audience of admirers. He seemed to be turning himself inside out. He had been the writer affecting a public personality, now he was a celebrity pretending to be a writer. Rather than creating new works of fiction, he exaggerated his personal exploits. He indulged in extravagant gestures and lavish displays. One night in Havana she had to stand for a public rebuke when he felt she had not been generous with her Christmas presents to the servants. He left her stranded while he drove away in his Lincoln. On another evening, when she insisted on driving her drunken husband home, he backhanded her across the face. Slowing down to ten miles an hour she decided to drive his beloved Lincoln 'through a ditch and into a tree, leaving him there and walking back home'. She could not bear to be on the *Pilar* with him. At the first port of call she would often hire a car to take her home. How could he waste himself this way when there was a war he should be writing about? She nagged him about it.

Ostensibly, Gellhorn's novel had nothing to do with her and Hemingway. It concerned a woman of colour kept housebound by her white husband. Liana gradually awakens to a sense of the world when she is taught to read by a French schoolmaster. Winston Guest, one of Hemingway's submarine-hunting buddies, remembers Ernest reading the novel in manuscript, making corrections and suggestions. Guest read parts of it. He thought the book related to Ernest's effort to incarcerate Martha in Cuba and that it was 'very gallant, very honourable of Ernest' to help improve the book. He saw Martha as something of a monster:

> I'll never forget Martha asking me what I thought of her choice of a husband. She explained to me that she'd picked Ernest because of his ability as a writer and possible remuneration from books. And I thought to myself, what a tough, mercenary bitch to discuss her husband with me, someone she hardly knew. She didn't imply that she loved him at all. She implied to me that she married him as a practical matter; it might help her improve her writing.

Gellhorn rejected Guest's memory as 'rubbish'. She never profited from the Hemingway name, she insisted, and never allowed him to support her. She had a well-established career before she met him. Yet she had sought him out, believing that she had much to learn from Hemingway, and she received attention from the press and from reviewers because of her marriage to him. Guest apparently exaggerated and blackened Gellhorn's feelings about Hemingway, but Gellhorn simplified and sanitized hers.

Christmas 1942. Gellhorn left Cuba again to spend the holiday with her mother in St Louis. Following her usual pattern, she wrote Hemingway about how much she missed him. She turned suicidal when she thought of him suffering any hurt during her absence. They had a wonderful life and so much to be thankful for – although she had to admit the last year had been awful. She had gone to church and lit a candle for him and his boys.

In mid-January 1943 Gellhorn, again in Cuba, laboured over *Liana*. Hemingway enjoyed reading the chapters as she completed them, 'like in the good old days when there were good magazines and good instalments'. He worked hard at editing her work, at taking 'every single thing of management etc. off your hands and keep your time free for writing. I tip-toe in the mornings, I make the servants be quiet, I tell people who want to bother you that they cannot see you, I ran the house and so forth when you were gone quite a long time at Christmas holidays and tried to have everything neat and clean and good when you came back, and I have had no greater joy than seeing your book develop so amazeingly and beautifully.'

Yet in March, when he had returned from one of his *Pilar* expeditions, she treated him 'as though I were some sort of villain of the piece. Bong I think you have me mixed up with some awful people you have been reading about or seeing in the movies or maybe the husband of the lovely mulatta.' Behaving like a 'prima donna', she took it out on everyone but herself when the writing did not go well. No one was trying to abuse her and he still loved her very much. Otherwise, why would he spend three hours writing her a letter about his feelings? Hemingway had forgotten his own trying behaviour during his arduous work on *For Whom the Bell Tolls*. Years later, Gellhorn told a friend that he had forbidden her to listen to the radio – even on the day in 1940 when Paris fell. 'I've got one book to write about the Spanish war, and France will fall again', he told her.

The pressures subsided when an elated Gellhorn finished the novel on 27 June. She could not stop talking. Then, at five in the morning, she woke asking herself whether the novel was any good. Was she deceiving herself? The last two weeks had been her best period as a writer, even though she was constantly tired and got a stomach-ache from smoking forty cigarettes a day. She steeled herself to the possibility that she might have to rewrite her work. How much better *Liana* was than *What Mad Pursuit*, she confided to Hemingway. *Liana* roused memories of her meagre existence in Paris in the thirties and she longed to be young again, to cancel things – the house, her reputation, her experience, all of it in exchange for the girl she once was. In what had now become a theme for her, she said to her husband that she wished they could start over again. She detested being sensible and cautious, dependable and settled. He craved marriage; she loved the role of misfit and wanderer. She knew he would not like this yearning for youth and its lack of attachments, but what kind of marriage was it if she could not speak to him of her profoundest emotions?

An appalled Hemingway replied that 'no one that chased their youth ever caught it'. Like Wells, who criticized Gellhorn for her lack of discipline – her refusal to write every day even when not inspired – Hemingway identified her real problem as an unwillingness to harness herself to writing: 'There never was a great race horse that could not be ridden nor that did not have to have a bit in his mouth on race days: and the thing that bridles and bits you and rides you and is your true master is the need to write truly and well.'

In one of his more jocular moods Hemingway declared: 'You're the writer in the family now, Marty.' According to Gregory, his father meant it. 'Marty was flattered at first, then amazed, and finally disgusted', he recalled. That her husband should think of retiring at forty-four revolted her. 'Let's give Marty a chance She deserves one', he would say. When Gellhorn got word from *Collier's* that she would be sent to London in the fall, she wanted Hemingway to secure a similar assignment. He hung back. The fights between them started again. After one of their petty and cruel exchanges, he wrote: 'Now I know how horrible I am because you rightly tell me. But otherwise I would have been unconscious as the way I liked to dance and thought I could until you told me how I couldn't and never could and never have since.'

Fred Field, an old friend of Martha's and Edna's, visited the Finca and witnessed some 'strange evenings' with the Hemingways. He did not know Ernest, but he admired his work. Things started off with heavy drinking. Soon Ernest ran out of ice. He called one of the servants. No answer. He shouted. No servants appeared. Enraged, he screamed. Field found such scenes distasteful and wanted to tell this son of a bitch Hemingway to stop 'browbeating servants'. Martha rushed in and quietly got a servant to supply the ice. Hemingway harangued Field for two evenings about cloud formations and machine-guns. Field did not see Ernest bait Martha. But an embarrassed Gregory admitted Martha was usually in the right.

Making love only aggravated their estrangement, Hemingway later confessed to Gregory. He never lost his physical appetite for her, but he was callous about her feelings. As she later said to an English friend, Hemingway's lovemaking was 'short and sharp'. Gellhorn tried to overlook the sexual failure of her marriage. One of her friends observed that her 'interest in sex was more literary than personal, that she was more excited by Hemingway the writer than by Hemingway the man, that ambition rather than passion had inspired her marriage'.

Gellhorn left the Finca on 20 September, novel in hand. Encountering Dr José Luis Herrera Sotolongo, who had attended her and Hemingway since their days in Spain, she announced: 'I'm leaving for Europe and I won't come back to the *beast*.' When he asked Ernest for an explanation, he said: 'She's from St Louis, Missouri.'

In New York Gellhorn revised *Liana* for Scribner's. Max Perkins promised that it would head the publisher's list in 1944. Movie producers and Book of the Month Club expressed interest. She wrote Hemingway a self-abasing letter: he had only to say the word and she was his. She wanted him to tell her what to do. She recalled their days along the Loing Canal in France, the setting for 'November Afternoon', her story in *The Heart of Another*.

Liana evolved out of buried feelings Gellhorn vented only after Hemingway's repeated attacks and his frequent references to 'the great unending battle between men and women'. In the novel, Marc Royer, a wealthy white businessman on a Caribbean island, marries a mulatto and changes her name from Liana to Julie. At the same time he is in love with his dead brother's widow, Marie, a middle-aged white woman who is as elusive and independent as Liana is available and dependent. Yet Liana rebels when she realizes Royer simply wants her as a sexual possession. She has been thrilled at the promise of becoming a white man's wife, visited by white ladies and dressed in European clothing. While Royer supplies her with finery, he keeps her at home and she receives no company. She locks her bedroom door and refuses his advances, for she knows he also beds Marie. Enamoured of her own beauty and having some sense of self-worth, Liana is bitter about her fate.

Royer is a man who is frustrated by women. Marie, for example, is indifferent to his visits and not at all concerned by her lack of good looks. She enjoys sex, but she does not let it rule her emotions. Royer is angered not to own women as he owns his business and much of the town. Liana's race simply makes it easier for him to indulge his craving for ownership. If he cannot possess Marie, he will find a way to bind Liana to him. His sense of sex is allied to his sense of power: the point is to be the dominant partner in all trans-actions. Liana figures it out for herself: 'She was something he had bought for use when he could not have what he loved.'

Royer is only really comfortable in the company of men, drink-ing with them and exchanging stories, but his marriage to Liana and his great wealth isolate him. This is why he conceives a plan to relieve Liana's boredom and provide himself with a male compan-ion. He pays Pierre Vauclain, the French schoolteacher, to give Liana lessons in reading. Not only does Liana learn quickly, she begins to have a mind of her own. She reads novels and starts to identify with the characters. She becomes interested in war news and what is hap-pening in Vauclain's beloved France. Suddenly it is her conscience and not the shape of the island that determines Liana's view of things. She presses Royer to show her precisely where France is on the map. In short, she begins to locate her own feelings.

Vauclain, a sensitive teacher, opens up the world to Liana. They become friends and are accused of being lovers. The very accusation prompts in them an awareness that their intimacy has been sensual as well as intellectual. Then they become lovers. Royer's discovery of the affair turns him against Liana, not Vauclain. For women have always thwarted Royer. He has coveted Vauclain's friendship all along and persuades the Frenchman that he must abandon Liana so that he can fulfil his desire to serve in the Free French army. Vauclain has been unhappy on the island and Liana – in spite of his passion for her – is not enough to deter him from his thoughts of home. Accepting Royer's offer to help him return to France, Vauclain abandons Liana, who has long since concluded that the island is too small for her. She must find a world commensurate with her maturity. Abandoned by her lover, ostracized by the island, repulsed by Royer, she commits suicide.

This is Gellhorn's only feminist book, in which issues of race and sex are paramount – indeed, they are identical, since it is the subjugation of human beings that is at stake. Like Liana, who must answer to Royer's 'Julie', Gellhorn was asked to answer to the Hemingway name. For her work she never used her husband's name, but in private letters she was 'Mrs E. Hemingway' or 'Martha Hemingway'.

Men behaved as though it were their world. What gave them the right to decide? Gellhorn had never asked this question in so many words. In a letter to Wells about *Liana*, Gellhorn admitted: 'I am very sorry for the girl in the book, but on the whole I am sorry for women. They are not free: there is no way they can make themselves free.' In *Liana* every page is suffused with feminist questions: why is it that women must stay at home? Why must they be sequestered from the action? Why should a woman's imagination be seen as second-rate, a product only of the emotions and not of the intellect? What is the evidence supporting the treatment of women as inferiors? Why should men be allowed to rule as the superior sex? Gellhorn was not writing a tract; such questions are implicit in the narrative. As one critic of *Liana* remarks, 'There is a truth of observation in the studies of Liana herself and of Marc ... the keen feeling for atmosphere, emotional as well as environmental.'

Liana did not become a Book of the Month Selection. Nor did it become a motion picture. But the reviews were good. In the *Nation*, Diana Trilling pointed to a 'perfect blending of intellectual and

emotional pitch'. In the *New Republic*, Mark Schorer lauded Gellhorn's handling of the two men, who 'come to understand, almost
to love, each other'. The utter exclusiveness of this male world causes
Liana's breakdown. Reviewers noted a certain weakness in character-
ization, in Gellhorn's tendency to draw her figures a little too
sharply and simply. Her work did not quite have that circumspect
sophistication of the finest fiction. Gellhorn seemed to find herself
all at once in the composition of this book. It could not have
escaped Hemingway: she had written herself out of his life.

12

W AR
1943-1945

WHEN GELLHORN left Cuba her first concern was to get to Europe and to cover the war, although that also meant sorting out matters with Hemingway. On 3 November 1943 she arrived at the Dorchester Hotel in London, breakfasted with Virginia Cowles and waited to get her official credentials as a war correspondent. Martha reported to Ernest that as his wife she was getting special treatment. How fine it would be if he would give up his phoney and foolish Cuban life and join her.

For *Collier's* Gellhorn wrote about RAF bomber pilots, thousands of whom left on missions in the moonlight, flying towards the fortified French coast, 10,000-foot mountain peaks and miserable winter weather. This exhausting, hazardous duty, performed by gallant men who called their work 'a piece of cake', cheered Gellhorn, relieved to be no longer on the sidelines. The English amazed her. Just a few short years earlier she had been outraged by their stolid attitude, when they seemed impervious to the devastating war about to be visited upon them. Now their self-confidence ensured that they would not surrender. Bomber pilots had to spend long hours waiting for assignment, yet their nerve never broke. They could sit in the mess at teatime, reading and behaving like obedient schoolchildren. After all the planes had returned safely from a night mission, there was only the briefest understated exchange of words between the pilots and their group captain, who politely asked about their trip as though they had come back from a casual outing.

Gellhorn reported on London's poor children, the Cockneys who worked 48-hour weeks for an average pay of $8. By the time they were fourteen, they were supporting families who had sent their older men to war. A rugged, spirited and clever lot, meeting in their own clubs to jitterbug, they asked Gellhorn if she knew movie stars like Humphrey Bogart. Few of them had any illusions about the war. They expected their lives to be just as hard when peace came. But they enjoyed arguing about whether the war would bring changes to their lives. They were proud and patriotic but had little sense of the war's meaning. These children numbered some 2 million, Gellhorn pointed out to her *Collier's* readers, and they were more vital to the survival of England than they realized.

In spite of a severe cold, Gellhorn trudged through badly bombed neighbourhoods and felt stimulated by these energetic people. Struck by how warmly Hemingway's writing was received, she felt attached to a 'mythical' being. She urged him to send her more cables, telling him she had his pictures on her desk and talked about him all the time. Yet he seemed so distant now and not quite real. She wooed him, coaxed him to come over where she said absolutely everyone felt he should be. His replies made it clear he would have none of it.

Interviewing three Poles in London, Gellhorn began to get first-hand reports of Nazi atrocities. Jews had been forced to dig their own graves and were publicly executed. Old people, Jews and the disabled were packed (130 to a cattle car) and sent to concentration camps to die. A ten-foot wall had been built around the Warsaw ghetto. More than a half million Jews were incarcerated, deprived of work and access to other parts of the city. Laughing German soldiers watched starving Jews struggling for the bits of bread tossed into the street. Shooting parties took aim at whatever Jew happened to be in sight. Corpses were left in the streets covered with newspaper and picked up later. Slave labourers were given barely enough food to survive and often had to work in wooden shoes with no underwear or socks. Their diet consisted of meagre amounts of potatoes, vegetables or soup, and bread. Diseases like typhus and tuberculosis were spreading. Poland was a cemetery. Already two-thirds of Poland's Jewish population (2½ million people) had been exterminated. The Nazis planned to make Poland 'German for ever'.

As hopeless as it seemed, Poland had not given up. Close to 100,000 children in Warsaw attended underground schools, with teachers paid, textbooks printed and students educated on every level, including instruction in the creation of explosive devices for sabotage. A clandestine government held meetings in shops and German factories, even though the penalty for such activities was death. As Gellhorn learned these things from Polish escapees, she marvelled at their composure. As with the RAF pilots, she saw the toll on their lives registered in weary eyes that had witnessed too much.

Interviewing Dutch refugees in London, Gellhorn reported further signs of resistance to the Nazis. Prisoners in solitary confinement in German jails used heating pipes to communicate with each other; cars commandeered by Germans were sabotaged by putting sand in the oil; and a general strike in Amsterdam protested against the deportation of 160,000 Jews from Holland. She highlighted instances of Dutch heroism and Nazi brutality: a boy caught talking along the heating pipes had had his eardrums pierced; the Dutch offered Jews places to sit on public vehicles and hid Jews, even though the punishment for aiding them was death. Like the Poles, the Dutch had an underground press thriving even as the Nazis deprived the Dutch of their leaders.

As she had done in Spain, Gellhorn visited military hospitals and did not flinch from reporting the gruesome consequences of war – severely burned and scarred men with unrecognizable faces. It was hard to say how old they were because their features had been destroyed. Only by their eyes and their voices could she sense their feelings. Most of the wounded men stayed a minimum of two months and some much longer, submitting to excruciating operations aimed at restoring their features. The doctors had done wonders and the men's morale was very high. They were encouraged to travel in pairs to London to get used to their new faces and to meet the gaze of others without self-consciousness, but nothing could quite still the anxieties of men whose wives, parents and friends broke under the strain of this disfigurement. Gellhorn noticed that they made a 'joke of disaster' and she implied that many of them had the strength to overcome the tragedy that war had made of their lives.

Though Gellhorn continued with her assignments, her cold had developed into an infection and other ailments she could not shake. Her weakened spirit seeped into her letters to Hemingway. She would not return to Cuba and still encouraged him to join her in London – if not to do his own work, then for a vacation. When she could not budge him, she followed up with a long letter on 12 December 1943 marshalling all her arguments: he was *the* writer to cover the war; no one else could write as brilliantly about its significance – indeed, his very career was at stake, not to mention their marriage. He was making a profound error and she regretted not being able to share the war with him. He would be the eyes for both of them. She followed up with all sorts of suggestions as to how he could get his accreditation as a war correspondent.

The very next day four letters from Hemingway arrived announcing his absolute opposition to leaving Cuba. Gellhorn tried very hard not to feel disappointed. She could not resist saying once more that he was making a mistake, but she promised not to hound him about the war any more. Instead, she wrote in self-justification, explaining that she had to act upon her convictions; otherwise he would be stuck with a woman who had no faith in herself. She had to see things for herself; she could not make them up like a Jane Austen or the Brontë sisters. She did not think he would really be content with her if she sat at home surrounded by a high stone wall.

Hemingway was not so sure. On Christmas Day 1943 he wrote to Archibald MacLeish that he was 'sick-lonely with Marty away. Like somebody with their heart cut out – loved Marty so much and to the exclusion of everything and all else that everybody who use to love me quit. So now I have no Marty and nobodies else. If anything happened to Marty – would be in a bad place. Just being absent is bad enough.' Yet Hemingway spent time in Havana's bars talking like a cowboy who would soon saddle up, ride after his woman and 'kick her ass good'. Stay home or go to military school – those were the alternatives, he said. Letters in which she called him her 'own' had not swayed him, especially when she admitted Cuba had become unreal to her. She had been out reporting on an English village, observing children wearing outgrown clothes and old men walking in cracked shoes, amidst the roar of Spitfires overhead and to the east. Meat was rationed, the village's young men were off to the war, houses were in disrepair, but everyone made light of the hardship in comparison to what their brave soldiers had to endure. When Gellhorn thought of Cuba now, she dreaded it. She apologized to Hemingway, but she could not resist comparing Cuba to being 'strangled by those beautiful tropical flowers that can swallow cows!'.

Edna Gellhorn wrote to Hemingway trying to console him. She wanted him to send her his 'gloomy letters'. They would not make her happy but she would rather have them than 'keep wondering' how he and his cats were managing without Martha. 'Men generally can't manage loneliness. Women generally are better at it, perhaps because traditionally men have gone and women have waited, so we learn about being left from our fairy story times straight through our lives', Edna suggested. Her efforts were not rewarded. Ernest wrote to Martha on 13 January 1944 that her mother in a 'sharp cold letter' thought he should 'exult in your being away'. He knew 'how good your reasons are and how sound and how much I need to see and partake and be a part of history … but you are like a patriotic nurse trying to handle an old tank'. By the end of the month he had almost capitulated: 'Just feel like old horse, good, sound, but old, being saddled again to race over the jumps because of unscrupulous owner. Will make same race as always, best that can make, but am neither happy, excited, nor interested.'

As for Gellhorn, she had managed to make it to Italy, the only active front in the war. In July and August 1943 the Allies had invaded and captured Sicily and by 3 September the invasion of southern Italy had begun. By 22 January Allied forces had landed at Nettuno and Anzio, and met with stiff German resistance. In February Gellhorn was driving in an army jeep through windy hills approaching an area held by the Free French (part of the British army) on her way to the blown-up town of San Elia. First it snowed, then it hailed, as the French driver tried to negotiate the narrow, curving roads. Up ahead the Germans held the higher mountains. To the right and left were Poles and Americans. She had come north from Naples, passing every sort of military vehicle, trying not to get stuck behind the long convoys that rumbled like herding elephants. Tents flanked the roadside, with men shaving and overhauling their vehicles. Houses looked sliced apart. Roofs were ripped off; homes were now reduced to rubble. Telephone wiring wound its way everywhere like the tendrils of exotic jungle plants. She could see children using old telephone wire to swing on and women doing their washing at an ancient stone trough. The pounding of the batteries, when she got near enough, created a pressure she could relieve only by opening her mouth and breathing hard. It was grim work prying Germans out of the rocky sides of cliffs. In a field hospital she spoke with two French soldiers who had been repairing a telephone line. One had had his leg virtually severed by a shell, and the other – blinded in one eye – stopped his friend's bleeding by making a tourniquet of telephone wire. Then he had to cut his friend's leg off, since it was attached only by skin and tendons. The blinded man refused all treatment until his friend got attention. It was ghastly for the French: poor food, bitter cold, no opportunities to relax and no replacements. As Italian refugees swarmed the roads, the French soldiers showed no sympathy, remembering their own refugees. The French fought on, giving the lie to people who said that France was finished.

Gellhorn's writing captured the feel of slippery, obstacle-strewn roads, where her jeep hit things before Burton (her driver) could see them. A windshield would crack, Gellhorn's and Burton's heads would snap back, their knees smashing the dashboard. 'I ain't had so much fun since the hogs ate my little brother', Burton exclaimed after they had a moment to react to the jolt. She captured the exhilaration, the camaraderie and the exaggeration of war, but also its incomprehensibility. American GIs did not hate Germans. In fact, they respected them as soldiers who dug in and refused to give up territory. This nettled Gellhorn, who wanted to see more anti-German fervour, but how could she dispute with men who were doing the fighting holed up on cold, barren mountainsides? Their feelings would have been different if they were dug in on their own land, they told her. The dispatches from Italy showed Gellhorn at her best. As Hemingway declared in the 4 March 1944 issue of *Collier's*: 'The things that happen to her people really happen, and you feel it as though it were you and you were there.' Despite this tribute, he sent her cables asking, 'ARE YOU A WAR CORRESPONDENT OR WIFE IN MY BED?'

On 27 February – just before leaving Italy – Gellhorn and other correspondents were shot at near a river crossing on the outskirts of Cassino. It had been her idea to go there and, according to correspondent William H. Stoneman, 'in a weak moment we volunteered to go along with her and check up on the situation'. At one point they had to make a sharp right turn and 'dash across a short stretch of road into a shelter of cliffs on the other side'. For more than half a mile the correspondents were 'under direct observation by the Germans'. It was, unquestionably, a 'hot spot'. Suddenly the Germans started shooting and Gellhorn 'hit a nice deep ditch at the same second' the other correspondents did. After fifteen minutes of shooting they ran across the road and took a jeep, flying around turns with shells dropping beside them. Somehow they managed to get out unscathed. Unabashed, Gellhorn wondered aloud why they did not advance on Cassino. 'Let her go on wondering', Stoneman concluded.

On a brief visit to the North African front and to Morocco Gellhorn's friend, Lady Diana Cooper, had her dazzle André Gide for a day. Jack Hemingway, on leave from the army, remembers staying for the weekend at a 'beautiful villa in the hills above Algiers', where Lady Diana's husband was installed as ambassador to the new French government. Jack presents Gellhorn as adding 'more than a touch of glamour' to a gathering graced by Lady Diana, 'one of the great beauties of her time'. In company that included Randolph Churchill, Sir Winston's son, 'Marty was in good form, though she scarcely mentioned Papa', Jack concludes.

In March Gellhorn returned home to Cuba to have it out with her husband. She had had a long, tiring flight from Tangiers, cooped up in the ice-cold innards of a bomber with some sick soldiers, but right from the start Hemingway was at her. He would not let her sleep. He raged that all she craved was 'excitement and danger'. She must be crazy. Where was her sense of obligation to home and husband? In Gellhorn's view, her true 'crime really was to have been at war when he had not'. The curious thing is that he finally gave in: okay, she wanted him at war. Then not only would he be there, he would take the choicest assignments and be her fiercest competitor. He contacted *Collier's* and agreed to become their front-line correspondent. Michael Reynolds points out: 'Ernest or no Ernest on their payroll, *Collier's* could not send Martha to the war as their front-line correspondent; had Colebaugh not hired her husband, he would have hired some other man.' True enough. Yet Hemingway, who had his pick of numerous offers from newspapers and magazines, obviously rubbed in his advantage by choosing *Collier's*.

In April the quarrelling continued in New York. Hemingway said he would be killed and he would have Gellhorn to thank for it. He hoped that satisfied her. 'My father was always much more frightened of getting killed than Marty,' Patrick Hemingway observed. 'He felt that he was entitled to stay behind, living in a place that he liked, and enjoying himself.' Gellhorn told Hemingway bluntly that his behaviour diminished her love for him. When she asked him to use his influence to arrange a flight with him to Europe, he replied, 'Oh no, I couldn't do that. They only fly men.' As a result, she embarked on 13 May, the only passenger on a freighter carrying explosives and no lifeboats. For two weeks she lived under blackout regulations, the ship zigzagging through murky, freezing and foggy waters, trying to avoid collisions with other vessels. After this long and dangerous trip she learned that Beatrice Lillie and Gertrude Lawrence had both accompanied Hemingway on his plane to Europe.

When Gellhorn docked in Liverpool on 27 May, reporters explained that Hemingway had been involved in a car crash after an all-night party. Thrown against a windshield, he had gashed his scalp and sustained a concussion. At the hospital she found him lying in bed, a huge figure lounging with his hands behind his busted head, with bandages wound round his scalp in a kind of turban, holding forth like a sultan and surrounded by his cronies. She saw champagne and whisky bottles under the bed. This was a sick man's room? He showed not the slightest concern about her frightful trip. Indignant, she told him their marriage was over. She would regard herself as free from now on. She had had enough of his taunts, his intimidation, his lying and bragging. She actually laughed at his warrior pose and walked out on him.

Two days later the hospital discharged an outraged Hemingway determined to make Gellhorn's life miserable. He got her on the phone and invited her to dinner. When she arrived at his room, he opened the door to expose his nakedness and feigned an attack on her as she retreated, weeping angrily. Ira Wolfert, a fellow correspondent, persuaded him to apologize and on the phone he got her to agree to meet him at her room. But before they got there he spotted Mary Welsh, whom he was already courting, and left Wolfert to escort Gellhorn to dinner.

Both Hemingway and Gellhorn used an uncomfortable Leicester Hemingway to deliver notes back and forth. Ernest alternated between aggressive and mournful moods. 'She only came to see me twice while I was laid up and hurting ... What a way for a wife to be', he complained to his brother. According to Leicester, his brother still respected Gellhorn's professionalism and spoke of her important assignment in the 'Mediterranean theater of operations'. As chief of correspondents, he tried to operate in a businesslike manner – even when it came to approving her expenses. 'He's worse than the government', Gellhorn told Leicester when she wanted him to intercede on her behalf.

D-Day. Like the rest of the press corps, Gellhorn was told in a morning briefing in London of the Allied invasion just hours after it had begun. An English press officer had stood up to announce, 'In five seconds the first communiqué will be given to the world. You may leave. Go!' She ran out, like the rest of the press, to send a cable. But as a woman barred from the combat zone, she really had nowhere to go. Hemingway, as a front-line correspondent, had been taken aboard landing craft, where he could observe troops wading ashore.

Determined not to miss this historic event, Gellhorn hid in the bathroom of a hospital ship scheduled to cross the Channel at daybreak on 7 June. The 'painfully white' vessel made an easy enemy target, although the Geneva Convention forbids firing at hospital ships. A lane had been cleared of mines but two previous ships had struck them. So far the damage had been slight.

When Gellhorn sighted the coast of France, the enormous size of the invasion forces overwhelmed her. Destroyers, battleships and transports converged to present the picture of a 'floating city of huge vessels anchored before the green cliffs of Normandy'. Smaller craft seemed to sport about in the water, but the distant gunfire reminded her of the treacherous sea full of mines and submerged tanks.

Drowned bodies drifted past her. Barrage balloons 'bounced' in the strong wind above the giant ships to the accompaniment of dance music coming from a radio on the beach. With planes buzzing high overhead out of sight, mines exploding, troops pounding out of barges on to the shore and tanks clanging into action, Gellhorn saw the most impressive orchestration of war ever attempted.

The ship moved in towards the French beaches and water ambulances were lowered into the water slowly to avoid mines. The stretcher-bearers' hands quickly blistered from carrying the wounded from the shore to ambulances to the ship and down the twisting stairs to the hospital wards. Four doctors and fourteen orderlies cared for 400 men on a trip that lasted twenty-nine hours – right through a night of examinations, transfusions, wound dressing and countless other medical procedures.

Gellhorn distributed water, food, medication and cigarettes, and carried urinals. On 7 June, after dark, she snuck ashore with the stretcher-bearers. On the Normandy beach head she manoeuvred her way around minefields and barbed wire. Having done everything through official channels, Hemingway found himself confined to watching the action from landing craft. He was angry at Gellhorn for actually getting ashore and even tried to deny that she did, claiming she could not have done so because she did not have the proper papers. In fact, she had shown more initiative than he had and he would never forgive her for it.

An impressed Gellhorn watched wounded men talking and joking among themselves even though they were near collapse. Many had not eaten for two days, but they remained professional soldiers. German soldiers were treated as well as the Americans, although the Germans were arrogant and complained loudly. The American hospital crew did not pause during an air raid, even when she could sense the anxiety of wounded soldiers immobilized during the attack.

In London Gellhorn noted the theatrical way a German officer carried himself, 'with his hands on his hips, registering scorn and indifference'. One American soldier marvelled at the sight of this German who seemed ready for a movie set. A captured German doctor termed the invasion a final desperate act. Black American GIs carefully carried these 'Aryans' on stretchers, never commenting on how defeated this 'master race' now looked, for most of the Germans were scrawny and in poor health. A Jewish doctor attended the wounded Germans conscientiously, although they were very noisy. He asked Gellhorn to tell them to keep quiet so he could hear his patients. Very courteously she relayed the doctor's message to one of them, who thundered, '*Ruhig*'. The absolute silence after the command made her feel as though she were in the Third Reich. She and the doctor exchanged expressions of 'contempt and despair', as if recognizing that these Germans knew only how to give or take orders. There was 'nothing in between'.

In a note to Hemingway, Gellhorn said she was happy he had returned from Normandy safely. She would follow the war in Italy rather than stay in the Dorchester, where on her return from Normandy she had discovered him in her room with a girl.

Then the American Army's PR office arrested Gellhorn for not having the proper credentials for a combat zone. Sentenced to confinement at an American nurses' training camp outside London, she was told she could fly with the nurses when they were ready to set up a base hospital in France. Gellhorn tolerated this discipline for a day, then hoisted herself over a wire fence, bummed a ride to a military airfield and got an unauthorized flight to Naples, telling the pilot a sob story about missing her fiancé in Italy.

Once there, Gellhorn functioned entirely on her own: 'No papers, no travel orders, no PX rights, nothing. I was a gypsy in that war in order to report it', she later told Bernice Kert. (How she was able to file her dispatches and get them through censorship without papers she did not explain). While Hemingway played soldier and big brother to younger correspondents, exaggerating his military exploits and holding back some of his best material from *Collier's*, Gellhorn threw herself into the lives of the French, the Italians, the Poles and the Americans who fought and coped with the war. Having no myth of herself to maintain, her reports surpassed his in concreteness, sensitivity and intelligence. Harold Acton, who reviewed correspondents' cables in the censorship office at the Hôtel Scribe, singled out Gellhorn's as 'the best-written and most vivid of the articles submitted' to him.

Already assessing the fate of Europe after the war and reporting on developments that augured an anxious peace, if not a cold war, Gellhorn travelled in July 1944 with a squadron of Poles who called themselves the Carpathian Lancers, because they had fled Poland through the Carpathian mountains. They had not seen Poland in five years. Assembled in 1941 as a cavalry regiment in Syria, they fought in the Middle East and the western desert. In Egypt they had distinguished themselves in armoured cars at Tobruk and El Alamein. For almost a year they had outlasted the intense heat of Iraq, protecting oilfields. By January 1944 they were in Italy, taking Cassino by May. They had now progressed 200 miles up the Adriatic, having to contend for every stretch of road, battling a magnificently trained enemy.

During a lull in the fighting on a nearly perfect day, Gellhorn decided to join the soldiers for a swim. But what to do about the mines? Like a troop of Balinese dancers they daintily trod over a wrecked bridge, careful not to disturb the split-up railroad ties. Down the road on the other side of the bridge Gellhorn pushed on with a companion who agreed they should walk together, since it would not be fair for just one of them to be blown up. As they swam, they could observe the Germans getting shelled. What if the enemy broke their way? The best thing to do, they thought, was to stay in the water.

In her dispatch on the Carpathian Lancers, Gellhorn reported the well-founded Polish fear that after the war Russia would dominate Poland. After all, Stalin had invaded from the east just after Hitler had entered Poland from the west. Many of the Lancers had relatives imprisoned in Russia, and no Pole could forget that his country had been partitioned and then obliterated by foreign powers for more than 200 years. Gellhorn tried to console them. Surely the Russians would have to respect Poland's autonomy. They would have to honour the sacrifices the Poles had made to fight the Germans. Sounding very much like Mary Douglas in *A Stricken Field*, Gellhorn knew she was expressing her Americanness, 'the optimism of those who are forever safe'. She realized she had no right to lecture them when Americans had come nowhere near the tragedy Poland had experienced. *Collier's* did not print Gellhorn's piece on the Lancers. In *The Face of War* she speculates that her article damaged the Soviet Union's standing – then at an all-time high in the US.

Polish soldiers told Gellhorn about escape via the Jewish under-ground, fleeing the country on the Trans-Siberian railroad to Japan, becoming slave labourers in German and Russian concentration camps. Here in Italy her love affair with Poland began. It would become one of her special concerns after the war.

From the Italian coast, Gellhorn followed the Eighth Army to Florence. Under German attack, the Allies attempted not only to defend the city but to preserve its art treasures. For Gellhorn this was a most telling point. The Americans could have shelled the city and turned it into a battlefield, thus shortening the time it took to drive out the Germans. Instead, the Eighth Army had chosen a more difficult and laborious route, and respected the rights of the Com-mittee of Liberation, which had been formed before the Allies arrived in Florence.

Gellhorn prevailed on a British officer to take her out in an armoured car to meet with partisans. She was impressed by very young men, constantly on the move, daring and resourceful in cap-turing weapons from the Germans. They fought well – now that they had a cause worth fighting for – and had lost a third of their men, wounded and dead, in ten days of intense warfare. She was awed by the unruffled, elegant Florentines, who coped so well with hunger, with the lack of drinking water and fuel, and with enemies both in and outside their city.

Staying with the Eighth Army in its historic advance across Italy, Gellhorn emphasized not just military feats but the implications for humanity of these victories. The Eighth Army seemed to include nearly everyone: Poles, Canadians, South Africans (black and white), Indians, New Zealanders, Englishmen, Scots and Irishmen. Some-how in this babel of languages – including numerous dialects of English – the soldiers understood each other. It amused her that this polyglot army got along so well. They had become 'neighbourly men'.

After leaving the Italian campaign, Gellhorn sped south through France, now occupied by both Germans and Allies, with a machine-gun escort of three companions she 'affectionately called madmen'. In between assignments she met with Hemingway in Paris. When she asked him for a divorce, he accused her of wrecking his life. He would certainly die in battle, leave his children fatherless and she had been the cause of it all. If she talked about a divorce any more, he would shoot her. Photographer Robert Capa found her crying in her room. Did she know about Mary Welsh? Capa asked. Why not call the Ritz and ask for her? Hemingway answered the call. 'Tell him you want a divorce', Capa coached her. Shaking all over, she did so. Hemingway started swearing. 'Tell him that you know all about him and Mary Welsh and that he *must* give you a divorce.' She did so and more of Hemingway's swearing followed.

Hemingway told his cronies that he had gone to war to catch up with his wife and claimed that 'whenever he showed up, she ran away from him'. He had finally wised up: 'When I got to know Marty, I knew she collected things. She collected bric-a-brac, oriental rugs, paintings; and it took me some time to realize that I was part of the collection.' On 15 September he wrote to his son Patrick that he had not had a letter from Gellhorn since June. She was a 'Prima-Donna', he assured his son:

> When head was all smashed and terrible headaches etc. she would not do anything for a man that we would do for a dog. I made a very great mistake on her – or else she changed very much – I think probably both – But mostly the latter. I hate to lose anyone who can look so lovely and who we taught to shoot and write so well. But have torn up my tickets on her and would be glad to never see her again.

On 17 September three battalions of the 82nd Airborne, led by daring General James Gavin, parachuted into Holland. General James Gavin, only thirty-seven, was eager to have the exploits of his men documented in war dispatches. One of three correspondents brought from Paris to cover the action, Gellhorn soon became attached to the men and their commanding officer. They had made history by parachuting into Sicily and Salerno, and they were among the first soldiers to hit the beaches of Normandy. That several Lincoln Battalion veterans were among the 82nd Airborne endeared it all the more to her. They had battled without respite or replacements and had never retreated from enemy fire.

Gavin had enlisted in the army at seventeen, earned a place at West Point and risen to the rank of lieutenant-general. Gellhorn judged him the ideal soldier, one who had a sense of history, fought

alongside his men, and showed unusual courage and creativity.
Tough and demanding, he fostered initiative and individuality, and
protected his soldiers in trouble. While training them in the States he
had stood up to a superior officer who had wanted to discipline a
paratrooper for having had 'sexual intercourse with a young lady on
the lawn of the courthouse in Phenix City' (outside Fort Benning,
Georgia). Gavin responded: 'In view of the fact that that young man
will be asked to give his life for his country in the next few months,
I suggest we give him a medal.' Gavin's men called him 'General Jim'
and saluted him as though they were shaking his hand. They liked
the 'cocky way' he wore his hat and they were 'fiercely proud' of
their fighting record under him.

Gavin led his men by jumping out of the lead plane. He slept
with them on the ground and believed a general should be at the
battle and get the 'odor of it in his nostrils'. He had scorned grand
strategists and 'set-piece' tacticians who stood still collecting forces.

Gavin had brilliantly devised the plan that had taken intact the
Nijmegen bridge, a huge modern structure that had explosives
cemented into it, Germans hiding underneath it, and machine-
gun nests, artillery and mortar fire trained on every access route. Tall
and thin, with a charming Irish face, he appeared dignified but not
pompous.

Gavin became Gellhorn's lover – one of several men she would
take to her bed during the war. When Gellhorn reminisced many
years later about her wartime amours, she confided to younger
British friends like James Fox and Nicholas Shakespeare that sex
grew out of friendship and compassion; it was a '"dessert" that you
had to offer occasionally to make the meal a success'. She told
Shakespeare about her 'one-night stands' in the war. 'It was my
Florence Nightingale act. They so desperately wanted it. It meant
nothing to me.' Of her coupling with an artillery officer she
remarked, 'It was as if I had a piece of bread and he was hungry and
I let him have it.' Tiptoeing on a mined beach, she made love in the
water with a Pole, one of those heroic Carpathian Lancers she
admired. 'It was wonderful for him – but it just left me cold.'

Gellhorn also admitted to Shakespeare that she was 'singing for
my supper with sex'. A Gellhorn friend during the war, Maxine
McClellan, assigned to General H. H. (Hap) Arnold's staff, told her

nephew Ernie Sibley that she and Gellhorn had made a 'friendly bet on which of them could sleep with the most Allied general officers'. They had 'carte blanche to officers' clubs and general headquarters all over the ETO [Eastern Theatre of Operations]'. The number 'approached three digits. ... Neither of them got Ike ... but my aunt was particularly proud that she got Monty and Gellhorn didn't', Sibley remembered. Certainly McClellan, if not Gellhorn, was probably magnifying her conquests, since the suggestion that Monty had an affair with anyone is about as startling as suggesting that JFK was celibate. Gellhorn appeared to regard sex as a catering job: it just seemed like something males needed.

Both Gellhorn and Gavin were discreet, and for the record he restricted himself to praising her quick wit and talent, her independence and analytical power. Rumours of a romance would not take very long to reach Hemingway, who knew several of Gellhorn's and Gavin's friends, such as Robert Capa and the correspondent Charles Collingwood.

Early in December 1944 an exhausted Gellhorn contemplated leaving the war zone. She had been badly bruised in a car accident. Her writing seemed inadequate to the enormity of the horror she had witnessed, she wrote to Charles Colebaugh. How could she imbue others with the indignation she felt over the atrocities she had reported? She had seen pictures of two bodies dug up with gouged-out eyes, the victims of Gestapo terror. An escapee from a German extermination camp told her everything: 2700 people a day were gassed and burned; everyone in the camp had their arms tattooed with numbers and their bodies shaved; Jews were forced to shovel the bodies of other Jews into the ovens. The stench of burning flesh permeated everything and made people retch. She had not spared herself in witnessing the worst human beings were capable of, but these last incidents had shocked her into an uncharacteristically emotional lament. What kind of civilization had created this insanity and was there anyone who could stop this vicious infection from spreading?

At Toulouse, Gellhorn managed to visit a French concentration camp, where refugees from the Spanish Civil War had been languishing for nearly six years. Many Republican soldiers and their families had been moved as many as six times from camp to camp. Men had untreated, unhealed wounds; some had been beaten; one child affected a toughness, the result of many hardships, but still wept when he was asked about his father. These were people without a country, sleeping on straw in frigid cement huts. Perhaps half a million Spaniards had fled to France after Franco's victory. Some 7000 had become slave labourers for the Germans; others had been put in the camps; still others had become part of the Maquis (the Resistance). The Spanish Maquis had sabotaged 400 railway lines, fifty-eight locomotives, thirty-five railway bridges, 150 telephone lines, twenty factories and fifteen coal mines. Even with poor military equipment they had managed to capture three tanks. In southern France, without the assistance of Allied troops, they had liberated at least seventeen towns. What Gellhorn wanted to say, and what she very much had to believe, was that after the horrible defeat in Spain, after years in the camps these Spaniards had endured, their spirits were sound.

On 16 December the Germans launched a surprise attack in the Belgian Ardennes and broke through the American front. General Gavin's 82nd Airborne was called in to force a corridor for the rescue of four American divisions. Stationed in nearby Luxembourg City, Colonel John Ruggles invited Gellhorn to spend Christmas Eve and Day with the 22nd Infantry, where Hemingway was stationed. Ruggles knew nothing about the couple's estrangement and mistakenly thought he was preparing a pleasant surprise. In effect, she was on her husband's turf at a time when he was still making it difficult to discuss their divorce. Well briefed by his buddy Hemingway, the commanding officer, Colonel Buck Lanham, took an instant dislike to Gellhorn:

> She was a bitch from start to finish and every member of my staff who met her – and most did – thought so, too. I turned over my room to her and went out and slept in this icy trailer, and almost froze to death when I did get to sleep that night. You never had a thank-you, you never had anything from her. They hated her guts. She was rude, just plain country rude. I was sitting next to her in the jeep. I always let Hemingway ride in the front seat next to the driver. She went on in French thinking I couldn't understand it.

Well, I'd gone to school at the Sorbonne in Paris in the 1930s, so I could speak French somewhat. She'd taken on what Hemingway always called 'a big Christmas counterattack'. He gave her hell and really made her just shrivel up when he turned on her and said: 'Now you've gotten through with all the privacies in your life speaking in French, it might interest you to know that Buck speaks better French than you do!' That shut her up.

Years later, in an interview with Dennis Brian, Gellhorn admitted, 'I'm sure that every word of Buck Lanham's is absolutely true.' She had behaved badly and felt embarrassed and powerless in the midst of what Hemingway called 'his' division.

On New Year's Eve, Hemingway's friend Bill Walton met Gellhorn for the first time and liked this 'tall girl with honey-coloured hair and well-fitting slacks'. She had the elegance and bearing of a 'fine race horse', he recalled many years later, and he was pleased when she accepted his dinner invitation. When Walton got back to his room, Hemingway was waiting for him, listened to his friend's account of Gellhorn and announced (with a grin) that he would join them for dinner. Hemingway loudly harangued Gellhorn – Walton's efforts to soft-peddle the conversation notwithstanding. The back and forth was like a hotly contested tennis match – although Walton remembers Gellhorn behaving well 'under the circumstances'. Back in his room Walton chided Hemingway for his boorish behaviour. 'You can't hunt an elephant with a bow and arrow', Hemingway replied. As if to complete his ridiculous big-game metaphor, he appropriated a chambermaid's bucket for a helmet and her mop for a lance, and paraded down the hall in his long underwear in a mock assault on Gellhorn's room. Behind her locked door she dismissed him, simply saying, 'Go away, you drunk.' After such incidents Hemingway would sometimes apologize. 'I feel the way a man would feel who had spat upon the Holy Grail', he remarked.

On New Year's Day, Gellhorn travelled along the road to Bastogne, seeing piles of dead Germans clumped together. Thunderbolts, the American dive bombers, swooped down on the enemy. The planes got so close to the ground that they left her breathless and thinking they would surely crash. At one point, before her visit, the 101st Airborne had been encircled by a German force outnumbering it four to one, yet the Americans had held on through intense bombing and shelling, and now seemed incredibly chipper about it – never conceding the gravity of their position. Strafed by two planes, Gellhorn and a companion took off for the front, thinking it could be no more dangerous than their present situation. In this confusing period American planes sometimes attacked American troops on the ground and the disposition of certain infantry units could not be immediately determined. The Germans were still capable of fighting tank battles and she was turned away at one section of road where as many as thirty German tanks were reported on the attack. Reluctantly, she left these gallant soldiers and made her way to the farmhouse headquarters of a tank commander, observing the way everyone instinctively ducked when a shell landed some distance away on the road. In spite of the continuing combat, she knew that the Battle of the Bulge (called that because of the bulge created within Allied territory when the Germans counter-attacked) was over. She took the rest of the day off, imagining herself among the millions who were disgusted with war, and went sledding with a dozen Luxembourg children.

The Thunderbolts – Gellhorn called them 'snarling bulldog planes' – fascinated her. She wanted to know what it felt like to fly in them. After so many gruelling assignments and disheartening dispatches, she found a way to relieve her tension by writing a report about her ride in a Black Widow night fighter over Germany. Titled by *Collier's* 'Night Life in the Sky' and reprinted as 'The Black Widow' in *The Face of War*, the piece begins with an army major advising her not to fly: the planes are tempting targets and are just as likely to come under friendly as enemy fire. Of course, she ignores him. As she puts on each piece of gear – pants, boots, jacket – her breathing becomes harder. Then there is the cumbersome oxygen mask that is not exactly designed for 'ladies'. With gloves in hand, packing a parachute and suffocating in her mask, she is deemed ready for flight. The trouble is she can hardly move. She keeps getting dragged down when she intends to stand up – the result of the hefty parachute attached to her bottom. It is so cold she feels like burying herself in her own clothes, but it is a marvellous-looking aircraft: its 'two long tails and the long narrow wings' remind her of a 'delicate, deadly dragonfly'. Just after she receives complicated directions about bailing out, the plane seems to hurtle into the sky without actually taking off. A veteran of unpressurized, bad-weather flying in China, she is still stunned by the few seconds it takes the Black Widow to jump from 11,000 to 22,000 feet. It feels like being pressed into some huge iron machine. The pressure is vise-like, her stomach apparently attached to her backbone. She would welcome any change now – just so she could catch her breath. The cold has made her nose run and the drainage freezes on her face. She has barely enough presence of mind to hear the pilot pointing out a fiery V2 rocket. Then her plane becomes the target of enemy flak and takes acrobatic, evasive manoeuvres before landing. In the pilot's view it has been a dull trip. Gellhorn could only marvel at men who took these missions (two or three a night) with such aplomb. 'Night Life in the Sky' is presented as a kind of lark, the *Collier's* lead caption noting that its 'girl correspondent sat on a wobbly crate and flew over Germany looking for enemy planes at night. ... They didn't down any Germans, but otherwise that's routine life for the Black Widow pilots.'

After the German counter-offensive failed, Gellhorn flew from Luxembourg to London. In March 1945, at the Dorchester Hotel, she saw Hemingway for the last time. He had come to say he was divorcing her in Cuba – the easiest way, since they were both residents there. She made no demands. His proposal was convenient, since she did not want to leave the war for weeks of residence in Reno, where Americans got their divorces in six weeks. She had taken to her bed with the flu and his visit was brief. He promised to attend to her affairs as though they were his own. She wanted her passport 'changed back to Gellhorn. I wanted above all to be free of him and his name; and step out of the whole picture fast', she later told Bernice Kert. Not yet realizing her integral role in the Hemingway myth, she badly underestimated its hold on her. Getting rid of him would prove to be an impossible task.

13

POINT OF NO RETURN
1945–1947

'SINCE 1943, London has been the one fixed point in my nomadic life', Gellhorn wrote in *The View from the Ground*, confessing that she had some explaining to do. After Munich, she had said she was 'finished with England. Never set foot again in the miserable self-centered country.' She associated it exclusively with Neville Chamberlain, a 'stick figure with a fossil mind … speaking to and for the meanest stupidity of his people'. But in 1943, she later commented in *The Face of War*, it was a 'new country, the home of a new people'. Calamity brought out the best in the English. The very qualities she had deplored before the war – 'slowness, understatement, complacency' – had been transformed into 'endurance, a refusal to panic, and pride'. The extraordinary discipline of Londoners under siege won her heart. She could live in London precisely because its people had known suffering; she could never return to America because the country – whatever sacrifices it had made – had come out of the war with its own land unscathed. Later, in her reports about Vietnam, she would express an overt loathing for Americans who, in her estimation, could not identify with the sufferings of others.

From London, in April 1945, Gellhorn returned to the war in Germany. Facing an American army of occupation, no one would admit to having been a Nazi. 'No one is a Nazi. No one ever was', Gellhorn wrote at the beginning of her *Collier's* article. ' "We Were Never Nazis." It should, we feel, be set to music. Then the Germans could sing this refrain and that would make it even better.' Indeed, everyone seemed to have a story about hiding Jews – 'all God's chillun hid Jews', she commented sarcastically. The Germans seemed to her to have suffered little: 'nice and fat too, and quite clean and orderly and industrious'. They led neat, disciplined lives and spoke in terms they thought Americans would approve. When asked what form of government they now desired, 'democracy' was the answer. Gellhorn thought she got a more candid reply from a group of women who said they did not care '*who*' was in charge so long as they prospered. This declaration confirmed her suspicions that Germans were authoritarian, and liked to give and to take orders.

The day Germany surrendered, 7 May 1945, Gellhorn was at Dachau. The camp's survivors, seen through the electrified fence on a sunny day, appeared to be skeletal figures examining themselves for lice. They all looked the same, ageless and featureless. In this place of plague and death it was hard to make out the countenances of these bony, shrivelled, tortured people. They had been the subjects of experimentation: deprived of oxygen to measure how long pilots could survive at high altitudes; submerged in freezing water to study the effects of prolonged exposure to extremes of temperature; injected with malaria to determine whether a vaccine could be developed for German soldiers. Others were castrated or sterilized. Gellhorn described these atrocities in detail, quoting a Polish doctor who found them incomprehensible. He was enraged but also mortified that the human race could be capable of such things.

Gellhorn found the horrors of Dachau unrelenting. When she could no longer listen to the stories, she visited other sights – torture chambers no larger than telephone booths; stifling, overcrowded barracks where starving inmates struggled for a bit of sleeping room; gas chambers where she was advised to cover her nose with a handkerchief because of stacked-up dead bodies the Germans had not had a chance to burn. Some inmates had died of their own joy when they were liberated; others had perished hysterically eating the food that had finally been made available to them; some had died on the fences rushing to their deliverers. Hearing the news of victory in Europe at Dachau made that place symbolic for Gellhorn. Ultimately the war was about places like Dachau. Victory had to mean the abolition of Dachau once and for all.

The German concentration camps marked a divide in the world's experience and in Gellhorn's own. There had been nothing quite like it in human experience, as she would try to make clear in *The Wine of Astonishment*, the war novel she would soon begin to write. The war had set her adrift.

Back in London, Gellhorn wandered the streets wondering what to do next. The city looked 'sad. Weeds and wild flowers grew on bombsites everywhere, and great beams shored up the sides of half-destroyed buildings.' Paint was not yet available to freshen façades. A tired people faced a cold winter and strict rationing. Yet Gellhorn could not think of a better place to live. She wrote to Wells that if the city after the war was as 'wonderful as it was during the war it seems to me a place where a permanently rootless one might take roots'. She visited plenty of rundown and damaged houses available at bargain prices and purchased a 'pretty little' one in South Eaton Place. She patched up the roof, suffering from 'terminal dry rot', and lived in her new home in the intervals between her travels in the next two years.

Gellhorn wrote to Hemingway on 27 May that she would spend the summer with her mother, then cover the Pacific war or return to Europe. The Pacific theatre sounded grim and she was not at all sure she wanted to report on the vicious Japanese. Her letter was kind and conciliatory. In a lot of ways the war was over. She had heard the good news that Hemingway's son Jack had been released from a prisoner of war camp and she wanted Ernest to know how well she had been treated by his military friends when she had visited Nuremberg. Their separation was now public knowledge, thanks to a Walter Winchell radio broadcast, but there had been no big uproar about it. Could he get started on the divorce and contact a Cuban lawyer? She hoped he had begun a new book, and she asked him to kiss Patrick and Gregory for her. She wanted to stay in touch with them. In a good mood she signed off with his nickname for her: 'Love, Mook'.

In an undated reply he never sent, a gracious Hemingway discussed his sons, including details of Jack's imprisonment, remarking that 'he loves you very much and we talk of you very affectionately. ... So don't ever feel lonely for him because you always have him.' He remembered their final meeting at the Dorchester as 'lovely ...

such a pleasure not to be enemies'. He let her know about the home in Cuba, assured her he had told columnists the story they had agreed on in London. He had been full of praise for her and she should have no fear of embarrassment. He saw no reason why they should not have the same friends. He had had a friendly exchange of letters with Edna and Martha's brother, Walter. Mary Welsh was with him and he did not hesitate to tell Martha about her, comparing Mary's recent accident with Martha's 'jeep spill'. Martha should not worry about her things; they were packed and in a closet 'regularly aired'. He wished her success for *Love Goes to Press*, a play she and Virginia Cowles were writing. He called her 'Dearest Mook' and promised he would get on with the divorce if absolutely necessary, although he preferred, for the moment, a separation. Writing was difficult in the aftermath of the war, but he vowed to 'write as well as I can to make up (there is no such thing) for all the things we lost'. He even offered to share the Finca with Martha and her mother. This long, rambling, repetitive letter marked the last time he would express his love for Martha in a straightforward, uncritical fashion.

On 23 July Hemingway wrote to Buck Lanham comparing Martha's behaviour in the 'Spanish' and 'D'american' wars. World War Two had spoiled her; women were scarce and very much treasured. In Spain, having a woman was about the same as owning a map case. She had lived with him in a truck, sleeping on a double mattress covered with canvas, and 'under bad circumstances behaved about as well as womens [*sic*] behave'. He admitted giving her trouble there and cited *The Fifth Column* as evidence of his dislike for her. Yet he had grown to love her intensely. Of course, he did not take her to the 'big fights', yet she stuck it out through the siege of Madrid. He had schooled her in war, but she had never learned such basics as reading maps. She had been in one '*real* action', during the time the fascists launched their drive to the sea and during the Loyalist defence of the Ebro. In fact, as he began to think about it, she had been magnificent during the retreats in the grim winding-down days of the war. He had pointed to her courage; she had shamed Catalan troops who seemed about to desert. She had taken it all in good spirits, and he loved her for her beauty and reliability. Buck should not think she had always been the bitch who had shown up on Christmas Eve at their headquarters. Hemingway could not resist putting her down by adverting to a meeting he had had with her in Paris, where he supposedly tore her apart in front of her friends, told her he was in love with another woman and pointed out she would never die in war because 'she never went where they were makeing [*sic*] deads'. She always showed up at times when 'civilians still thought things were bad'. Indulging his fantasies again – what had he ever been but a civilian? – Hemingway allowed his misogyny full expression. After trying to be judicious – Marty was great in Finland, awful in China, 'very good in Singapore and Dutch East Indies' – and insisting she should not be blamed for the stupid mistake he made in marrying her, he concluded: 'Buck we are so fallible we should always pity women.'

On 22 November 1945 – just one day after her fifth wedding anniversary – newspapers announced MARTHA GELLHORN SUED FOR DIVORCE. In a petition filed in Havana, Hemingway charged her with abandonment. In affidavits accompanying the divorce suit he described their married life as 'peaceful and uneventful' until his departure for London in 1944. As one newspaper account put it, 'Mrs Hemingway subsequently informed him she had decided to continue her writing independently.'

For part of the fall and winter of 1946 Gellhorn returned to London – its dilapidated condition a welcome, familiar environment for a displaced war correspondent. She and Virginia Cowles worked on *Love Goes to Press* in between trips to ruined Berlin, where the 82nd Airborne was stationed, and to Portugal and France, where she drafted her war novel.

In January and February Hemingway wrote to Buck Lanham complaining about Gellhorn's letters from Europe. She was having 'tantrums', claiming that she once loved him but that she could no longer abide his behaviour – even when he was 'cold sober'. She accused him of never taking her anywhere; they never went dancing, and he expected her to be bound by convention and by the demands of his career. She wanted the freedom to rove as a reporter. Plainly disgusted, he took her correspondence as a ploy to get him back. Even if he shaped up (so Hemingway told Lanham) and stopped drinking and gambling while perfecting his manners and sensitivity, it would not be enough, for he believed she persisted in attacking him for thoughts he neither held nor implied. In short, this was an impossible women who wanted everything to run smoothly all the time. She would not be pleased, he concluded, unless he could hire for $35 a month 'a butler with the probity of Cardinal Newman and the organizing capacity of Henry Kaiser'.

On 10 June *Love Goes to Press*, by Martha Gellhorn and Virginia Cowles, opened in Eastbourne at the Devonshire Park Theatre for a week of previews. Then it transferred to the Embassy Theatre in Swiss Cottage. Gellhorn and Cowles nervously watched the audience from the balcony and then fled, not able to cope with their success as the actors took a dozen curtain calls and the audience called for the authors. The *Spectator* reviewer praised the play's 'gusto, astringency and much skilfully applied local colour'. If a certain air of unreality pervaded the plot, it made 'little difference to our enjoyment of a most competent play which is admirably acted and produced'. *The Stage*, a weekly theatre newspaper, noted that 'at times the humour rises to brilliance'. On 22 July the play moved to the Duchess Theatre in the West End of London for another forty performances. The play opened at the Biltmore Theater in New York on 1 January 1947 and closed after only four performances. American reviewers were shocked by its farcical treatment of the war. 'London audiences knew about real war; they had lived through it, either in uniform or as embattled civilians. Knowing the real thing, they were free to laugh at this comic, unreal version of war', Gellhorn later explained in the published introduction to the play.

Gellhorn afterwards called it 'frivolous', a 'joke' she and Cowles had confected in about ten days. Initial reports in American newspapers of the play's reception praised its humour and liveliness. It is set on the Italian front and it focuses on the romances and rivalries of war correspondents. The two female heroines, Annabelle and Jane, bear some resemblance to Gellhorn and Cowles. They are good-looking, brave and competent women who know how to get stories and how to manipulate military officers. The male correspondents, on the other hand, are competitive and covetous of each other's work – and quite willing to steal a story or a woman if the opportunity presents itself.

Many of the lines in the play could have been stolen from Hem-

ingway, who had written sketches involving two women war correspondents during his wartime stay in London. He referred to them
as having 'the manners of whores du combat and the morals of lady
woodchucks'. Hemingway had Gellhorn in mind in his description
of Janet Rolfe, an elegant blonde, walking with a bold strut, knowing
what a good backside she has as her luscious hair swings heavily just
above her nearly perfect shoulders. Blakely, the narrator of one
sketch, refers to Rolfe as one of those 'old, badly laid mines' that
turn up from the last war. She replies 'well laid', but dismissing his
'literary' language, she mentions that he has never liked the way she
talks. Later she explains to another male character that Blakely is a
'conceited bastard' who expected her to give him a child because
she had said she was madly in love with him.

In *Love Goes to Press*, Hemingway's brand of bitterness is played
for comic effect. The male correspondents distrust women, and
accuse them of not working hard for their stories and relying on
their looks. Any decent woman, one male correspondent argues,
would be at home. Annabelle is out to save the world (she calls it her
'mother complex') and is angry about the restrictions put on her in
battle zones, but she can switch in mid-sentence to complimenting
Jane on her hair. Annabelle prides herself on her fashion sense and
knowing how to dress for war. Obviously, Gellhorn and Cowles are
getting in their licks, but the play also suggests the wish – especially
strong in England at the time – not to dwell (not yet, at least) on just
how debilitating six years of war had been.

On 5 August 1946 Hemingway's own coda to the play took the
form of a letter to Gellhorn he decided not to send. He was irked at
his ex-wife's 'ungracious' letter to Mary, provoked, he decided, by a
'sudden rush of either success or failure to the head' (Gellhorn's
London hit and New York flop). He would never forget how many
times he had rewritten her work so as not to sound like him. While
he 'hand-carried the wounded' in the war she rode around in captured German jeeps, the darling of army officers. 'One money
makeing [*sic*] ride at night in a Black Widow doesn't clear that'. Her
fiction would never succeed because she produced melodrama with
simple black-and-white characters: this 'over-writing comes from
your always being your own heroine which, since you are not terribly sound about yourself makes your characters sooner or later quite

silly unless someone corrects them'. Now an ageing beauty, 'a product of beauticians', she was a 'career bulldozer' with a 'phony accent;
much more phony each year'. Unable to practise his renowned talent for understatement, he continued: 'Won't put anything in about
your physical make-up, your thousands of rubbers, pots, pans, jars,
capsules, grease guns, mud packs, bust lifters, mustache removers, flat
foot aids, pessories, or other aids to beauty. Congratulations on your
thatched roof cottage in the country. Why don't you try thatching
the roof with yourself?' He conceded only two good qualities: *The
Trouble I've Seen* had one 'wonderful story' and she was 'usually
excellent about children'. He signed off, 'Good night, Marty. Sleep
well my beloved phony and pretentious bitch.'

When Gellhorn's 'Cry Shame' (an attack on the House Committee on Un-American Activities) appeared in the 6 October 1947
issue of the *New Republic*, Hemingway wrote to Charlie Scribner
expressing his approval: 'She is at her best when angry or moved to
pity.' She was 'at her worst when dealing with daily life or, say, more
or less natural life without runnings away or atrocities'. War had
spoiled her by feeding her vanity. She seemed to regard it as a 'sort
of very highly organized tribute to her own beauty and charm in
which, unfortunately, people were killed and wounded'. He wondered whether she would have continued as a correspondent if her
earnings had not been tax free, or if war ceased to be the big drama
'in which there was a satanic enemy fought by Our Side'. He
claimed she was upset about her assignment to a nursing outfit during the Normandy invasion because she could not go over to France
on 'a glamour basis'. Hemingway remembered her writing about
the beauties of Rome when 'we were not yet out of the hedgerows
in Normandy'.

Hemingway was warming up for the attack he would make on
Gellhorn's character a few years later in *Across the River and Into the
Trees*, where he would emphasize her mean-spirited competitive-
ness. He wrote to Lillian Ross that he had to let Gellhorn '*almost* win
[at tennis] for her to be happy. If you *let* her win she became insufferable. You had to let her win sometimes insufferable or not.' She
was a good player, he admitted, and 'quite handsome to watch. But
was lead-footed.' She hated people watching her and her game
would deteriorate. She was much better when she could play alone

with him or with the Basques, who praised her 'Bryn Mawr serve
... built her up and made her shine'. Gellhorn would retaliate years
later in London regaling her chaps with stories about what a poor
tennis player – and equally poor sexual partner – Hemingway was.

When Buck Lanham wrote to Hemingway about rumours that
Gellhorn was about to marry James Gavin, Hemingway replied on
17 November with nasty descriptions of Gellhorn's sexual parts and
suggested she had misrepresented herself, claiming she was not Jewish when, in fact, Hemingway found out she was. He still would
have married her, since the Virgin Mary was also Jewish, but he
would have appreciated getting at least an approximation of the
truth. He said that she had had two abortions before he met her
(when, where and who the men were Hemingway did not specify).
Without discussing it with him, she had had an operation aimed at
improving their sexual relations. In Hemingway's view this made
matters worse and he had terminated their intimacy with a gross
remark that was far worse than his alter ego Blakely's comment
about badly laid landmines. He would heartily congratulate any man
who could now fill in for him and reward that man with a Louisville
Slugger and other tributes to his potency. Judging from the tone of
Lanham's letters, it seems Hemingway suspected Gellhorn of spreading damaging stories against him. He was counter-attacking
and reminding Lanham of their encounter with Gellhorn during
Christmas 1944, when (Hemingway claimed) he had rejected her,
saying his one devout wish was to see her dead and to be allowed
the opportunity to refuse to speak at her funeral. She had written
him letters trying to get him back, saying her love for him was
stronger than ever, but he had flatly told her there would be no second chance. For her part, Gellhorn tried to abort any definitive
assessment of Hemingway's claims by burning their correspondence
shortly before she died.

Hemingway's 17 November letter is couched in cryptic, quasi-
military language. He refers to himself as an 'operative' and to Gellhorn as if she were his assignment in an attempt to distance himself
from her, to dehumanize her and to enlarge his own martial image.
Lanham, who despised Gellhorn and never changed his opinion of
her as a 'certified bitch', was nevertheless appalled by his friend's animosity, admitting many years later to biographer Carlos Baker that

Hemingway 'wanted to write the worst about her and to him this was the worst that could be said about any woman'. Hemingway wrote an obscene poem, 'To Martha Gellhorn's Vagina', in which he compared her sexual parts to the wrinkled neck of an old hot-water bottle. He declared that he read it to any woman he could get into bed with him.

Hemingway regarded James Gavin as the hero Gellhorn had always wanted and failed to get in Hemingway himself. He thought Gavin would get a bad bargain, but military heroes were often not very smart off the battlefield. Yet Gellhorn had been able to fool him, so he had to give her credit. If she had revamped herself once to catch him, maybe she could do it again to get Gavin.

A week later Hemingway's mood had shifted from all-out attack to a condescending interpretation of Gellhorn's need to snare Gavin. After all, Hemingway had kicked her out 'on her ass', so she had to marry a finer, more courageous man, good-looking, highly decorated and (on the evidence of *Infantry Journal*) a good writer.

For six months Hemingway had been building up his case against Gellhorn – much of which seems to have been stimulated by a letter from his publisher. In June 1947 Hemingway had written to Charlie Scribner, asking for a report about Gellhorn and remarking that he had a new housemaid named Martha whom he enjoyed ordering around. He figured his ex-wife must be forlorn without a war to write about. Scribner replied with news on Gellhorn's novel, anticipating the reactions of several male reviewers who marvelled at the novel's 'masculinity'. How could a woman know men's minds so well; how could she know so much about combat? the publisher wondered. Scribner foolishly thought, however, that Gellhorn should play up the wartime romances in her novel. The last third troubled him – all that grim stuff about Dachau. Maxwell Perkins had already talked her out of what he deemed to be a depressing title, *Point of No Return*, in favour of a biblical prayer for healing a land broken by war.

Obviously disturbed over the advance praise accorded Gellhorn's war novel, Hemingway conducted a campaign against her that reached epic proportions (at least in his own mind). He cut off communication with her, refusing to answer her letters and letting her know through a third party that he would ship the 'junk' she had asked for. In the meantime, he was stuck with paying storage on the rest of her furniture. He rehearsed all his favourite charges about her never having seen real battle and added a few new ones – including a story that she had lured him to Europe by falsely assuring him she had a job lined up for him. Just lately he had heard a story about an Englishman who had handled a real estate transaction for her in London. The poor man got screwed out of several thousand pounds when she reneged on her promise to divide the profit from the sale of her house. Hemingway got so worked up that he even fantasized about shooting Gellhorn in the small of the back – one of the worst possible places to be hit, he assured Lanham. He pictured running her like an animal before he brought her down. He was playing a 'slow game' with her and spooking her. He 'hated her ersatz kraut guts'. He was sure her war novel would not make any money.

'Beauty show-offs, like Gavin, show-off in front of Marty. ... When she came up with us 2 she didn't even know we were fighting or had ever fought', Hemingway wrote to Lanham. He seemed to have forgotten that Stephen Crane (one of his literary models) had not seen the Civil War engagements he described. A year earlier Gellhorn had written to Charlie Scribner, lavishing praise on her old friend, Stan Pennell, who had just written a brilliant Civil War novel published by Scribner's. Pennell, she pointed out, had never been to war. Indeed, he had spent many lonely and impoverished years in Junction City heroically working on his novel. Several years later Hemingway himself praised Pennell's book to Charlie Scribner. Gellhorn freely admitted inventing combat scenes that were praised by many reviewers when the editor of the *US Infantry Journal* wrote to her requesting information about the dates and locales of the actions she described.

Hemingway was pleased, however, when he learned that Gavin had married a twenty-three-year old girl just as the 'age-conscious' Gellhorn was turning forty. Peeved about a 'snotty letter' Martha had written Mary, he decided not to answer her letters and to treat her like General MacArthur would, dealing with her through a 'neutral power'. She was already 'whining up the back alleys of friends' about his uncooperativeness and he had written advising them to tell her he was so mad that they were afraid to approach him. She was now the enemy and he felt entitled to slur her: 'And since she had that Prussian blood mixed with the Juden know how to really clip her in her krautism.' He knocked a recent story of hers that appeared in the *Atlantic Monthly* and hoped she would write 'even worse' stuff.

Hemingway got so steamed up about Gellhorn's war novel he wrote her a letter he did not send. He jeered at the book jacket's description of her 'extensive career' and claimed she had trespassed on the territory he and Buck Lanham had covered during the Battle of the Bulge. He was still upset about their Christmas jeep ride, when he had tried to compliment her by saying she had seen almost as much war as he had. 'She replied, I've seen more than you, unless you count the first war of course.' Coming from a thrice divorced man, his words of dismissal were pretty lame: 'Well she is a three time loser now. She lost to Bertrand de Jouvenel, to me, to James Gavin.' Hemingway even took offence at her use of the term 'deads' in her war novel, since he felt the Hemingway–Lanham clique owned that one. He charged that by 1944 Gellhorn was completely 'un-nerved' by the war. He had trouble appreciating her 'nervous situation'. After all, he bragged to Lanham, he had been off on his daring submarine expeditions.

As Jeffrey Meyers suggests, Hemingway's separation from Gellhorn was the most 'traumatic' of all his marital disturbances. None of his other wives had shown such a strong will or an intellect and imagination that matched his own. Hemingway's letters to Lanham reveal that he regarded Gellhorn as a competitor. When she published a story in the *Woman's Home Companion*, he took that as a sign of her decline as a writer, working now only for the money. While he took full responsibility for leaving his first and second wives, he felt abused and victimized by Martha. He had to accuse her of conniving ambition in order to salvage his pride. He was used to hurting women. It was a new and devastating experience to have a woman walk out on him and publish a war novel before his own appeared.

In spite of Hemingway's claims that Gellhorn poached on his war preserve, the setting of her novel is not in Hurtgenwald – where he and Lanham were stationed – but Luxembourg. *The Wine of Astonishment* takes place during the last winter of the war. After the Normandy invasion, the Allies had driven the Germans back across the borders of several countries. The war was clearly won, yet the

Germans fought on, reluctantly giving ground. The battle would not be over until they were thrown back across the Rhine. During a lull in the fighting, weary American soldiers begin to speculate that the 'krauts' are all played out. Lieutenant-Colonel John Dawson Smithers, commander of the 277th Infantry of the Twentieth Division, a conscientious soldier admired by his men, begins – as they do – to think about the coming peace. His life has been transformed by leading men into combat. He is no longer a small-town salesman from Georgia and wonders how he can possibly go back to his pre-war career, where his lack of class and clout showed, where he hungered after but did not dare approach the town's most desirable women. They were out of reach – too rich, too conscious of society to have anything to do with him.

Smithers has the prejudices of a small-town Southerner and reacts with distaste when he learns that his new jeep driver is Jacob Levy, a Jew. There are no Jews in his outfit. Yet Levy proves to be a regular guy, reliable in combat, a good driver, discreet and absolutely loyal to Smithers. To Smithers' mind, Levy is no different from his other good men. In other words, Levy does not behave like a Jew.

Although Smithers remains a major character in the novel, attention quickly shifts to Levy, who senses what it would mean if he were typecast as the 'Jewboy'. As he puts it to himself, 'A Jew had to earn being left alone.' In effect, this means suppressing any acknowledgement of his Jewishness – a tactic he long ago learned from his father, a shop owner who always advised his son not to associate with many Jews. In short, Levy knows little about what it might mean to be a Jew. In fact, he does not know much more than Smithers.

Both Smithers and Levy find women to love. Dorothy, a Red Cross volunteer, is a sophisticated war-weary woman who disconcerts Smithers with her forwardness and her seeming lack of vulnerability. He wants a woman to lean on him and to look up to him. She is a gratifying woman to be with, since her type is only attracted to officers. He could not have had this kind of woman in Georgia. Käthe, a Luxembourg girl, delights Levy because she is so submissive and so eager to please him. He has no trouble fitting her into his dreams of a shack in the Smokies where he can live on his own off the land. But when she asks him his name, he panics and tells the

Catholic girl he is John Dawson Smithers. Shocked at just how much of a liability his Jewishness is, Levy is not prepared to see how he has never been willing to acknowledge his true identity.

Gellhorn makes a point of how elegant, even princely, Levy can look. He can easily pass for a Gentile, although he has never explicitly thought in such terms. This handsome and graceful man, whose appearance is admired by men and women, fantasizes the circumstances in which he will tell Käthe about his real name and background. Like Smithers, Levy contemplates acknowledging his origins while dreaming of transcending them.

Levy is from St Louis, and the people in the Luxembourg restaurant where he meets Käthe remind him of Germans back home. There are no scenes set in St Louis and not much is made of Levy's St Louis background – leaving a certain vagueness in his character reminiscent of Gellhorn's own vague St Louis German-Jewishness, a Jewishness never acknowledged or confronted. Half the novel hovers over Smithers and Levy, over their uneasy lack of fulfilment and grandiose plans for the future, and over the stagnant front, where the soldiers have nearly convinced themselves the Germans are about to give up. Gellhorn's pacing is exquisite. She captures both the boredom and the anxiety of a stalled infantry campaign, the camaraderie of combat soldiers and their private daydreams. Her narrative's smooth, engrossing surface is pricked by subtle hints of trouble to come. With the sudden unpredictable onset of war itself, her novel explodes with action:

> Then with a suddenness the High Command could never quite explain, the Germans attacked this tissue paper front. The weather went over to their side and a thick dripping cloud settled low above the trees. It was iron cold and snow began to fall, as if to order. The Germans attacked through the snow, the pine forests, across the rivers and over the dumpy hills. Nothing like this had been seen; it was no counter-attack. They seemed driven by a final and furious hope. The front broke.

The rhythm of this passage – the precise reporting of weather and terrain, the feeling that nature (at least momentarily) was on the Germans' side, the sheer crazed quality of the enemy's drive and the sense of confused defences snapping – rivals Gellhorn's best reports on the war.

The sudden summons to combat is also what changes Jacob Levy's life, making him the novel's focus. Watching his best friends being maimed and killed by the German thrust, he realizes he has not given the war serious attention. If the Germans continue their penetration, they will retake Luxembourg City, where Käthe lives. Suddenly Levy feels he has a very personal stake in the war. What happens to her, what happens to his buddies, now is of overwhelming importance, for he has a share in their fate. Similarly, Dorothy has become Smithers's symbol for everything he has earned to set him apart from his small-town self. Losing her in Luxembourg would mean a retreat to the background he has overcome.

Slowly the Americans gain back lost ground. Levy and his fellow soldiers overrun German towns, do some looting and begin to see how Germans have lived. They visit a doctor's home and imagine his family life to be similar to their own until they see pictures of him in an SS uniform – a family man and a murderer, they realize. For Levy, the profound shock comes at Dachau, where he follows much the same route Gellhorn took. Heinrich, an inmate for twelve years, recounts in a matter-of-fact voice the tortures and mass exterminations. For Heinrich, this has become an everyday reality. For Levy, it is the recognition of a destiny that could have been his own – simply because he is a Jew. The families he sees at Dachau could have been his. Although he had been vaguely aware of the extermination of the Jews, he never knew the extent of it, never identified with their humanity. Indeed, he realizes that he did not take any of it seriously. His whole life had been built on the illusion that if he behaved like everyone else, he would survive and even prosper. But what about all these Jews leading normal lives? They had died simply because they were Jews. The Germans have acted as though they have a right to rule everyone.

Back in his jeep after visiting Dachau, Levy sees a group of Germans in the middle of a wide road, not moving at the sound of his horn, acting just like they own the world. He runs them down and crashes into a tree. He recognizes his action as murder. He also views it as a symbolic act. He has finally accepted his Jewishness. The novel ends with the suggestion that Levy will be let off with a suspended sentence for involuntary manslaughter. More troubling to Smithers is the depth of Levy's emotions. He did not know how his driver felt about being Jewish. Levy, of course, did not know himself. Unlike Smithers, he does not try to rationalize his action, but he is, in a way, reconciled to humanity when he learns that not all the inmates of Dachau were Jewish. Having thought himself doomed, having given up any hope of a post-war life, he begins again to hope, reinterpreting his murder of the Germans as an act of solidarity with all people, not just his own.

Gellhorn had poured her intense hatred of Germans into the novel. She had also chosen a hero who typifies the American blindness she decried. Americans did not feel they had a personal stake in the war. The concentration camps, the battles, were not on home ground. Americans knew they were returning to an undefiled country. Only by reaching a point of no return, by seeing his world shattered, is Levy able to empathize with the lot of humankind.

Is this what Americans needed: some kind of overwhelming disaster to make them see their place in world history and accept responsibility for others? Gellhorn's novel is the work of an expatriate. Like Smithers and Levy, she had seen years of war that made her wonder what was left for her in America. In fact, she would live the rest of her life abroad. She had reached a point of no return. Her native land was large, well-off and secure. It could attend to itself.

For Gellhorn, World War Two ended with the Nuremberg Trials (November 1945 to October 1946). Of the twenty-one defendants, only one, Hermann Goering, seemed undefeated and undaunted. Passionately believing in the trials, Gellhorn treated the Reichsmarschall as a has-been actor, described in the past tense: 'Goering's terrible mouth wore a smile that was not a smile, but only a habit the lips had taken.' Goering's puffy performances rebounded off Gellhorn as though she were granite. All the defendants were similarly diminished: 'These twenty-one men, these nothings, these industrious and once-confident monsters were the last left alive of that small gang which had ruled Germany.' Except for his 'terrible mouth', Gellhorn gave Goering no dominating characteristic – indeed, she did not describe him at all.

Lord Justice Geoffrey Lawrence, president of the tribunal, spoke in a 'slow, careful, and immensely quiet voice'. Listening to him 'reading without haste or passion ... You felt the dignity and

modesty of the man.' Indeed, 'everything about the trial at Nuremberg was unique in history; everything happened for the first time.
Everyone present seemed to know that history was being made;
everyone seemed to feel that responsibility and find it heavy.'
Gellhorn had no illusions that Nuremberg would make the world a
better place. But it was the least that could be done. By the end of
her report, Goering was an evil memory, the flaws and failures in the
court proceedings were not even mentioned. Rather, four nations
demonstrated that they could 'work patiently together to brand evil
and reaffirm the power and the goodness of honest law'.

14

A PRIVATE GOLDEN AGE
1948–1952

FTER THE WAR a change of editors made *Collier's* a less hospitable employer for Gellhorn and her reports from foreign parts became harder to place. 'I don't think we will be as much interested in international things as we were', the *New Yorker's* Harold Ross wrote to her on 29 March 1946. She planned to economize by living cheaply in Mexico and by placing her fiction in well-paying publications to make up for the $1500 per article that *Collier's* had paid her. She would place some of her lesser fiction in women's magazines, disappointed that the *New Yorker*, where 'I've always wanted to have something published', consistently rejected her stories. 'I seem to lack wit and to be on the whole a gloomy and earnest type of writer', she confessed to Katherine White, the magazine's fiction editor, in June 1948.

Martha Gellhorn called her four years in Mexico (1948–52) her 'private golden age'. She rarely read a newspaper or listened to the radio. 'Am practising to become a Tibetan hermit', she wrote to John Gunther. A neighbour phoned to make sure she knew about the start of war in Korea.

Half a year of drought, half a year of nightly rain, every day aglow with sun. An elemental sense of enchantment soothed one's troubles. In Mexico's gleaming atmosphere poverty did not seem quite so painful. From a village café Gellhorn watched craftsmen, merchants, begging children on the square and the handsome, slim Indians. She avoided the grungy bars and associated with foreign residents in a comfortable, unchanging environment that seemed 'preserved in amber'.

At the end of the dry months foreign residents tired of the heat, chafed each other, developed imaginary illnesses and fantasized about getting away to Europe. Like the trees, everyone seemed to sag in this land of dust, but she loved the climate, in which people indulged their peculiarities and took long siestas. After the evening rain the land the next morning seemed reborn, smelling fresh and shining. The earth sprouted around her – exotic trees blooming in hues of orange and red, plants in luscious pinks and lavenders, snow-white flowers and purple morning glories enveloping everything in a riot of colour. Lawns and gardens were perfect green arbours. Residents who had left for the season returned with news from foreign parts; suddenly everyone perked up with gossip and visits to each other.

Through her heroine, Susanna, in *The Lowest Trees Have Tops* (1967), Gellhorn evokes her own joy: sunning in the afternoons on the lawn, gazing in reverie at the sky, imagining herself a world explorer, a renowned scientist, or a celebrated, fashionable woman. The 'real world' seemed far off, full of strife and devastation, while in Mexico history had stopped, apparently absorbed into the warm, radiant air.

After the rainy season, in October, the clear, moonlit nights were studded with stars; the unclouded days were a pure blue and gold. This was the 'sober season', when Mexico's foreign residents took stock of themselves and each other, feeling that perhaps something should be done to better themselves.

Mexico beguiled Gellhorn because she could make her life from scratch. People talked about freedom and peace, she wrote to her mother, but she actually had it: the great challenge of facing each day afresh, with nearly total liberty to do as she wished. There were no wars, no political controversies, no jockeying for position, authority or prestige; she could concentrate on her own feelings.

Gellhorn enjoyed planning her life as though it were a military campaign. She had a strategy, what she called an 'eight-point scheme'. It depended on the sale of what she called her 'bilge' stories, which she hoped would replace her journalism as a source of income. Mexico served as her base, from which she planned trips to Europe, especially to Italy, where she wanted to investigate the plight of children made homeless by the war. She had ambitious plans not only for a book but for the 'babies' she wanted to bring home with her and educate – sending them to a local school and perhaps supplementing their studies herself until they were ten or twelve.

During the summer of 1949 in Rome, Gellhorn reported on a country buoyantly recovering from war and yet neglectful of its orphaned children, sequestered from the amiable façade of daily life, collecting cigarette butts and begging in the streets, suffering from tuberculosis and undernourishment, wasting away in dull, authoritarian orphanages and terrorized by their memories of the war. To most Italians her quest to adopt an Italian child seemed quixotic, the vagary of a wealthy American.

Gellhorn's friends did not share her enthusiasm for adoption. A single woman, used to frequent travel and independence, should not take on such an overwhelming commitment, especially to a child of a foreign background. One of Edna's friends, Anna Lord Straus, accompanied Martha on a tour of the milk stations set up for orphans. Writing to Edna afterwards, Straus reported the sight of Martha's weary yet dogged persistence, sitting on the side of a dusty road with a flat tyre while her companions fled to the bus. Gellhorn knew the odds were against a single parent, especially one who depended on an uncertain income from writing. Yet what were these worries worth next to the obvious need these children had for loving, caring parents? Better to have one parent than none at all.

Finally, in an orphanage teeming with unusually active children, noisy, rowdy and 'comfortably dirty', she found her boy, 'a blond fatty' in a flour sack, lying on his back, 'counting his toes'. He appeared to be blissfully by himself in the contentious crowd of children. She extended her hand and he watched her with affable curiosity. Then he took her hand, holding it while they exchanged smiles. Soon they were beaming at each other. With 'wide green-brown eyes', a 'button nose', square hands and a 'strong little chin', the affectionate fifteen-month-old child seemed sturdy and fearless – and to Gellhorn perfect.

Born Sandro, he would always be Sandy to her. He had almost starved before being brought to the orphanage from a nearby village in the hills. She spent a week playing with him, delighted to see his interest in every little thing, even weeds and pebbles. It took more than two months of paperwork and negotiations, and the assistance of Eleanor Roosevelt, the American ambassador to Italy, the Italian ambassador to Mexico and the Bishop of Missouri, to get her boy. Then there were hurried preparations for the trip to New York, with Gellhorn going through a crash course in motherhood offered by an Italian nurse. Then Sandy had bronchitis, then measles, and Gellhorn got the flu. Furiously reading books on childcare, she was terrified every time her child cried. Was he dying? Was he getting enough to eat?

Finally, amid a heap of luggage and baby care equipment, mother and son took off on their plane for New York. Diapering Sandy while flying over the Alps unnerved a clumsy Gellhorn, who dreaded that her fumbling would wreck him for life. Motherhood seemed much tougher than reporting on war and to Gellhorn mothers now seemed like uncelebrated heroes. The plane terrified a teething Sandy, who cried and slept his way home in the strange, dark, tunnel-like environment of the aircraft.

It had taken Gellhorn eight months to find her baby. Back again in Mexico, she realized how ridiculous her fantasy of motherhood had been, yet there he was: soundly asleep, his head in her lap, his feet on her feet, and she gave way to more fantasies. They would be happy for ever in a modest white house surrounded by a walled garden and tall velvety trees. This would be Sandy's quiet kingdom, where he would trudge around the garden making speeches to himself in his own secret language, friendly and confident with the neighbours and the natives, and delighted by the movement of the birds, bees and buses that passed by his house. Gellhorn watched him bloom like a flower, at peace with himself. She felt as though he had adopted her.

Although she worried that child rearing would end her writing career, it went on smoothly. Sandy made comical progress with English and Spanish vocabulary. His nurse bathed him. His mama played with him. He liked crawling all over her and practising faces. By the end of February 1950 Sandy had started nursery school, coming home with new crayons, which he used on the walls proudly to show his mama he was working. 'I adore him in the most foolish way', Gellhorn wrote to Mrs Roosevelt.

Tied down to a very domestic existence in Mexico, Gellhorn kept in touch with friends through her letters and enjoyed occasional visits from Dorothy Parker and others. She had struck up a correspondence with art connoisseur Bernard Berenson, during the course of which he asked her about Hemingway. She acknowledged her ex-husband's genius but deplored his decline into self-serving and egotistical writing, which brought him, no doubt, a fine income.

Gellhorn doubted she would ever marry again. She liked living alone. She would have her flings – romances that would remind her she was a woman and 'not some sort of dried seed pod'. But she tired of these affairs. She did not say so, but clearly the men in her life would have to accede to her terms. She wanted no part of another Hemingway.

By May 1951 Gellhorn had a suitor – the charming Dr David Gurewitsch – a close friend of Eleanor Roosevelt. He was forty-eight years old and Roosevelt (at sixty-three) doted on him. He took women seriously and they were drawn to him. Slim and elegant, with a shy smile, he would gaze at a woman, kiss her hand and initiate an intimate conversation. A sympathetic listener, he was irresistible. He resembled the attractive males Gellhorn portrayed in her fiction of this period: cultivated European exiles cut off from their homelands but making their way admirably in a new world.

Born in 1902 of Russian parents, Gurewitsch had a Jewish father, a mystic and philosopher who had surrendered his life by submerging himself in a Swiss Lake (to be at one with the elements). His mother was a powerful doctor with 'psychic healing gifts'. Gurewitsch spent his youth in Russia, leaving at the time of the Revolution for Berlin. There he became romantically involved with actresses in the new film industry while pursuing his medical studies. A young Zionist, he left Germany during Hitler's rise to power and worked as a doctor in a Jerusalem hospital, before coming to the United States in 1934, where he studied pathology at Mt Sinai Hospital in New York City. On his way to the States Gurewitsch met an attractive Scottish woman, Nemone Balfour, and fell in love. Soon he was having second thoughts about Nemone, but he made good on his promise to marry her, heeding his mother's injunction: 'Gentlemen do not walk out on such pledges.' But Nemone suffered from depressions and Gurewitsch from his susceptibility to the charms of other women. Nemone had given birth to a child, Grania, in 1940. By the time Gurewitsch met Gellhorn, some time in 1950, he was seriously thinking of divorcing his wife.

Gellhorn described Gurewitsch as a son on whom Roosevelt could 'lavish her devotion, her care'. Roosevelt worried about his diet, his tendency to overwork, his career – indeed, everything concerning him became her obsession. Joseph Lash intimates Roosevelt's attachment to Gurewitsch was romantic. Gellhorn rejected the idea, once threatening to '*choke*' anyone who spoke of a Roosevelt–Gurewitsch love affair, but Roosevelt's letters reveal that for a brief, uncomfortable period she found herself competing for his love with Gellhorn.

Roosevelt revelled in the younger man's attentions and fretted when he did not spend more time with her. She acknowledged the disparity in their ages, yet she hoped her very maturity would help to guide him 'over the rough spots that come in all lives'. She encouraged him to 'lean' on and 'cling' to her.

Lash suggested that Roosevelt kept her equilibrium so long as Gurewitsch remained married to Nemone. Roosevelt advised him about his troubled married life. But when he became interested in Gellhorn, Roosevelt regretted abetting a romance about which she had profound misgivings. Gurewitsch proposed they visit Gellhorn in Mexico. Roosevelt did not accompany him. She realized that he would be the perfect man to listen to Gellhorn's troubles, but she worried that he would no longer have time for her.

By the middle of July 1951 Roosevelt wrote to Gurewitsch that she was unhappy. First, he had to decide whether or not he would divorce Nemone. Anything less would not be 'worthy' of him. Then, without mentioning Gellhorn by name, Roosevelt noted that 'because a woman offers to go on a holiday with you and you want to find out if you can stop thinking of Nemone does not to me seem good enough'. Gurewitsch had not said, she observed, that he 'wanted to be sure ... if this was a real and deep love'. Rather, he had acceded to Gellhorn's casual invitation to a 'three-week holiday'. To Roosevelt 'a night now and then' was understandable, 'but three weeks of constant companionship either is very good or no good it seems to me'.

Roosevelt offered herself instead: 'Just now the care and love that it would be a joy to me to give might make you happier with yourself in making your final decision.' She implied that Gellhorn, like other women, chased after Gurewitsch and consequently he was 'spoiled by pursuit', never confronting what he really wanted.

Roosevelt could not understand why Gellhorn did not join Gurewitsch in New York. To her it meant that Gellhorn did not love him and was unprepared to commit herself to another marriage. Some years later she confided to a close friend her astonishment at Gellhorn's selfishness. Roosevelt felt that as a writer Gellhorn could live anywhere, whereas Gurewitsch, who had been a stateless person most of his life, would not find his place in Mexico.

In Mexico Gurewitsch hesitated: 'Cannot commit myself to an expression of how I feel, not even to you – I imagine this is because I do not know myself.' Gellhorn charged ahead, then drew back. 'Martha understands that her gift and her inclination to make plans have to be held back just a little at the moment', Gurewitsch wrote to Roosevelt. By Christmas Gurewitsch had retreated from Gellhorn, spending his time with Roosevelt. Although Gellhorn said she was in no hurry to marry, Lash noted a 'willfulness that comes from having been desired by many men'.

Gellhorn wrote to Roosevelt that she was unwilling to accompany Gurewitsch and Roosevelt on a trip they were planning to take to Israel and the Middle East. She declared her romance with Gurewitsch over. He lacked for nothing except her, she said, but his desire for her had diminished. Mrs Roosevelt should persuade him to see it this way too, Gellhorn concluded.

The Gellhorn of this period disappointed Roosevelt, who could not have found much to admire in Gellhorn's trite *Saturday Evening Post* stories like 'Lonely Lady', featuring a beautiful woman who dies unloved, or in travel pieces with inane titles like 'Everybody's Happy on Capri', which extolled a life of ease 'without fuss'. For Gellhorn, an article on Washington socialite Perle Mesta, 'Party Girl in Paradise', or 'Strange Daughter', a simple-minded story with a Mexican locale, helped pay the rent.

The Honeyed Peace (1953), mostly a selection of Gellhorn's best fiction since 1948, finally brought her out of this creative trough. The title of the volume has an ironic thrust, for her stories reveal a post-war world that has soured even as its survivors try to convince themselves of their good fortune. They are people who have lost faith but cannot quite abandon their convictions. If there is honour in this rather grim, grey world, it derives from deeply felt emotions – like Evangeline's unshakable love for Renaud, her French collaborationist lover in the title story. Gellhorn shows remarkable sympathy for Evangeline, who is a gossip more interested in fashion than in politics. Evangeline's devotion to Renaud is shown to advantage against the political opportunism of the French, who behave as though they had not colluded with the Germans.

Evangeline's friends worry about her sanity should Renaud come to harm in prison and Anne wonders 'if any man ever felt for any woman as Evangeline did for Renaud: did any man ever die of fear for a woman?' Like Gellhorn, Anne has never had such an overwhelming feeling for a man and wonders what she has missed. When it is announced that Renaud has committed suicide, Anne thinks of how Evangeline's world is destroyed. The story is a surprising tribute to romantic love and not just an ironic counterpoint to Longfellow's sentimental poem.

The Honeyed Peace is full of female characters who read like echoes of Gellhorn's past. Lily Cameron in 'Weekend at Grimsby' is well-travelled, having lived since the war in an Italian villa, a Paris flat, a London house and a New York hotel suite. She has even been to China. Homeless and practically stateless, she verges towards self-pity but brings herself up short, revolting against a picture of herself as a 'female Flying Dutchman or Wandering Jew'. She has been to war and shown a stylish competence. Like Anne in 'The Honeyed Peace', Cameron cannot forget the war and cannot help contrasting the straitened circumstances of her Polish émigré friends in Great Britain with their heroic behaviour in the Italian campaign. For Cameron her best days were spent with these crazy Poles, when she knew exactly what she wanted. It had been a time to treasure the joys of day-by-day existence. Now her Polish friends live in Grimsby, which is as grim as it sounds, and she has to force herself to see its greyness as a thing of beauty these Poles have come to accept as their new home.

Divorced immediately after the war, Cameron's feelings are close to Gellhorn's. Her life now has no definition and the peace seems ugly – as ugly as the thick, stocky legs of her Polish friend's girl, as ugly as the fiftyish newly married couple Cameron observes on a train, happily unaware of a grotesqueness that should have consigned them to a 'solitary life in a cellar'. Cameron speaks for the side of Gellhorn that cannot forget the war, the side that Hemingway claimed was now in trouble because there was no war to fight. Cameron's problem is that she perceives these gallant soldiers in peacetime as being no more than shadows of themselves, working and living in circumstances beneath the bravery that should have been rewarded with a better future. The Poles, however, see it another way. They have made a new world – nothing like the one of their native land, of their ancestral estates – but one in which they have found love and labour that is satisfying, if not ennobling.

One of the stories in *The Honeyed Peace*, 'A Psychiatrist of One's Own', suggests how Hemingway continued to dog Gellhorn. He knew of her correspondence with Bernard Berenson and had begun his own, initially presenting himself as a chastened ex-husband wanting to set the record straight. He hoped that Gellhorn was happy, but he cautioned Berenson not to believe her bitter stories. He should not have been so impressed by her ambition and good looks. Hemingway jibed at Gellhorn's lack of taste, her ignorance of the arts, while recounting his own faults and praising her command of French. She was a beauty, but when he took her apart he noticed her nose lacked the right proportions and her 'wrinkled, crèpelike neck' betrayed her affinity with other ambitious women. She was a stylish Harriet Beecher Stowe, profiting from the phoney romance of war. He had been a fool to treat her badly, even if she did love all the 'paraphernalia' of war. He felt that his guilt over leaving Pauline and the children contributed to his unhappiness with Gellhorn and had led to his drunkenness. The sight of her always moved him and he was envious of Gelhorn's friendship with Berenson, telling him he was not to speak about what Hemingway had told him.

Hemingway admitted to Buck Lanham that in *Across the River and Into the Trees* (1950) he had given it to 'Miss M. in two paragraphs and pretty well for keeps. Don't think she will be able to sleep good even with her glorious war record when she reads it.' Charlie Scribner worried over Hemingway's libelling her. 'If Miss

Martha were to take umbrage', she better be prepared to fight it out with him, was Hemingway's pugnacious reply.

In *Across the River and Into the Trees* Gellhorn appears only faintly disguised as Robert Cantwell's estranged third wife, an aggressive journalist, a sort of mean Dorothy Bridges: 'She had more ambition than Napoleon and about the talent of the average High School Valedictorian.' Cantwell's wife marries him only to 'advance herself in Army circles'. She is too 'conceited' to feel sad about the break-up of their marriage, especially since getting a good story – even if she has to steal it from her husband – is her primary concern. Cantwell claims that if they were to have another run-in, 'I'd look straight through her to show her how dead she was'. Other passages on the way Cantwell's ex-wife sleeps and on her inability to provide him with a child are unmistakable hits at Gellhorn. Hemingway had interpreted her refusal to try for one as a rejection of him in favour of her career. She told a friend after the war, 'There's no need to have a child when you can buy one. That's what I did.' Hemingway told a friend that Gellhorn could not have a child because of her many abortions. Gellhorn responded that she so loathed Hemingway that she had aborted their child without telling him. This ex-couple's multiple versions of their marriage ricocheted in books, letters, stories and gossip among mutual friends and lovers.

Hemingway's view of Gellhorn was later seconded by Robert Joyce, an American diplomat who saw a good deal of the Hemingways in Cuba. He and his wife Jane believed that Gellhorn used her sexual attractiveness to advance her career. Jane went so far as to call Gellhorn 'frigid'. Jeffrey Meyers links their testimony to this passage in a Gellhorn story 'The Fall and Rise of Mrs Hapgood':

> After the beginning, which was painful and awkward ... she could not say she liked or disliked the sexual act. She liked being tender, she liked knowing that this too was part of her usefulness to Luke, she liked (it had to be admitted, it had to be seen at last) feeling noble. ... She made no effort to conceal passion; the passion, not being in her, did not show.

Hemingway attributed this lack of sexual appetite to her privileged background. 'She was not built for bed,' he confided to Bernard Berenson, 'but few nice people are.' To his son Gregory, Hemingway reported that the problem was partly anatomical: her narrow vagina inhibited her sexual enjoyment. A vaginoplasty had widened her, Hemingway wrote to Berenson, and he compared entering Gellhorn with 'coming into Penn Station'.

In her letters to Berenson and in conversations with male friends in later years, Gellhorn confessed to having experienced very little hunger for sex. She described herself to Berenson as both male and female, an aloof androgenous creature who could not return the ardour of her third and last husband, T. S. Matthews.

During an interview with Robert Manning in 1954, Hemingway showed off his collection of Gellhorn photographs and exclaimed, 'There's my beautiful Martha. Isn't she beautiful?' Manning thought she would be pleased to hear of Hemingway's admiration, but her only comment was 'That son of a bitch!'. She did not want to be anybody's 'beautiful Martha' – least of all this braggart who acted like he still owned her. When Bernard Berenson wrote to her implying that her visit to his villa might coincide with Hemingway's, she refused to come, declaring she did not want to feel his 'hot jungle breath on my pretty little neck'.

In Gellhorn's 'A Psychiatrist of One's Own', Hemingway figures as Matthew Hendricks, a good-looking American novelist in his forties who has lived all over the world, including the Caribbean and Montana. Her story is an excruciating prediction of Hemingway's decline and a warning Gellhorn gave herself to be wary of the kind of writer's life that is self-isolating and irresponsible. Hendricks wakes up in Paris one day and finds he cannot write. Until now, he has gone from novel to novel, from one success to another. Writing has been a daily occupation and his stories have flowed effortlessly. He has not had much contact with reality. His wife has arranged everything around his writing schedule. All he has had to do is write. Yet this freedom from daily cares, from family responsibilities, from social and political concerns, has resulted in a monumental writer's block. Suddenly nothing he tries to put on the page seems worth saying. He does not understand why this is so and blames his inability to concentrate on external disturbances like the weather or the quality of the household help.

The unreality of Hendricks's writer's world has been developing for some time and has arisen out of the very conditions which he thinks have made him happy. He likes climates where there are no seasons. He finds the rain in Paris distasteful. Although he is not conscious of it, the change in the weather is a sign of changes in his own life. He leaves home, moves from hotel to hotel, considers an affair, but nothing works. He has lost his conviction as a writer, his pride in his 'discipline and skill'. He has been hallucinating and at odd times he has been visited by a figment of his imagination, a psychiatrist, whom he calls Dr Raumwitz. The psychiatrist silently observes Hendricks and refuses to engage him in discussion. Hendricks's hallucinations continue even after his wife arranges for his treatment by a psychiatrist. For Hendricks, only his invented psychiatrist will do. He resists treatment and flatters himself that somehow he and Raumwitz are co-conspirators. And so they are. For together they constitute the writer's dialogue with himself, a dialogue that is impervious to influences outside itself.

But the story was also about Gellhorn, restless and adrift, with no conflict to confront except the one within herself.

15

OPEN MARRIAGE

1952–1960

DOUBTS ABOUT SCHOOLING Sandy in Mexico sent Gellhorn to Italy in the summer of 1952, where she found a large farm less than a half-hour from Rome, in which she and Sandy could live quietly. She wanted him to grow up on the land with animals, far away from the atom bomb culture of America. She sent him on a bicycle every day to a Montessori-type kindergarten. In this safe, peaceful environment she wrote and indulged her obsession with Rome.

Italian worldliness and cynicism had their appeal for Gellhorn, who found Americans too cheerfully innocent and the English insufferably smug. But the elaborate deviousness and chiselling characteristic of Italian society troubled her. 'It's the little cheating that they do. If they just wouldn't cheat you just a little *every time*!' she complained to a friend. Italians expected her to take their charm as her recompense. She dropped Italy like a love affair with no repercussions but plenty of fond souvenirs.

Gellhorn spent much of 1953 in London, her post-war base from which she would 'roam freely and return' – rather like an 'open marriage'. But this constant moving about was hard on Sandy and it made Gellhorn's friends question her devotion to motherhood. She realized that Sandy longed for a more permanent home and it was draining on Gellhorn to act as a single parent.

She had been seeing Tom Matthews, whom she had known but

not seen much of since 1929. 'He was my first boss on the *New Republic*, my first job when I was twenty', she explained to Bernard Berenson. He had recently retired from the editorship of *Time*. He was fifty-three, wealthy, elegant and an Anglophile looking to retire in England to write the books he had postponed working on for far too long. He was a poet, though Gellhorn doubted his gift and worried that he seemed too conventional and scholarly for her taste. He had the chiselled, austere features of a founding father. Gellhorn did not pretend to understand Matthews. 'The most obvious sign of madness is his bulldog, not to say tigerish, determination to marry me.' He found support in Sandy's persistent demand for a father.

Gellhorn admired this well turned-out man with exquisite manners. But she did not have the physical craving for him that had made her affair with David Gurewitsch so passionate – indeed, Gurewitsch seems to have been the only man she found sexually irresistible. In July 1953 she had encountered him in Yugoslavia travelling with Mrs Roosevelt. No man had ever provided such sexual excitement. Calling him the love of her life, she realized she nonetheless could not marry him and tolerate that 'ugly slave life' in New York. Perhaps it was just as well, Gellhorn speculated, since she could not imagine living erotically day to day. Any kind of settled, domestic life – however sensual – did not appeal to an adventurer, a traveller always certain that the next destination offered new delights – or at least the diversion that she could not live without. She wrote to Mrs Roosevelt, acknowledging the 'silence' between them and vowed never to speak of Gurewitsch again.

Matthews would do for the everyday, especially since he promised not to interfere with her career or with her penchant for travel. They were married in London on 4 February 1954. 'We all got the general impression that Martha wanted to be in charge', a Matthews confidant said years later. She had predicted to Berenson that she would tire easily of family life, but Sandy liked his new daddy and Gellhorn found Matthews companionable enough in the first phase of their marriage.

Gellhorn and Matthews spent part of the summer of 1954 in New York. Establishing a pattern that would hold for the entire marriage, she saw many of her friends (like Leonard Bernstein and his family) separately. Later in the summer she and Matthews visited

Edna, whom Matthews adored, then they split up – Tom going to Princeton to visit old friends and Martha and Edna taking a vacation together at the Delaware Water Gap. Later, at a party in New York for the newlyweds, Martha ignored Tom's friends and spent her time with Robert Capa's brother, Cornell. On other occasions she could be downright rude. 'She didn't suffer fools, and she had a wider category of who she thought were fools than most people have', suggests one of Matthews' colleagues, who was so incensed he thought of sending Tom a wire saying, 'When you get back to England, your friends will still be here.' Over the years Matthews's friends never knew what kind of reception they might get from Gellhorn. As one of them recalls: 'She was very moody. If you were coming for a visit, it would be agreed that the four of you would be having dinner. Then you'd get there and find out she'd gone, and you wouldn't even see her.'

Few of Matthews's intimates and acquaintances ever got close enough to Gellhorn to understand why he became so enamoured of her. To be sure, they appeared a handsome – even awesome – couple to Stanley Flink, a young writer at *Life* who remembers what an urbane, attractive pair they made at parties. The tall, trim and athletic Matthews had no trouble keeping up with his active wife. She looked crisp and intellectually interesting. Although they were both born in the Midwest, their speech had a cultivated mid-Atlantic accent that made it impossible to identify them with any particular region.

For Matthews, Gellhorn represented an ideal independence he had never achieved. He had always wanted to be his own man. He had been born a parson's only son in Cincinnati at the turn of the century. Educated together with his sister at home, he grew up a guilt-ridden, timid boy, learning to be 'afraid – not only afraid of outsiders and of the outside world but most of all afraid of being judged and found wanting'. He had never measured up to his father's standards, but he had remained his mother's 'dearest hope'.

Like Gellhorn, Matthews travelled abroad at an early age. He developed a fondness for England and for poetry, but he lacked her confidence and outgoing nature. At school he behaved like a 'shy and pious misfit'. Not until he attended Princeton and met Schuyler Jackson, a brilliant undergraduate poet, did Matthews find an outlet for his 'adolescent bitterness'. Jackson spoke with such force and quickness he bowled Matthews over, convincing him of poetry's superiority over all other forms of writing, and of the poet's unique place in the literary world. Poetry was 'the essence, the distillation of writing itself'. Long after Jackson failed in his mission to be a great poet, Matthews worshipped him and the very idea of the archetypal writer who was above all pettiness, aloof, creating his own standards and excellences.

With Jackson aiming so high, it was perhaps inevitable that Matthews set his own trajectory much lower. He doubted the value of his own verse. He had a good ear and his lines scanned well, but by his own account his poems were rather sentimental and self-pitying. Matthews's Princeton class voted him 'Worst poet' and Jackson 'Most brilliant'.

When Matthews left the *New Republic* to join *Time* in 1929, Edmund Wilson, his mentor, told him *Time* was not 'respectable journalism ... *Time* is dirty ... And it's getting dirtier.' Wilson never spoke to him again. Ashamed of having become a company man, Matthews later confessed that he could not take *Time* seriously, calling the staff 'just bright, young, conceited college boys, who really didn't know a damn thing'. Yet he endured twenty-four years of 'servitude'.

Matthews's departure from *Time* signalled his disaffection with his country. 'This is not my day in America', he announced in *Name and Address* (1960). Like Gellhorn, he deplored an America obsessed with national security and the 'Communist threat'. Gellhorn encouraged his tendency to reject American vulgarity. He felt drawn to a woman who had trusted her own instincts and had lived by her own authority.

Matthews liked strong women. In the 1930s he had been under poet Laura Riding's spell until she married his beloved friend, Schuyler Jackson. Max Gissen, one of Matthews's colleagues at *Time*, remembered that he 'loved women ... to the point of silliness. An attractive woman could do outrageous things to Tom.'

Matthews fell in with Gellhorn's plans and there is perhaps nothing so attractive as an adoring lover who will do one's bidding. She could have everything she wanted and marriage too. Their differences entertained him – her need to be in control; his capitulation

to fate; her lively reactions to life's possibilities; his intense accept-
ance of 'doom'. He had money. They would live comfortably. He
had his own writing to do, but he did not look upon her as a competitor. It would be a congenial life, with Matthews providing a
soothing sense of security which the high-strung Gellhorn appreciated. As one of Gellhorn's friends put it, Matthews had the subtle
intelligence and the exquisite delicacy to calm Gellhorn without her
even realizing it.

Gellhorn gave Matthews quite a kick by taking on the world –
reporting for *The Times* of London in September 1954 about the
Senate hearings investigating Joseph McCarthy and noting that no
one had the nerve to censure McCarthyism itself. Outrage in a
beautiful woman could be very appealing. Matthews got her access
to his friend Adlai Stevenson, to whom she could vent her feelings
about Israel, the Gaza strip and Arab refugees. Her trips to Israel and
Poland reflected her restlessness. Yet she missed Matthews and marvelled at how bound she felt to him. On her own, she seemed
incomplete.

In Gellhorn's trashy, well-paying fiction (read her *Collier's* story
'The Good Husband') and in her journalism she developed considerable fondness for marriage and other domestic institutions. In her
most settled period she practically doted on the calm, articulate and
sensible English electoral system. In 'Spies and Starlings' (the *New
Republic*, 28 November 1955), she commended Parliament for discussing the spy cases of Guy Burgess and Donald Maclean in a sane,
good-humoured fashion. It seemed wonderfully refreshing to
observe the English steadfastly refuse to give way to anything like
American hysteria about Communism: 'What was new to our ears
these days, and thrilling to hear, was the steadiness and justice of
those who spoke, the absence of panic or exaggeration, the quiet
insistence on legal processes as opposed to trial by suspicions.
McCarthyism so repelled the English that they take special care not
to be infected by it.' Anyone reading the British press at the time
might have been astonished, however, that she took such a bland,
naïve tone. The Burgess and Maclean case was a major embarrassment to the government and brought into question the reliability
and effectiveness of its security services.

Gellhorn had long since tired of explaining to her friends why she lived abroad, but she took one more humorous stab at it in an article for *Harper's*. In earlier pieces she had mentioned her delight in the clarity of English public speech. Now she remarked on her fondness for the stately language of the London *Times*. The paper's soberness soothed her mornings and helped her prepare for the day. Like so much else in English life, the newspaper created no fuss. It used to be that she hated the grey, rainy weather. Now she was grateful to slop around with the rest of the population in old clothes and rain gear. It so eased the mind not to worry about fashion, said this most fashionable of women. It would have been truer of her to say that just now it suited her fancy to hear the English compliment her on an ensemble she had worn 'four years running'.

Gellhorn did not minimize the inconveniences of London life. For example, the English had never got 'the hang of central heating'. Her furnace had exploded more than once and the electrical system seemed to date from Edison's day. The plumbing was none too good (causing the ceiling to fall) and the shops were none too efficient in filling her orders for things like writing paper and food. But she made it all sound pleasantly 'daft' – an English word she treasured. The English had quaint terms for this survivable incompetence, such as 'muddling through'.

The English could be wildly eccentric and no one seemed to take particular notice: 'So he's getting married again? His fifth, is it? Well, well, never say die.' Through the years Gellhorn had derived much pleasure from her dear friend, Lady Diana Cooper, whose incredible variety of ailments and propensity for expecting the worst had not prevented her from savouring a long, successful life. After one of Lady Diana's trips, Gellhorn wrote to her:

> If I hadn't heard you were safely back at Chantilly, I would be fran-
> tic for fear you were dead as a smelt. ... Have all the pains and
> anguishes gone? Was it anything like the year you decided your
> heart was weak or the year you had cancer? It's awful to enjoy your
> ailments as much as I do, but they've always been so wonderful, so
> fatal and so sad that I cannot help liking them.

Gellhorn believed the English ignored eccentricity out of politeness. She had never known a more varied vocabulary of graciousness. The 'background music of life in London' was this 'chorus of please, thank you, may I, would you, so sorry, how kind of you, no trouble at all' and so on. To her delight, Sandy had picked up this behaviour, adding to his mother's order 'Go to bed now, darling' the word 'please'. London was restful and cosy, and the large number of English expressions Gellhorn quoted in her article and would use in her collection of stories, *Two by Two* (1958), suggests how completely she immersed herself in English life.

Two by Two is dedicated 'To Tom, With Love'. It is Gellhorn's most carefully constructed collection of stories. Each one is about a marriage and takes for its theme a phrase from the marriage vows: 'For Better for Worse,' 'For Richer for Poorer', 'In Sickness and in Health', 'Till Death Us Do Part'. The mature expatriate shrewdly assesses the Italians, the English, the French, the Americans and other nationalities. While she is sympathetic to her characters, the ironic stance of the well-travelled observer pervades her stories.

In 'For Better for Worse', Kitty, an American woman, devotes her whole life to her Italian husband, Andrea, the heir of a large estate who feels useless – a captive of his inheritance who must patiently await his father's relinquishment of authority and endure the German occupation of his country. Then the Americans arrive and Andrea offers himself as an interpreter, abandons his estate for a tour of duty with the American army and returns home as 'Andy' – a new man planning a new life for himself and Kitty in Montana. At first, Kitty is frightened by this change of character, then she sees that her very devotion to Andrea has abetted his passivity and she welcomes his transformation. And then she dreads the return of his fatalism as he becomes mired once again in the post-war conditions of his estate.

As in all the stories of *Two by Two*, love itself is not enough. What counts is how that love is expressed in different temperaments and in different circumstances. Gellhorn is not a determinist; people are capable of changing their lives, but these changes are accomplished at great cost. Kitty's kind of unqualified love both debilitates and invigorates Andrea, and that is the paradox of their marriage, a paradox she has grown to appreciate but is powerless to resolve.

'For Better for Worse' reveals how the themes of Matthews's life entered Gellhorn's creative work. She did not use him as a character or herself as a narrator, but the portrait of Andrea tied to an ancestral home, dominated by his authoritarian father, dogged by his sense of doom, recalls Matthews's old-world mentality. At any earlier age Gellhorn would surely have had less patience and interest in the fatalistic aristocrat of her story, but now the pull of home, family and tradition had more of a place in her imagination. She could actually see it: how a son would feel bound to the role history had cast for him. Like Matthews, Andrea yearns for a great change in his life, seems on the verge of making it, then mournfully acknowledges it is too late for him to become a new man. As Matthews would later write in *Jacks or Better*: 'I quit my job in New York twenty-one years ago and went to live in England, "to learn to write" – but it was too late or I was too lazy.'

'For Better for Worse' has a romantic, yearning quality that barely escapes sentimentality. By contrast, 'For Richer for Poorer' is refreshingly astringent, with lots of sharp dialogue. The story concentrates on Rose Answell, an ambitious women who schemes to make her pliable husband, Ian, a Cabinet minister. She has a great love of position and no love for Ian after he realizes his marriage and family life have been a sham. She abandons him as soon as she sees he is serious about retiring to farming. Much of the story's interest comes from observing Rose's manoeuvres in England's high social and political life, and in her dealings with ladies whose 'beauty was a public service'. They are 'elegant, serene ... able and sportingly willing to please', and find Rose's conniving progress to the top beyond what their conventions will allow. Gellhorn conveys their feelings through the tone of their dialogue – as she does with Rose, whose cold-heartedness needs no explanation after this cutting exchange with Ian:

> 'I thought Chloe was looking a treat,' Ian said.
>
> 'Oh, did you? I thought she seemed rather haggard. And she never varies, does she? I find that tiddily talk quite exasperating in the long run.'
>
> Sensible and funny and generous, Ian thought, what more could anyone be? But there was something more and better, and he did not know exactly what it was.
>
> 'She's a very good friend.'
>
> 'Oh, Ian, what a *pointless* thing to say.'

Gellhorn avoids melodrama in her depiction of Rose by showing how Ian and other men have allowed themselves to be manipulated by her. When Ian realizes Rose is all ambition, he leaves her and she easily switches to another man whose credentials for the Cabinet she can brighten.

'For Richer for Poorer' is set in a highly polished world of surfaces that Gellhorn knew well from her friendships with Lady Diana Cooper and Virginia Cowles. The story begins with Lady Harriet Adderford frowning at 'the exquisite curve of her mouth' in a mirror. She is unhappy about her lipstick. The seemingly trivial detail is precisely the point of Gellhorn's art: ladies and gentlemen in this society build their reputations by attention to aesthetic details, to form and fashion. Rose Answell irritates Lady Harriet primarily because of her style, which reflects aspirations that threaten to upset polite society.

'In Sickness and In Health' is the least satisfying story in *Two by Two*. It is a rather maudlin study of a man who cannot bring himself to leave his childlike wife, a woman who has suffered over many years with a heart condition so severe the couple have not been able to make love. Originally published as 'The Smell of Lilies' in *Atlantic Monthly*, its excessive emotionality is uncomfortably close in spirit to Gellhorn's commercial stories, but it does provide a counter-balancing tone to the piquancy of 'For Richer for Poorer'.

'Till Death Us Do Part' is the most haunting episode of *Two by Two*. Based in part on Robert Capa, who died in 1954 photographing the war in Indochina, the story demonstrates Gellhorn's most complex treatment of autobiographical material. A world-famous photographer, Bara, as Capa is called in the story, has had one true love in his life and, in turn, is loved by a woman who regards him as her one true love. Helen Richards cannot have him – not all of him – because he has never stopped loving Suzy, his unfaithful yet ideal soulmate. Suzy, also a photographer, has died in Spain just as Capa's beloved, Gerde, did.

The first part of 'Till Death Us Do Part' is about Bara's death and Helen's attempts to cope with it, to understand her attraction to him and his inability to reciprocate her love. The second part constitutes the testimony of Lep, Bara's closest male friend, who explains to Marushka (Martha) Bara's (Capa's) life in terms of her own. Marushka is the pet name Lep and Bara have for correspondent

Mary Hallett, who amuses them because of her anger. She is 'angry to pop', Lep reports to Bara, in describing her reaction to the extreme casualties sustained by allied soldiers invading Italy. In her fondness for Poles, in her obvious happiness in war and sharing the men's vulnerability, Hallett is a dead ringer for Gellhorn.

Marushka and Bara see each other only for brief periods, yet Bara calls her my 'sister *and* brother' since she reflects both his male and female sides. Capa was Gellhorn's twin. Both were noncombatants, aggressive on their assignments, willing to risk their lives to witness war, but still not wholly a part of the action. Capa never pretended – as Hemingway did – to being a soldier or an intelligence agent. Capa's pictures and Gellhorn's dispatches were important, but they never overrated their celebrity or influence and never made themselves the main event.

There is something childish in Marushka's discontent with the world, which recalls Gellhorn's. Marushka often behaves like a frantic child who sees the world collapsing on her head. It amuses Bara that she should take human suffering so personally. Who could live with the weight of the world always present on one's shoulders? No wonder they often find themselves on opposite sides of the street, furious with each other. How can he take seriously a woman who is always so serious about the world's fate? How can she take seriously a man who seems to take nothing seriously? In his view the world will never change, but she insists on progress and deliverance. She has this 'major tic' about injustice and does not understand that injustice is not an aberration but something built into the very nature of things. To him, it seems futile and foolish to be constantly hectoring the world to reform itself.

Gellhorn knew how well Capa understood her. In 'Till Death Us Do Part' this realization became Bara's observation that 'Marushka loved humanity ... but people made her nervous'. She had been taught to embrace the world on such a large scale that individuals, sooner or later, bored or irritated her. How could she make a life with one man when the whole world beckoned to her? For Capa, as for Bara, the world was lost. Know that and perhaps you could enjoy yourself, find love and be contented with your friends. For Bara, there is almost something insane about Marushka's badgering people to come to the immediate aid of others. Certainly Hemingway had felt this pressure to take on the world and resented never really having Gellhorn to himself.

Capa thrived on his disagreements with Gellhorn. His quarrel with her, like Bara's with Marushka, was a family spat. They never stopped talking to or amusing each other and their politics were the same even when they disagreed on the ultimate effectiveness of politics. She admired his winning personality. A likeable fellow and a healer, he brought people together and accomplished social comity, whereas for all her grand plans she actually produced – to use Marushka's word – 'nothing'. Bara is deeply worried when Marushka's visits to concentration camps destroy her faith in human perfectibility. When she no longer expresses her anger, he is unnerved, for he has always counted on the energy of her outrage as fuel for his own accommodation with life's disappointments. To a large extent they survived on their memories of Spain. As Lep puts it, Spain is the 'home' of Marushka's heart. It is where 'everyone was poor and friends', fighting passionately for 'the rights and dignity of man'.

Gellhorn had resolved to cover war no more, but it remained a preoccupation. In *The Face of War* (1959), she collected her *Collier's* dispatches, with an introduction and autobiographical glosses on her decades of war reporting. She recalled her youthful belief in the 'perfectibility of man, and in progress', which journalism as a 'guiding light' would support. She termed her pride in her professional prowess 'absurd'. As in *The Honeyed Peace*, she expressed some guilt in surviving the wars, calling herself 'a special type of war profiteer'. She still professed the educational function of journalism, but she no longer believed it had much to do with making the world a better place. But at least journalism kept the record straight. Carefully done, it exemplified a 'form of honorable behavior'.

The advent of nuclear weapons had convinced Gellhorn of the ultimate idiocy of all wars. The world now had the power to destroy itself and perhaps only the memory and imagination of other wars could prevent it from annihilating the future. *The Face of War* earned her the best reviews of her career. In the *New York Times*, Herbert Mitgang called it a 'brilliant anti-war book that is as fresh as if written for this morning'. In the *New Statesman*, Nigel Nicolson called

The lotus-eating life in Cuba in 1942 and 1943. *Above:* beside the pool where Martha would join Hemingway and his friends for drinks and a swim.
Below: Gellhorn, however, soon started complaining that nothing ever happened in Cuba and compared her life there to being 'strangled by those beautiful tropical flowers that can swallow cows'. (*John F. Kennedy Library*)

◁ Gellhorn at work. At home in Cuba between January and June 1943 she was writing *Liana*; Hemingway enjoyed reading the chapters as she completed them. (*John F. Kennedy Library*)

The high life. Hemingway and Gellhorn share a toast at the Stork Club in New York City. (*UPI/CORBIS*) ▽

New York April 1944. By now things were far from well with the marriage. Hemingway was sure that he would be killed reporting on the war and that Gellhorn would be to blame. She warned him bluntly that his behaviour was destroying her love for him. (*John F. Kennedy Library*)

Back to war. Gellhorn talks to troops on the Italian Front in 1944.
(*Hulton Getty Picture Library*)

◁ General James Gavin (right), intrepid commander of the US 82nd Airborne Division and Gellhorn's lover; seen here talking to Major General Matthew B. Ridgeway in Belgium shortly before the end of the war. (*Bettman/CORBIS*)

Hemingway, too, had his loyal admirers among the US officers in Eisenhower's army. He is seen here inspecting a captured German gun with a military crony, Colonel C.T. Lanham, who was later to describe Gellhorn as 'a bitch from start to finish'. (*Princeton University Library*) ▽

Merry Xmas
Happy New Year
from
Sandy and Martha

Martha's adopted son. He was sturdy, affectionate and fearless and his name was Sandro – but to Martha he would always be Sandy. (*Franklin Delano Roosevelt Library*)

◁ By May of 1951 Martha had a new suitor, Dr David Gurewitsch, seen here with his friend and mentor Eleanor Roosevelt. But, although he probably meant more to Gellhorn than any of her other lovers, ER's hopes of a marriage were not to be realized. (*Franklin Delano Roosevelt Library*)

Gellhorn's third husband, T. S. Matthews, at his editor's desk at Time Inc. Although she compared his chiselled, austere features to those of a founding father, the marriage soon fizzled out in apathy. (*UPI/Corbis*) ▽

◁ Martha Gellhorn at home, London, 1977. (*Magnum Photos*)

The Welsh cottage which was Gellhorn's much-loved rural retreat during her later years in Britain. (*Author*) ▽

◁ Martha in 1987. Though very much the grande dame, she continued to cast her spell over a coterie of young admirers until the end. (*Ginger Sharp*, Lansing State Jounal) her 'one of the best correspondents whom the War produced'. Like Mitgang, he praised the immediacy of her reports. They seemed to write themselves. But he found a curious contradiction in her condemnation of war. He noted how intensely Gellhorn identified with the Spanish cause, the nobility she found in the Finns and in the Chinese who fought to repel invaders. He was responding, in fact, to her own contradictions (she used the word about herself in the introduction), which friends had pondered for years. 'Martha was always talking pacifism and couldn't wait to get to the front-line trenches', one of her friends recalled.

Each year with Matthews and family proved to be more of a strain. Gellhorn did not get along with his children especially well and she hated holiday gatherings, the exchanging of presents and entertaining people. Matthews proposed an American tour and a jointly authored book. Gellhorn rejected the book idea but brightened up when he suggested they take her mother along on their ride across the American continent.

The threesome travelled from Denver to Seattle to Portland to several parts of California, Arizona, New Mexico, Texas and Florida. Martha exploded with heated generalizations – a sign of her Germanic blood, she thought. American women, for example, were hardly better than 'Arab females' slavishly devoted to their husbands. Edna 'sighed, lightly'. American women were chauffeurs for their children, cooks and housekeepers, and spent the rest of the time building up their husbands' egos. 'If I had to work as hard as most of the women I see, and notably the young women, I'd go into a decline', Martha asserted. 'Yes', Edna remarked, keeping her voice neutral. Even worse, what time American woman had to themselves was wasted on shopping sprees, Martha claimed in a lengthy monologue. 'Oh, my child', Edna interjected in the space between her daughter's long speeches. Martha wanted to know what her mother meant by the expression. 'I was thinking about generalizations', Edna replied. 'And how difficult they are.'

Back in England, Gellhorn brooded on a marriage that seemed to have lost its point. In *His Own Man* (1961) and *Pretty Tales for Tired People* (1965), her male and female characters circle around the issue of commitment to each other. There are well-married, happy couples in her fiction, but they are a rarity and serve only as fixed points in an unstable marital universe, where the most urbane couples take lovers and treat marriage as a form of convenience, as a necessary – even comfortable – institution, but seldom as a permanently romantic or inviolable union. There is a personal bitterness – as one interviewer (mentioning Gellhorn's divorces) pointed out. She was startled: 'I never thought of the stories like that. Now you mention it, I suppose they all are about divorces.'

What went wrong between Gellhorn and Matthews? In a word, she was 'a traveller in life', a word that Jessica de Camberges applies to Ben Eckhardt after he abandons her in *His Own Man*. He is from Milwaukee, but it might as well be Martha Gellhorn from St Louis. Speaking of Milwaukee, Ben explains, 'I had a perfectly okay time, living the way everyone I knew lived, but it ran on rails. I couldn't see anything in it.' Ben tires of women because he tires of having things expected of him. He has trouble staying put and feels trapped. Years later Gellhorn called the marriage to Matthews 'perfectly ludicrous and boring and hopeless'. She chafed at 'not doing anything' and at Eleanor Roosevelt's assumption that she lacked for nothing with a husband to look after her. In tears, Gellhorn said, 'You think that all these years that I've loved you because I wanted something? I never wanted anything; I just love you.' Mrs Roosevelt could not see what use she could be now. Gellhorn, feeling abandoned, flung her arms round Roosevelt and said, 'You can't do this to me; you really cannot do this to me!'

Gellhorn felt inauthentic 'married to quite a rich man and [living] in a splendiferous house'. For his part, Matthews had tired of tagging along on her trips. Friends saw increasing signs of his impatience with her. To live a life by phases – first in one place, then another – did not appeal to him. Gellhorn now seemed to lack gravity. The convivial, if 'acid', Matthews – as one friend of later years described him – would later thrive in the country with a wife who cosseted him.

The couple did not divorce until 1963, but by the spring of 1960 she stepped up her reporting assignments and began to eye a life alone in Africa, determined once again to discover her beautiful exile.

16

HEART'S DESIRE
1960–1963

G ELLHORN SPENT THE spring of 1960 in Poland. She
could no longer abide London. Life there now seemed too
easy. She had in mind the conventions of marriage and of
maintaining a large establishment in Chester Square. Yet she would
never forsake the city as her home base, for there were times when
she had to return home to recover from arduous travels and often
from disappointment in a world that did not, in the end, fulfil her
dreams. London would always prove to be reliable and comfortable,
even if she often spurned it as dull and damp.

Poles represented to her the nobility of overcoming hardship and
suffering. For them, the war had not meant victory but rather the
deadening grip of Stalinism, which they resisted with great spirit.
The inept and destructive Communist regime nevertheless fostered
education and tolerated culture. All over Poland she discovered theatrical companies and an interest in the arts that astonished her. In
one hideous Silesian mining town a theatre performed Arthur
Miller's *A View from the Bridge*.

Poles yearned for a look at the West. It delighted them to think
of people like Gellhorn free to travel just about anywhere. It pained
her to see how little contact they had with the outside world. Consequently, she used her own money to endow what she called the
'Polish Fun Fellowship' – to be used by a Pole to visit as many
museums in France or Italy as the time limitations on a Polish passport would allow. Surprisingly, the Polish government acceded to

this wacky plan and the first 'Fun Fellow' lived up to her hopes, but the government subverted her intentions by sending a second who took the Communist line.

A year later Gellhorn visited Arab refugee camps. Everywhere she encountered the same opinion: Israel should not exist. It should be driven into the sea. She listened to wild reports of massacres perpetrated by merciless Israelis. That Israel had won two wars meant nothing. It should be forced to give up everything, even though the refugees had made it clear that if the Arab nations had been victorious, the Israelis would have been massacred. Finally, Gellhorn got angry with her Arab informants and shouted terrible things about Israel's right of conquest and its historic claim to Palestine. In the end, she could not identify with the refugees because they were unable to identify with the suffering of others. They pitied only themselves and had shown no mercy towards others. In 'The Arabs of Palestine' (*Atlantic Monthly*, October 1961) her condemnation of Arabs is as absolute as her condemnation of Germans:

> Arabs gorge on hate, they roll in it, they breathe it. Jews top the hate list, but any foreigners are hateful enough. Arabs also hate each other, separately and en masse. Their politicians change the direction of their hate as they would change their shirts. Their press is vulgarly base with hate-filled cartoons; their reporting describes whatever hate is now uppermost and convenient. Their radio is a long scream of hate, a call to hate. They teach their children hate in school. They must love the taste of hate; it is their daily bread. And what good has it done them?

In May and June of 1961 Gellhorn attended the Eichmann trial in Israel. Incensed by world opinion that ignored the trial's moral and historic importance, she admired the Israeli judges who proceeded in a coherent, orderly fashion, with profound respect for 'rules of evidence'. She focused on Eichmann's effort to minimize his role in the Nazi bureaucracy of extermination. In his glass booth he sat virtually impassive, giving spectators little to observe other than a taut mouth and a small tic beneath his left eye, better prepared than his attorney and voluble on the intricacies of his job. He was, in Gellhorn's estimation, 'the greatest organization man of all time', identifying absolutely with the Nazi state, doing what he was told and justifying the most heinous crimes by deferring the consideration of all moral issues to the nation's leader.

Gellhorn wondered whether post-war Germany had managed to surmount the legacy of Nazism. Her trip there in the early winter of 1962 was not reassuring. She felt uncomfortable about German obedience to authority and about the closed climate that made it difficult to discuss ideas. Many students she met seemed to think it unpatriotic to criticize their government. But the younger generation did reject militarism and appeared to have no attraction to the dress and paraphernalia of war that Hitler exploited so successfully. Even so, these young men and women did not seem to understand the purpose of the Nuremberg trials and treated them merely as a national humiliation. Similarly, the import of the Eichmann trial eluded them and she deplored their inability to empathize with the plight of others.

German women bothered Gellhorn. She called them the 'Arab women of the West'. Their submission to authority was even greater than what she had observed and deplored in American women a few years earlier. In general, Germans had little notion of civil liberties and Gellhorn doubted their capacity to create a genuine democracy.

An underlying theme pervaded Gellhorn's writing during this period. Like her mother, she cared deeply about being a good citizen, about taking responsibility for one's own actions and calling one's government to account when it failed to serve the public welfare. Citizens had an obligation to be aware of more than themselves. They had to know about the greater part they played in community and world affairs. This was, in large part, why she wrote. As she explained in a letter to President Kennedy, since World War Two America had lost its purpose and failed to understand the tenor of history. With Kennedy's election the country seemed to have revived.

Kennedy was the first American president since Roosevelt to stir Gellhorn's imagination. She had met the President and his wife, and had confided to James Gavin (still one of her close friends) her fondness for them. She had very personal reasons for feeling grateful to the new President. for he had used his influence to obtain American citizenship for twelve-year-old Sandy. With Kennedy's support,

Senator Stuart Symington of Missouri had introduced a bill in the Senate that waived residence requirements for the child who had spent his school years in Switzerland and his vacations in America. Gellhorn had written to Symington that Sandy 'adores America and calls himself American'. At his Swiss school he had fought with a classmate who claimed the United States 'would not admit Italians'.

Sandy was Gellhorn's hope for the future. She wanted him to have a cultivated background and to attend Harvard. Kennedy, a Harvard man, represented her highest hopes for America and she regarded it as her personal mission to defend his administration. In November 1961 she was outraged over a newspaper item concerning a 'subhuman' Dallas publisher who attacked Kennedy's foreign policy. She did not like 'Texas-type bomb waving' and wrote to the President to say that millions of people were on his side and approved of his diplomatic efforts. She signed the letter 'your solid adherent'.

In the first three years of the new decade, Gellhorn left London to travel for business and pleasure to France, Spain, Italy, Israel, Germany, Mexico, Switzerland and Africa, with brief stopovers in New York and St Louis, where she would sometimes leave Sandy in the care of her relatives. If her son was to understand her world, he would have to know languages and get used to shuttling across continents. He had a formidable mother with high expectations, easily disappointed in people and places, and impatient with conventional arrangements and expectations. What if he did not want to be so adventurous and independent? Tensions between mother and son inevitably developed as he matured and she realized that he had a nature quite different from her own. Sandy was just entering his teenage years when his mother embarked for Africa in late January 1962, beginning a new phase of her life at the age of fifty-three.

Gellhorn planned to cross Africa from west to east. She set off with less knowledge of the continent than one might acquire from reading a few entries in a standard encyclopaedia. Her doctor thought her trip sheer lunacy and injected her with antitoxins to ward off exotic diseases. For a three-month trip she packed a suitcase with a hot-water bottle, wool clothing, cotton dresses, a few pairs of dress shoes, a big straw hat, a cosmetics case with drugs, paperback thrillers and books by Jane Austen and William Shirer.

In Douala, Cameroon, Gellhorn's first stop, she found exactly what is described in the *Columbia Encyclopedia*: 'swamps and dense, tropical rain forests' with one of the wettest climates in the world, not the golden land she had conjured in her imagination. In the early morning hours of 24 January she staggered off the aeroplane into the stifling heat, feeling drained after so many hours of sleepless flight. Gellhorn laughed loudly when she remembered her hot-water bottle.

How was it that Isak Dinesen had written about Africa so composedly? Gellhorn wondered. She felt sweaty, greasy, swollen, and infected. She could not overcome her repugnance at the reeking Africans she met. Was it the climate or the lack of soap (an expensive commodity) that accounted for an odour that seemed to be a mix of urine and perspiration? Ashamed of herself, she regretted the damage she had done to her convictions about 'human brotherhood'.

Gellhorn scorned the European conceit of having brought civilization and religion to the continent. Christianity had not been practised very well in the West and who had the right to say that Europeans were justified in tampering with African culture? Whites deplored African incompetence, but what else could be expected when a young African boy had to deal with complex machinery that an American child grew up taking for granted? Nevertheless, Gellhorn had to rein in her impatience when an African official (who may not have been able to read) turned her passport every which way for long laborious minutes.

Gellhorn encountered jungle tom-toms beating out a sinister rhythm just like in the movies. In visits to leper colonies she observed people without noses and with limbs worn away by the disease drunkenly dancing and cavorting. She found her own biases reciprocated: Africans thought whites had a revolting smell – something akin to rotting corpses. Gellhorn wanted to escape civilization, only to find that she could not relinquish her habits and blend into the natural surroundings.

On the morning of 1 February she fumed over her two guides, Ali and Ibrahim. Their tardiness meant she would miss the elephants coming for their morning bath. They seemed lost in the habitat; she distrusted the show they made of examining elephant droppings, the position of twigs and the wind direction. Then, less than sixty feet away, she spotted a silent elephant herd. She just managed to steal a retreat without riling the female elephants protecting their babies.

Gellhorn made mistakes with her African guides and never learned how to treat them properly, yet the Westerners she met had little practical advice to offer other than their conviction that a woman should not be out alone travelling with Africans. She deplored the wretched West African hotels and the ruinous roads. African women, she observed, were not much more than sexual objects and childbearers. She watched barbers shaving the inside of their customers' nostrils with a sharp knife in fascinated horror.

East Africa, on the other hand, had weather like Cuernevaca, people who did not stink and wonderful game parks where she could indulge her main interest, nature watching. She wanted a driver and translator so she could enjoy the view and question the natives. When the prissy, dainty-looking Joshua offered his services, she overrode her instinctive doubts and hired him, for she hungered for the real Africa (the one of her dreams), not the one of celebrities like Robert Ruark and Kirk Douglas who set off from Nairobi on their white hunter safaris.

Joshua turned out to be a pious and priggish city boy. He could not drive but would not admit it, conning Gellhorn into taking the wheel with a number of excuses: he could show her the way better if she drove; his licence was not good in certain countries; the authorities would be hard on him if he had an accident; he would be better than she at watching for holes in the road from the passenger's side of the Landrover. His Swahili was barely serviceable; he had never been out of Nairobi. Gellhorn had to cajole, threaten, ridicule, amuse and comfort Joshua. Or, as she wryly put it, he made a man out of her.

Yet to jettison Joshua meant relinquishing her illusions. She wanted to believe him. She wanted to think she could reach an accommodation with this African and he had his endearing moments. When they observed the elegance of giraffes, huge and glossy with long eyelashes, Joshua remarked, 'Oh, *nice*' and laughed, making Gellhorn realize she was showing him his country for the first time. Then she got stuck in the middle of nowhere, aware that her maps offered nothing more than a guess as to how to get through Africa.

Bitten by tsetse flies, stuck in the mud, crossing flooded areas in an aged Landrover that took four hands to put it into four-wheel drive, Gellhorn ordered the whining Joshua to '*buck up*'. More fussy and fastidious than she, he put his handkerchief over his nose and said Ugandans sweated 'dirty'. When she upbraided him he sulked and played the 'offended damsel', and made her out to be the bully. Even so, she had gloriously happy days watching African animals in their natural environment. She thought it charming that one of her European hosts had a garden regularly visited by hippos who munched her flowers and seemed to like them even better with the pepper the gardener thought might put them off.

Gellhorn managed to foist Joshua off on a white couple travelling to Nairobi, but her journey remained a disaster. Her Landrover had to be pulled out of a stream after it had got stuck on a rock and her wonderful day of swimming on the African coast turned wretched when she returned to her hotel with massive sunburn. This last calamity made her wonder whether she would ever grow up. Apparently she lacked the 'mechanism' that prevented adults from making fools of themselves. Yet Africa gave off glimpses of itself as the land of her 'heart's desire'.

Of course, Africa could never fulfil Gellhorn's hopes for it. She studiously avoided the Africa of Ernest Hemingway. She did not come to shoot big game but to explore the land and the wildlife, which she hoped would offer a panorama of adventure. Gellhorn was beginning to glimpse, though, just how futile her adventuring had become, how absurd, really, it was for her to seek salvation in travel. It would be another fifteen years before she would be able, in *Travels with Myself and Another*, to wrest the comedy from her complaining about her trips. Even then, the thought of another jaunt, another destination, always beckoned.

In *Travels with Myself and Another*, Hemingway appears as UC, unwilling companion, and it is the only time Gellhorn was able to write about Hemingway with humour and unqualified admiration. On 2 July 1961 he had killed himself with his own shotgun. Gellhorn refrained from any public comment on his suicide. Privately she expressed her belief that the Mayo Clinic had made 'terrible mistakes' in its treatment of his depression and that his wife Mary compounded the problem by not having him institutionalized. Her opinion, shared by Hemingway's son Patrick, with whom she had kept in close touch, and by several other Hemingway intimates, took into account his own opposition to institutionalization. But to Gellhorn he had become 'quite insane'.

Like Mary Hemingway, Gellhorn now began to confront legions of scholars and biographers starting on their post-mortems. In April 1963 she met with Carlos Baker, Hemingway's authorized biographer, at the Hotel Gladstone in New York City. At fifty-four she appeared 'tall and slender, with her blonde hair just beginning to turn grey'. She had a bold, open face and a distinctively British manner of speaking. The biographer had conscientiously investigated Gellhorn's career, read her books and gave her an opportunity to comment on drafts of chapters. In an early draft she came out looking little more than the great author's appendage.

Baker wrote that in January 1937 'Hemingway spent two weeks in New York, carrying on his love affair with Martha Gellhorn by long distance telephone.' Gellhorn underlined 'love affair' and commented: 'No love affair: *not* lovers, never spoke of love; not even a courting. Not even a kiss! Interest of great author for young one, shared interest in Spain. I was much more anti-Fascist, politically aware etc. Get this right.' Baker wrote of Pauline who 'did not yet fully appreciate the threat to her marriage posed by Ernest's growing infatuation with Martha Gellhorn, who was soon to follow Hemingway on the *Ile de France*'. Gellhorn underlined 'growing infatuation' and 'soon to follow Hemingway', marked Baker's manuscript 'urgent' and wrote on the reverse side: 'Carlos: This is wrong, in tone & implication, an injustice to us both.' She recapitulated her own political history in Germany and her anti-fascism. She was her own person, writing a novel, concerned about her mother after her father's recent death. She would have gone to Spain regardless of what Hemingway had done. Certainly he found her 'a pretty female' and he was unquestionably her 'literary hero'. They were 'not lovers & marriage, as an idea, was not mentioned for a year'.

Baker took his information from Sidney Franklin, who adored Hemingway and hated Gellhorn. Herbert Matthews, who also annotated Baker's drafts, commented 'you cannot trust Franklin *at all*'. Franklin claimed to have eased Gellhorn's way into Spain. It was a lie and she resented 'this beautiful darling aspect'. She became so incensed at Franklin's lies that she wrote 'Balls!' in the margin of Baker's manuscript. She did not have 'sandy hair', she wanted Baker to know, but she admitted 'the blonde bit was what always confused the issue: luscious blonde or serious writer?'.

Gellhorn denied that she and Hemingway were '*open* lovers' in Spain. She challenged a description of her as a 'sleek woman with a fair halo of hair'. 'No one ever thought me sleek.' Baker had her in bed with Hemingway while he tried to think of words that captured the sound of shelling. She commented: 'So odd, this picture. It wasn't like that. We never could sleep together – sleep in the same bed! Ah well, I see I'll have to grin and bear it.'

Baker wrote that Hemingway secured permission for Gellhorn to visit forward command posts. 'Such rot,' she wrote. She went 'everywhere' with Hemingway and Matthews, and needed no special authorization. Often she went off on her own. 'Honestly! Have you ever read *my* Spanish reporting? ... I'm *hating* this job of reading the mss.'

In Baker's draft Hemingway glided with ease from one episode to another with no recognition that Gellhorn was, in her words, the 'leg-woman', the one who worked hard to get a showing for *The Spanish Earth* at the White House. Over and over, Baker left Gellhorn out of important battle scenes in which the intrepid Hemingway appeared. Over and over, Gellhorn would insert her name, finally remarking 'and me (or does it matter?)'. She hated being typed, circled the biographer's reference to her as Hemingway's 'paramour' and asked, 'Must you use that word?'

After the interview with Baker at the Hotel Gladstone, Gellhorn refused any further co-operation, forbidding the biographer to 'acknowledge her contribution'. She thought she could put a period to the story of her life with Hemingway. In fact, she would never be able to shake his hold on her imagination.

17

A NEW KIND OF WAR
1965–1969

AFTER GELLHORN'S DIVORCE from Matthews in 1963 she tried to resume her career as a foreign correspondent. She was now in her mid-fifties, and though she had continued to work as a freelance reporter, she had no regular affiliation with a newspaper or magazine, and much younger men and women had claims on editors for assignments. Gellhorn had lost her 'place in the queue' – as she would put it to friends.

By the autumn of 1965 Vietnam had become an everyday event on television screens. Gellhorn's opposition to the war was instantaneous: the very idea of napalming poor villagers appalled her. She would expose American contempt for other nationalities and races in *The Lowest Trees Have Tops*, a novel set in Mexico but with a subtext that grew out of her anger over Vietnam. During a brief visit to New York she made herself most unpopular by suggesting she and her friends who protested against Vietnam would in the future be known as 'good Americans', just as people talked of 'good Germans' who protested against fascism.

Having completed *The Lowest Trees Have Tops* by the summer of 1966, Gellhorn tried to get a job covering the war in Vietnam. She was considered too old for a war being covered like a 'sports event', with accounts of 'kill ratios' and 'body counts'. But she wanted to report on the devastation inflicted by the war on Vietnamese civilians and no newspaper in Britain thought this a newsworthy subject, except the *Guardian*, which Gellhorn's feisty agent, Elaine Greene, persuaded to commission Gellhorn.

Out of Gellhorn's brief stay in August–September 1966, she produced six newspaper articles of enormous power, originality and
unity, which the *Guardian* reprinted in booklet form. In retrospect
she admitted to having censored herself – the reality was far grim-
mer than she could write – but her very restraint (in part the result
of not wanting to be accused of writing Communist propaganda)
makes the articles magnificent examples of tightly controlled, evocative reportage. Although napalm was often mentioned in news
reports, Gellhorn described the

> jellied gasoline, contained in bombs about six feet long. The bomb,
> exploding on contact, hurls out gobs of this flaming stuff, and fierce
> fire consumes everything in its path. We alone possess and freely use
> this weapon in South Vietnam. Burns are deadly in relation to their
> depth and extent. If upwards of 30% of the entire thickness of the
> skin is burned, the victim will die within 24 to 48 hours, unless he
> receives skilled constant care.

Skilled constant care did not exist, 'since the hospitals have neither
staff nor facilities for special burn treatment'. Children were often
the casualties because of the constant day and night bombing. In
such passages Gellhorn made clear she had gathered facts from
Americans on the ground – an American surgeon, a photographer, a
housewife from New Jersey, visitors and workers in the country
who had anguished over America's indiscriminate destruction of a
people and a country. 'The use of fire and steel on South Vietnamese
hamlets, because Vietcong are reported to be in them (and often
are not), can sometimes be like destroying your friend's home
and family because you have heard there is a snake in the cellar', she
concluded.

What made Vietnam a new kind of war? It was not so much a
war of strategic objectives, of territory to be captured, as it was of
winning 'the hearts and minds of the people of South Vietnam'. This
is how an American government briefing document put it, and
Gellhorn's first report began by citing this apparently humane
statement. Yet American bombing killed countless civilians. While
military casualty figures were acidulously reported, civilian wounded
went unrecorded, she noted. How could the hearts and minds of
a people be won if their daily dying made no impact on the

Vietnamese or American governments? And why did the richest
South Vietnamese never visit the hospitals and never attend the
wounded and the dying? The well-off had no conscience, a nun in
one hospital told Gellhorn.

Although the United States sent millions of dollars to help Vietnamese civilians, little of it reached the people. Civilians did not dare
to criticize their government; the politicians and the military
thought only in terms of ideology, of Vietnam as a 'second Spain',
the advance battleground for World War Three. Self-proclaimed anti-
Communists reaped a fortune in Saigon. The overstaffed war com-
mands of the South Vietnamese and the Americans concentrated
their fire power on ridding the countryside of Vietcong – a nation-
wide search-and-destroy mission that pushed the peasants off their
land. While the Vietcong had been accused of assassinating somewhere between 6000 and 13,000 village officials, American bombing
had killed and displaced hundreds of thousands of villagers. American propaganda exaggerated the menace of the Vietcong (after all,
millions of peasants remained on their land and grew their crops
with no evident fear of Communists) and falsely extolled the
strength of the South Vietnamese.

An air of unreality pervaded virtually all aspects of the war,
including the reporting done by several hundred correspondents –
almost none of whom thought to cover the civilian tragedy. While it
has often been said that Vietnam was the most reported war ever and
that its daily presence on television helped move the American people towards opposing the war, Gellhorn emphasized that famous
pictures like the one of a naked girl sheathed in napalm fire running
down a road appeared rather late in the war. Most graphic reports
about the way napalm melted human flesh were not published. Only
Gellhorn's tamest pieces appeared in the *Ladies Home Journal* and the
St Louis Post-Dispatch, but they provided relentless eyewitness
accounts of human suffering: the abominably dirty hospitals served
often by only one doctor and nurse; with patients (usually two to
one narrow cot or bed on boards) being cared for mostly by their
homeless families; with bathrooms overflowing with human excrement; with at best one meal a day; with children looking out at
Gellhorn with maimed and lopsided faces, with missing limbs and
eyes. This overpowering eyewitness testimony put Gellhorn on a

South Vietnamese blacklist. After just this one brief trip, she was never able to get a return visa to Vietnam. And no wonder. How many readers of the *Ladies Home Journal* would forget her descriptions of children who looked at her with agony and confusion? This was a war of sheer terror, and the hospitals were full of women and children who had gone insane. These were crimes against humanity. What had happened to the principles of Nuremberg? Gellhorn asked.

Spending the spring of 1967 in St Louis, Gellhorn wrote a piece comparing the war in Vietnam to Lyndon Johnson's war on poverty. She quoted his election year statements that insisted Vietnam was not a war American boys should have to fight. Yet Vietnam and the obsession with Communism had eclipsed the fight to help the poor. By one estimate it cost $400,000 to kill a *'single'* enemy. The total budget of just under $4 billion for non-military aid to Vietnam equalled the amount spent on the war on poverty in a country fifty-seven times larger than Vietnam. The bureaucratic definition of poverty and the inadequately funded domestic programmes were evidence to Gellhorn of a country deficient in insight and mercy. As she noted in a postscript to her Vietnam reporting (published in 1988), more bombs were dropped on Vietnam than on 'all theaters of war by all air forces in World War II'. The Vietnam bombings were not the 'surgical strikes' touted by the military. Even worse, she pointed out, the retrospectives and movies on Vietnam did little to show the war as the Vietnamese experienced it. The media created the impression that Americans had suffered most from the war, she concluded.

For Gellhorn, Vietnam was another Spain – in the sense that she believed its people had a right to determine their own destiny instead of becoming proxies for superpower battles. She strongly identified with their quest to settle things on their own and her reports are filled with admiration for the beauty of the Vietnamese people. They had a gentleness and refinement that profoundly impressed her. Compared with their diminutive elegance, 'we are overweight, unlovely giants', Gellhorn wrote. It was not just an excess of feeling that made her also write that if she were a generation younger, she would have gone to Vietnam and 'joined the Vietcong'.

In 1967 a new edition of *The Face of War* appeared that included Gellhorn's six Vietnam reports for the *Guardian* and her commentary on them. She could not get over the sight of American streets 'bombed by poverty' and the massacre of Vietnam. Driving her through a city slum, listening to her excoriate the government for spending over $2 billion a month while allowing its own cities to deteriorate, a plaintive taxi driver summed up the public paralysis and hurt: he could not believe his own nation had done 'wrong'. This bewildered taxi driver was a world away from the proud army major in Vietnam who showed Gellhorn colour photographs of his kills. These dead Vietnamese were Vietcong – he was sure of it. Why not stick their heads on poles to encourage others? she asked him in disgust.

By the late 1960s Gellhorn saw hopeful signs of massive public protest against not only the war but against Cold War politics. She had attended a protest meeting in which the young and middle-aged, black and white, got together to review the history of Vietnam, to call for peace and to demand a decrease in spending on weaponry in favour of investment in social welfare. Julian Bond was the star speaker. Twice he had been refused his elected seat in the Georgia legislature because of his opposition to Vietnam. She liked his slim, elegant 'Negro' looks, his quiet articulation of the issues and the total integration of the audience, which was inspired by his fortitude and wisdom. It seemed as though public opinion had swung Gellhorn's way when the audience rose to applaud Bond's concluding sentence: 'It's not our job to make the world safe for democracy, but to make American democracy safe for the world.'

In January 1969 at the Paris Peace Conference, Gellhorn reported on Madame Binh, one of the North Vietnamese negotiators, a slight, diminutive, weary, but indomitable woman who demonstrated exactly why the United States had not been able to prevail in Vietnam. This frail, modest figure had a belief in her cause and an endurance that would outlast all foreign invaders. She had been imprisoned, tortured, separated from her family and bombed, but nothing had deterred her fight for independence. Most remarkably, she revealed no hatred for Americans and she could conceive of being on good terms with them just as she was now on good terms with the French, Vietnam's former European masters. Similarly, Gellhorn was amazed at the exuberant, polite, gentle nature of the young American protesters who had come to Washington to demonstrate against Nixon's widening of the war to Cambodia. This was after Kent State, where students had been shot simply because they were dissenters. These young people in Washington were well organized. They picked up after themselves and were generous with each other, determined to make the system work for them. Gellhorn found something liberating in their joyful laughter, in the 'Fuck Nixon' chant, soon replaced by the more rhythmic 'Fuck you, Agnew'. Even a cop was prompted to compliment a young girl on her smile. This was the generation of youth John F. Kennedy might have understood and valued, she concluded.

Having been away from the country so long, Gellhorn never imagined so many thousands of young people could assemble at such a good-natured and serious event. It was not an America she could have dreamed up and certainly not the country she had thought of so contemptuously during her African and English years.

As in Spain, however, Gellhorn refused to deal with the political nature of war. Did the Vietcong really represent a more humane alternative to the Americans – any more than the Soviets served as a better alternative to the fascists in Spain? The ruthless future the Vietcong would bring about had no place in it for Martha Gellhorn when she updated her comments on Vietnam in the 1988 edition of *The Face of War*. Her outrage remains compelling, her role as passionate, campaigning journalist is admirable, but she also revealed a wilful ignorance of the larger canvas of history.

18

HOPE AGAINST HOPE
1967–1972

NEVER AN ALL-OUT PACIFIST, Gellhorn rejoiced in Israel's victory in the Six Day War. Nasser had vowed to destroy Israel and announced on 30 May 1967 that Egypt, Jordan, Syria and Lebanon had armies prepared to invade their enemy. In addition, he boasted that Iraq, Algeria, Kuwait and Sudan – indeed, the whole Arab world – had declared its opposition to Israel's existence. The next day Cairo radio broadcast the chant: 'Slaughter, Slaughter, Slaughter.'

Gellhorn reported that Israel had less than 50,000 soldiers, including its reservists. The four principal Arab powers had three times as many tanks and planes. While Israeli territory was a mere 8000 square miles, the Arabs controlled 677,000 square miles. It was 46,100,000 Arabs in Egypt, Jordan, Syria and Lebanon against 2,300,000 Jews and 350,000 Israeli Arabs. These were the figures Gellhorn counted up. Yet in six days Israel had vanquished its enemies with a minimal loss of civilian life (less than 200 casualties). She did not exaggerate when she called this victory an 'unparalleled military achievement'.

Gellhorn did not arrive in Israel until 10 June, the fifth day of the war. In the Sinai, where much of the fighting took place, she observed the rotting, stinking bodies of Egyptian soldiers, mounds of mines, abandoned gun lines pointing at Israel and burned-out tanks. Flies swarmed over bodies that resembled bunches of rags and on to the living, darting into eyes and mouths dried out from the heat and the glaring sun. In this carnage she met the reservists, the 'citizen army' of Israel – young men and women already being sent home just days after victory. There seemed to be almost no sense of hierarchy; everyone addressed each other on a first-name basis. Officers wore no insignia and did not salute. Everyone seemed to know his or her job, so there were few orders issued. It was a unique army because of its lack of uniformity and regimentation. Men wore beards, moustaches, sideburns, ducktails, and just about any kind of khaki clothing served as a uniform. Gellhorn observed two female soldiers wearing 'soft black ballet slippers'. They were radio operators in the Signal Corps.

This democratic and humane army had stopped returning Egyptian prisoners of war when they saw them being shot by their own army. Gellhorn found a virtual absence of personal animosity towards Arabs, even though Arab propaganda had been producing Nazi images of Jews as fat and swarthy with great hook noses and dribbling lips. Surveying the Golan Heights, from which the Arabs had shelled Israeli villages for eighteen years, Gellhorn reaffirmed her conviction that the Israelis had been fighting for their very existence.

After the first days of victory a dismayed Gellhorn watched support for Israel evaporate. It was treated like just another occupying power and not like a small nation that had brought off something akin to a biblical miracle. Her Six Day War articles reported how careful Israel had been in minimizing civilian losses. Arab propaganda alleged atrocities in areas she had visited and which had actually sustained minimal damage. She tried to sit calmly and listen to Arab charges that Bethlehem had been constantly bombed. She could see it was not so and she could find only one incident in the entire war where Israel had dropped ten or fifteen small bombs on a Syrian town holding troops. This was not like Vietnam; this was a battle of armies incurring very few civilian casualties, but the Arab peoples had been taught to hate Israel and to imagine their defeat in terms of human massacres. King Hussein had urged them to murder all Jews, even if it meant attacking them with bare hands, nails and teeth.

Gellhorn called for a census of the refugee camps and a realistic effort to relocate the displaced that was not predicated on Israel's destruction. After all, she argued, there were at least 35 million refugees worldwide, not counting the Arabs, and many of them had quietly and courageously created new homes and careers.

After her stint in Israel, Gellhorn returned to Africa. For thirteen years, beginning with her first trip in 1962, Gellhorn would spend part of each year on the continent. By the end of 1967 she had found her spot on top of a mountain (Longonot) in Kenya. She wrote to Raleigh Trevelyan, her editor at Michael Joseph, that she hoped to construct a 'very small house' and spend seven months a year 'looking at a large empty world and circumambulating animals so as to recover from what I feel to be the unbearable disasters of the present'.

To some extent Gellhorn's residence in Africa formed part of her plan to resurrect her writing career. Although her fiction continued to be published by Simon and Schuster, and Dodd, Mead in the US in the 1960s, her work did not sell well and Michael Joseph did not continue her on their list. Her production of first-rate journalism had dwindled and she had always found it difficult to write fiction. Finding the ideal spot in Africa, she hoped, would provide her with new stimulus.

Gellhorn did not tell the story of how she acquired her African home. She admired and befriended the journalist Alan Moorehead, author of *No Room in the Ark* (1959), *The White Nile* (1960) and *The Blue Nile* – books about African animal life and nineteenth-century explorations of the continent. Moorehead had written to Jack Bloch, a very hospitable hotelier, asking him to take special care of Gellhorn. 'Well, you had to be kind to Martha. She was so entertaining to have around', remembered one witness to this period.

> She got quite friendly with Jack and asked him if she could build a little cottage at the top of Longonot Mountain. Jack said, 'Martha, I don't think you should. There's no road going up to the mountain. If you build a house, you're going to have all the problems of getting the stone up, travelling up, travelling back if its raining hard. It's going to be a horrible skiddy road. In dry weather you will have terrible dust'. But she wouldn't be dissuaded.

While Bloch was travelling, Gellhorn got his farm manager to begin work on the cottage, explaining that she desperately wanted a secluded place to write. When Bloch returned he faced the inevitable: 'She's done it', he said. He admired Gellhorn extravagantly. They shared an enthusiasm for the state of Israel (Bloch's mother was a Sabra). 'It was a darling little house, furnished all in limey green and white. Never had much furniture. No clutter. She had chairs, the odd painting', a Kenyan friend recalled. In the end, Gellhorn did little writing on her mountain top. The altitude bothered her.

She did battle with creatures creeping along her interior walls or residing beneath her dining table, or dodging a black mamba (snake), jabbing at it with sticks, or whacking away at a tarantula with a rolled-up magazine. As in Cuba, she raged against the inconveniences of her dishevelled household and the incompetence of workmen. She wanted exposure to a rougher-edged world, but brought along two sceptical Spanish servants to provide the comforts of home. While they complained about the encroaching wildlife, Gellhorn enjoyed the noise monkeys made on her roof. Bat invasions terrified her, but she indulged passions for tree-pruning and 'goggling' at the underwater sea life so abundant and so near her coastal residence.

Gellhorn delighted Bloch, his family and friends. No one had to make conversation because Martha was her own show. Indeed, she wanted no competition. The legendary Beryl Markham lived nearby, but Gellhorn saw her only once – later saying regretfully, 'I wish I'd spent more time with her.' She talked about T. S. Matthews, who like all men seemed not up to her standard. Martha dominated parties and others rarely put in a word. 'Doesn't Lady K ever talk?' Martha asked.

Gellhorn was not, of course, always cheerful. Indeed, she did go on about how difficult life was, especially for her. 'She was a bit of a moaner', recalled Pauline Neville who saw Gellhorn both in Africa and London. Gellhorn spoke often about how dreadfully the Germans had treated the Jews. And she was always looking for a new place, a new destination, for places, like men, sooner or later let her down.

Gellhorn often discussed Sandy. They did not get on terribly well. She went on and on about how she had found him. She advised her Kenyan friends about bringing up their children, who should not be pampered. To be on your own at an early age – that was the ticket.

Worried about Sandy, Gellhorn sent him encyclopaedic letters trying to convince him that he was not going to die in Vietnam. (He had been a student at Columbia for a while before being drafted.) He had trouble settling to anything and was a puzzle to many people, including Tom Matthews, who kept up with Edna and promised he would write to Sandy, whom Matthews found unpredictable. His adolescence had been made all the harder by weight problems and Martha had harped on how fat he had become. Tom Matthews had referred to him as a 'hefty will-o'-the-wisp'.

The previous month Edna had taken a bad fall, breaking her hip, and was expected to stay in hospital for at least three weeks recovering from surgery. But she had been released early, prompting Matthews to send her a cheerful letter about outwitting pessimistic physicians. For many people Edna had been a beacon, a source of assurance and a touchstone. In a poem about her after her death, Matthews called Edna a 'wise old lady' who had kept 'the same expectations she had as a girl'. She had a freshness that delighted everyone who knew her. Her growing frailty frightened Martha.

Two or three times a week Martha wrote lively letters to her mother, but she could write little else. She tried a change of scene, travelling to London in late June. She fretted about Sandy, who was evidently writing letters to Edna complaining about Martha. 'You realize Sandy's letters to you are outpourings of a sick boy, with perhaps not the best heart', Martha wrote to her mother. Sandy had said to her, 'I feel I have disappointed you.' Martha agreed, calling him selfish and egotistical. Sandy was 'weak', she told her mother.

By 12 July Sandy had got a medical discharge from the army and was living in Martha's new London flat in fashionable Cadogan Square. She loved her new digs but as usual her disorderly and incompetent household help and workmen upset her – as did her troubled relationship with Sandy. 'I am so sorry for Sandy who doesn't know what it is to love his mother', Martha wrote to Edna. He seemed 'pitiful and alarming' to her.

Ten days later, with Sandy's psychiatrist's 'blessing', she had given her son 'the boot'. He was off, 'knapsack on back', to explore

Europe. At twenty-two he had barely got over his adolescence, Martha thought, but now he would have to start making his own choices. As for her, she began cooking lessons with ironic reverberations – generations earlier her grandmother had run classes in cooking for the children of the poor.

On 9 August, Martha wrote her mother a long, reminiscing letter. She had been tacking up family photos in her bedroom and had found a lovely portrait of Edna, holding her head high in a beautiful and elegant fashion. Martha thought her childhood pictures always made her out to be a scold or a protester, the most serious and irritated of the Gellhorn children. All this talk of family made her think of Sandy, who had had no real home in his teen years. She regretted that her preference was to live by herself.

Edna Gellhorn died on 24 September 1970. Martha had made frequent trips home in the last few years of her mother's life – usually refusing to see her friends, but occasionally making an exception for Mary Hall, who worried about the possibility that her son would be sent to Vietnam, or for Martha Love Symington, who helped to protect Martha's privacy. 'I'm here to see my mother', Martha would announce as a way of declining most social invitations. She would often stay with Symington, using her own key to come and go as she pleased. She also resented the claims people made on Edna's time, but then Edna was far more giving in her daily associations with people than her daughter ever could be. Martha had never had much use for St Louis anyway. 'The reason I talk so much when I'm in St Louis is that everybody's so boring. I'm the only interesting person here, so I might as well talk and listen to myself', she told Mary Hall on one of their long walks together. The St Louisans Martha really cared for were people like William Julius Polk and Martha Love Symington, people with 'great character', Mary Hall observes.

On Martha's last visit to her mother she told Symington that she was leaving the next day. 'My mother is definitely going to die, and I don't want to be here when she dies. I want to remember her as she was.' Symington thought this very strange: 'I think you must stay if you think your mother's going to die. You have a responsibility.' Martha replied, 'I'll leave my brothers to do that.' In fact, her brother

Walter's wife, Kitty, took care of most of the funeral arrangements, as she had taken care of many things for Edna through the years. Martha was 'skipping out before the real nitty-gritty happened', observed Symington, who remembered Martha standing on the staircase in her home, predicting the very day her mother would die. After her mother's death she called Symington to ask what day she had said Edna would die. When Symington told her, a heart-broken Martha kept saying, 'I knew it. I knew it. I knew it.' When Symington looked back on it, she could think of other occasions when Martha would duck out on the really 'unpleasant things'.

Martha's absence at her mother's death and memorial service troubled many of her St Louis friends and acquaintances. 'I think I'd want to be right there when the person I loved made that passage', Mary Hall suggests. Martha's absence seemed less than courageous for a woman who had always shown so much fortitude. One of Edna's close friends doubts that Martha could have lived through the memorial service. 'I don't think anybody could have said what she thought should be said', remarks Mrs Aaron Fischer, who spoke at Edna's service. In one of Martha's last letters to her mother she made a veiled reference to some family tensions ('stupid internecine offspring bits'). Gellhorn never talked about family tensions, but certainly her mother's friends were aware that the family thought her the odd one out. Edna refrained from criticizing Martha, and mother and daughter remained close. Indeed, Martha treasured her mother and simply could not bear to share her special sense of her with others or to make their grief her own.

Edna's death prolonged a 'paralysis' brought on by an interminable war that had 'gripped' Martha's mind. She could not write, except for vivid letters to friends and occasional vituperative responses to scholars soliciting information – usually about Hemingway. On 29 February 1972 Professor A. S. Knowles queried her about the trip to China in 1941. Hemingway had told Malcolm Cowley that a forced landing there had for the first time since 1917 'cured him of his fear of death'. Gellhorn replied that there were no forced landings in China and the tale was 'balls'. But she agreed to his visit, even though it would be a 'waste' of his time. On 22 May Knowles entered Gellhorn's flat in Cadogan Square and greeted a sixty-four-year-old woman – still slim, blonde and attractive in a Bryn Mawrish way and she clearly knew it. She managed to be both patronizing and coquettish. They talked for about an hour and a half over drinks as she reviled Hemingway. The fame of this fraud had obscured her. People knew her as his third wife – a dirty trick. Yes, his early work had merit, but *For Whom the Bell Tolls* was a phoney book describing guerrilla fighting that had not occurred in the Spanish Civil War. Only once did Knowles remember her relenting, when she admitted Hemingway had a certain flair. She told a story of their flying on a transport plane in China that hit an air pocket and took a terrific plunge, sending everyone sprawling. Hemingway had been about to take a slug of gin in his dixie cup just before the plunge. When the plane stopped falling, the rest of them, scared out of their wits, started pulling themselves together only to find him, unshaken, swallowing his gin and grinning, saying proudly, 'Didn't spill a drop!' She admitted that this gave them all a laugh and dispelled their fright. She would later recount this incident in *Travels with Myself and Another*, but to Knowles her story did not seem a tribute to 'hard-won grace under pressure, but only as a certain boyish bravado that Hemingway could manage on occasion'.

Knowles felt that Gellhorn wanted to flirt and have him echo her denunciation of American imperialism. Instead, this eager academic ignored her own career, her opinions and her attractiveness, and saw her only as a resource for some Hemingway research. Later he realized that his visit must have been trying for her.

In a funk, Gellhorn looked for inspiration, for that 'one grand person', and finally found it in the work of Russian dissident, Nadezhda Mandelstam, the wife of a great poet, Osip Mandelstam. Her book, *Hope Against Hope* (1970), had profundity in every line, and courage. It explored her struggle after her husband's disappearance and death in the Soviet labour camps. She fought to preserve her husband's poetry, often combating government bureaucrats and agents determined to break her spirit. She narrated her life with earthiness, humour and scorn, producing a masterpiece of autobiography.

When a book moved her, Gellhorn had a habit of sending off an admiring letter to the author. In this case the admiring letter led to correspondence that eventuated in Mandelstam's inviting Gellhorn for a visit. The invitee felt morally obligated to a person in her seventies who had so effectively shown what it was like to live day to day in a horrifying authoritarian society. How could Gellhorn refuse a writer who had such a quick, sharp style? To Mandelstam the invitation may have been purely hospitable. It was characteristic of Gellhorn, in other words, to create an air of expectation and duty about her trip which Mandelstam most likely had not intended.

On 3 July 1972, with much foreboding, Gellhorn set off to meet her esteemed author. The trip proved worse than Gellhorn's first journey in Africa. In heavy clothing she sweated her entire week in Russia, not believing the weather reports that had put the temperature in the nineties. Rather than accept as a matter of course that travelling in a secretive, rigidly controlled and backward society would be inconvenient, Gellhorn chafed at everything: the laborious process of changing money, broken elevators, the lack of a city telephone directory, restaurants with dirty tablecloths and inedible food, and dour public manners. She missed London, where just recently a bus ticket inspector had given back her ticket and said, 'Thank you, my blossom.' There was little civility in Moscow, taxis drove recklessly and she felt the pressure of a state that snooped on its citizens relentlessly. In some sense she had known it would be like this for her and had only come for Mandelstam.

That, too, was a disappointment. Mandelstam held court in her apartment every day, where a peckish Gellhorn had trouble following chaotic conversations and grabbing the morsels of greasy fried mushrooms, strawberries, tomatoes and cucumbers passed round at intervals. It unnerved her to hear Mandelstam talk of possibly leaving Moscow for London. Gellhorn could see her future: one of constant attendance on this great woman – doing her bidding. Then it occurred to her that all this talk of living abroad was a diversion, meant by Mandelstam to rile her friends. The final disillusionment came in an argument about Vietnam, when Gellhorn found that Mandelstam and her friends supported Nixon. Gellhorn blew up. She had spent six years of her life opposing the war, she told them, and accused them of not being able to identify with other people's anguish. These Russians did not seem to know that the war was the most appalling event in her country's history.

In 'Stalin-Gothic' Moscow, Gellhorn became paranoid, fearing she would never get out of this 'claustrophobic prison-land'. E. M. Forster was right, she observed. Democracy deserved its two cheers.

In the fall of 1972 Gellhorn decided to campaign for George McGovern, who represented the liberal hope of the Democrats doing battle against their *bête noire* Richard Nixon. In Cambridge, Massachusetts she drove about with a bullhorn in a voter registration drive. One friend of hers thought she sounded apocalyptic, like one of the gods exhorting the people to realize the end was nigh. Yet she rang doorbells and stood on street corners distributing McGovern buttons just like any other volunteer.

Martha Kessler, a volunteer working at the New York City McGovern headquarters, stashed in a crummy old brownstone in the East 30s, watched Gellhorn walk in, dressed in stylish slacks and looking nowhere near her sixty-four years. Kessler knew about Gellhorn from her doctoral work on the Spanish Civil War, and older McGovern workers active in New York Democratic Party politics recognized the Gellhorn name and were pleased that someone of her importance had arrived who could be shown off to the staff. Kessler was working in the speaker's bureau and remembers Gellhorn being very concerned about getting the right people to make speeches on McGovern's behalf. Many of the big names already sensed that he did not have a chance of getting elected. So everyone welcomed Gellhorn's help, especially since she did not have a star's haughty manner. She wanted to put her few days in New York to good use, which meant doing the typical 'shit-work' of political campaigning – calling people, stuffing envelopes and so on.

Approaching the age when many people think of retirement, Gellhorn still wanted to be in the thick of it. With the prospect of another four years of Richard Nixon, she did what she could to change history. It seemed like her last chance to do so and to feel part of a country that had disappointed her so often. James Gavin, whose own views had been greatly influenced by hers, called it her 'last hurrah'.

19

THE LEGEND OF
MARTHA GELHORN
1972–1998

AFTER THE MCGOVERN campaign's failure, James Gavin believed Gellhorn had given up America for good. She kept her hand in, though, writing in December 1972 to the *New York Times* attacking Nixon's 'peace with honour' policy and his political and financial support of the South Vietnamese dictator Thieu. During the deadlocked Paris peace talks Vietnamese villages continued to be bombed each day, she pointed out. By July 1974 she was back stateside awaiting the impeachment of Richard Nixon. She wanted to see him tried, so that the record of criminality – as in the Nuremberg and Eichmann trials – would constitute a 'lesson for future generations'. She regretted Nixon's resignation as an action that forestalled the public examination of this sorry episode in American history.

Gellhorn resumed writing when the Vietnam War ended. In her own words, she had been released from a kind of prison and walked out into a suddenly expansive world. She produced two books, a collection of African stories and a travel memoir, between 1975 and 1977. *Travels with Myself and Another* had been written, appropriately enough, all over the world. She drafted *The Weather in Africa*, on the other hand, in her London flat at 72 Cadogan Square. She preserved her 'spacious white, spartan sitting room' for answering friends' letters. 'Upstairs in the attic' she donned her 'working uniform of blue-jeans and turtleneck', seated herself at a 'flat table' and pounded out her stories on a manual typewriter. When she needed inspiration, she could always gaze out through the short, wide window or at the picture of her mother. In this unheated room, with only an electric heater to take out the dampness, she wrote as much as fourteen hours a day, with several drafts going into the wastebasket.

In *Travels with Myself and Another* Gellhorn confesses her frustration at never getting close enough to Africa. She thought that if she had had an African occupation, if she had been a botanist or a farmer, she might have come to some fuller understanding of the continent. She might have been thinking of Beryl Markham, whom she visited once in the early 1970s in her sturdy 'settler' furnishings. Like Gellhorn, Markham still had a glamorous physical presence and clothing.

Wary of women like Markham and Isak Dinesen, Gellhorn admitted: 'I had to love *Out of Africa* despite what I felt to be a certain parvenu quality in the author's mind.' Gellhorn the reporter distrusted writers who appropriated foreign lands as their own, although this very reluctance to absorb the environment into her own imagination accounts for her inability to write great fiction. The very ego she deplored in Dinesen – the 'most insatiable tapeworm that exists' – probably made great fiction possible.

Nevertheless, in *The Weather in Africa*, three interlinked novellas – 'On the Mountain', 'In the Highlands' and 'By the Sea' – Gellhorn approaches an identification with a land that had eluded her in her daily experience of it. As Victoria Glendinning suggests, the book is about the 'inner and outer weather of Africa', and it presents a narrative that itself is a projection of what it feels like to live there.

'By the Sea', the third novella, is based directly on an incident in Gellhorn's life, when her car struck and killed an African child. The accident was not her fault, she told Hemingway's oldest son, Jack, but she was forced to leave Kenya.

In the story Mrs Jamieson, on vacation to forget her failed marriage and the death of her young son, takes a car trip to get away from civilization, to observe some of the native species. Suddenly she is involved in an accident. Her car has run over a black child. Naturally she identifies with the black child's mother. Isolated in her hotel room, grieving over this misfortune, she is visited by a hotel employee who tries to extort money from her by exploiting her sense of guilt. Her hysterical response is to throw herself from the balcony, an act of despair which is heightened by the story's closing line lamenting that this unfortunate woman should have come to Africa.

Gellhorn had also lost her home in Kenya. When the Blochs sold their extensive holdings, she was forced to vacate her cottage. She did not own the land and became furious when Jack Bloch offered her a sum that she deemed inadequate for the improvements she had made. She never spoke to him again, although in typical fashion she befriended other members of his family who became her champions.

By the early 1980s Gellhorn had found a replacement for her Kenyan redoubt. Now in her seventies, she chose a cottage in Wales near the English border. It seemed remote enough to give her that feeling of splendid isolation in which she could write without interruption, yet it was also close enough to London and her flat in Cadogan Square.

Much of Gellhorn's writing in the 1970s and 1980s took the form of reminiscence, as she revisited old haunts and took up old themes in new settings. In early 1976 she travelled from London to Spain to witness the end of Franco's rule. Arriving just after his death, she was glad to see that in spite of Franco's tyranny, a new generation had grown up ready to establish a democratic state. Although censorship and bans on public demonstrations existed, the ideals of Republican Spain had not perished.

At Christmas 1976 Gellhorn investigated lives of the unemployed in Britain. The Labour government was beginning to confront the breakdown in consensus about the welfare state that would eventually bring Margaret Thatcher to power. A deeply troubled economy was racked by labour disputes. In 'Doomed to the Dole' (*Observer*, 2 January 1977) Gellhorn wrote: 'A political face on TV announces: "We must expect increased unemployment next year." As if talking about bad weather, not doomed people. ... Officialdom is hostile to inquiring outsiders', she declared. 'For two weeks I have been trying to break through the wall of silence, and simply *see* unemployed people in their homes. It was far easier to meet dissidents in Russia and the underground opposition to Franco', she complained. She found welfare regulations nearly impossible to decipher and the amount given disgracefully low in spite of government propaganda that implied the unemployed were coddled. As in her Depression era reports, she found the poor resourceful, honest and even cheerful. When Gellhorn tried to visit a hostel for homeless women in north London, she was refused entrance. Handed a telephone on the steps of the hostel and given the phone number of the manageress, she called and asked the woman what gave her the right to act as a censor. 'I was angry enough to make *her* angry so that finally she said, "I've signed the Official Secrets Act and so have my staff. There's nothing more to say." The unemployed, the homeless are *an official secret?*' Gellhorn asked.

This encounter provoked her to request information about herself under the US Freedom of Information Act. Her FBI file consists mainly of blacked-out lines, so that the names of government informants are not disclosed. Her *New Republic* article attacking the House Committee on Un-American Activities had been clipped. She was listed as a member of six Communist Front organizations – all ad hoc groups she had worked with to aid refugees from the Spanish Civil War. The file began in 1941 and detailed her contacts with Communists and fellow travellers in the US and Mexico. One report stated that 'there is no information available indicating that she has knowledge of the Soviet intelligence activities of the Sterns' [a couple the FBI were investigating] or that she would be co-operative in an interview'. Her marriage to Hemingway and her friendship with the Roosevelts were duly noted.

Interviewed about the Roosevelts on 20 February 1980, Gellhorn remarked that the United States was a different country during the Roosevelt administration. She condemned a recent book by Doris Faber, *The Life of Lorena Hickok, Eleanor Roosevelt's Friend*, which suggested that Hickok and Roosevelt had been lovers – a contemptible speculation that should not have been published. The country, never very cultivated, did not deserve Mrs Roosevelt. The Roosevelts had given America some style. Why did Faber's book even have to be reviewed? Mrs Roosevelt had a 'girlish' side and would write warm letters about hugging you, but that hardly justified the implication of sexual intimacy. Gellhorn called Hickok a huge, ugly woman 'built like a tank', with an emotional life equivalent to that of the 'captain of the girls' hockey team'. Gellhorn could not imagine that anyone had ever taken much notice of 'boring' Hick except the 'terribly nice' Mrs Roosevelt. Gellhorn made no mention of Hickok's role in helping to secure her job in the Roosevelt administration or of her own 'girlish' letters to Hickok.

Gellhorn's rewriting of the past paled beside those she considered the 'apocryphiars': falsifiers of history who built up themselves or denigrated their famous subjects. Are apocryphiars acting out of resentment? she asked. Were they trying to secure a better place in history or had their conceit got the best of them? Her mission, she announced in the *Paris Review* (spring 1981), was to admonish the apocryphiars and instruct future historians. Her immediate targets: Stephen Spender and Lillian Hellman, both of whom (in her view) had claimed important relationships with Hemingway that the facts did not support.

Gellhorn denied Spender's story about the lunch he had had with her and Hemingway during the Spanish Civil War. Spender reported that Hemingway said he regarded his participation in the *causa* as a test of his courage. Gellhorn thought Spender demeaned Hemingway whose support for the Spanish Republic was selfless. Spender replied that Gellhorn simply disliked the emotional colouring he had given to events. She seemed, moreover, oblivious to her own Hemingwayesque style. He remembered the 'banter between Hemingway and her in the style of dialogue in Hemingway's early novels, in which she addressed him sometimes as "Hem" and other times as "Hemingstein" '. Her article on apocryphying was written in the same 'manner', Spender added. Indeed, the article featured her ex-husband's tough-guy, swaggering and patronizing idiom: 'Built-in falsehood, children, is bad', Gellhorn began in a fair imitation of Papa.

Gellhorn's defence of Hemingway revealed a good deal about herself. There was the good Hemingway ('selfless') and the bad Hemingway (selfish). This melodramatic view of the world makes Gellhorn's journalism and letters vivid, but it vitiated her political commentary and understanding of herself. She could not countenance Spender's idea that Hemingway brought his big ego to his sincere support of Republican Spain any more than she could acknowledge the size of her own ego and the way she projected it on to the world. Thus her fierce resentment of biography and of biographical commentary had to do with her refusal to examine her own motivations and the psychology of her life – a necessary subject for the biographer.

Rather than psychologizing about Lillian Hellman, for example, Gellhorn checked the dates in *An Unfinished Woman*. She demonstrated that Hellman's travel itinerary for 1937 contained so many internal inconsistencies that Hellman could not have been in all the places she claimed to have visited. Gellhorn confuted Hellman's story about reading the proofs of *To Have and Have Not* in Spain. Hemingway had actually read them before leaving for the war. Hemingway and Gellhorn could not have stood on their balcony in Madrid watching the fireworks from bombing (as Hellman claimed) since the bombs in Spain did not give off light.

Gellhorn demolished Hellman's 'first-hand' description of an air raid. Though Hellman has children screaming and women running, Gellhorn recalls how impressively quiet Spaniards were in dangerous situations. Is the policeman who pushes Hellman under a bench for protection during an air raid an 'imbecile'? Gellhorn asks. What kind of shelter is afforded by a park bench? This could not be Hellman's attempt at humour, could it? Gellhorn wanted to know.

Of Hellman's description of a plane dropping down and setting loose a bomb that 'slowly floated … like a round gift-wrapped package', Gellhorn remarks that the planes over Madrid flew at a 'prudent height', were not dive bombers and the bombs did not come one at a time floating 'like an auk's egg, or a gift-wrapped package'. At the most, Hellman had spent three weeks in Spain. In Gellhorn's memory of their brief meetings she was a grumpy, sullen presence and no match for her splendid companion Dorothy Parker, who showed none of Hellman's conceit. Gellhorn considered most of Hellman's scenes in her memoirs between herself and Hemingway to be sheer inventions, especially the one in which Hemingway compliments Hellman on her courage, saying she had '*cojones*' after all. 'In my opinion,' Gellhorn concluded, 'Miss H. has the *cojones* of a brass monkey.'

Gellhorn warned Marion Meade, Dorothy Parker's biographer, not to trust a word Hellman had to say on Parker. Gellhorn wrote to me that Hellman was cruel and false to Parker, and proceeded to elaborate the conviction that she could not be a true friend to any woman because she was 'ugly'. Of course, Gellhorn conceded there were ugly women like Golda Meir and Mrs Roosevelt who had been endearing, but these were the only major exceptions to the theory.

Gellhorn also wrote to Mary McCarthy, then confronting a libel action launched by Hellman after McCarthy had called her a liar on the Dick Cavett television programme. Gellhorn offered her support to McCarthy because Hellman had violated an 'ancient and noble tradition of writers, which is to call each other any names they like, in print, insult not law being the proper behavior'. Gellhorn then proceeded to offer 'tips' on doing the investigation that would expose Hellman as a 'self-serving braggart'. True to her own experience as a journalist, Gellhorn advised McCarthy to fasten on 'specific details, wherever she actually names a place, a street, a fact: simply prove it cannot be true'. Gellhorn's letter cited numerous examples culled from her own research. 'As a reporter', she told McCarthy, she regarded apocryphiars such as Hellman and Spender as 'wicked, deforming the news and the facts'.

In her later years Gellhorn confessed to immobilizing rage attacks. Asked to describe Gellhorn at college, one of her Bryn Mawr classmates said, 'Not quite so angry as she is today.' She stopped an interview: 'This conversation is so boring I think I'm going to faint.' She wrote to friends about 'suicide' days and attacks of 'nervous disintegration'. Life now seemed 'like playing chicken with oneself'.

Although Virago Press helped keep Gellhorn's fiction in the public eye – publishing *A Stricken Field* and *Liana* in 1986 and 1987 – she said, 'Virago has put me off women publishers in a big way.' She disliked tags for writers: 'Feminists nark me. I think they've done a terrible disservice to women, branded us as "women's writers".' She 'slashed' women who wrote to her in support of the cause. Men, she pointed out, were not saddled with such labels.

Nothing aroused Gellhorn more than talk of Hemingway, one of those 'killer men', whom she gave in to and then had the 'sense to flee'. Bernice Kert, at work on *The Hemingway Women*, had to make several 'pacts' with Gellhorn, including one that stipulated she could not write about Gellhorn's life before meeting Hemingway, except as it seemed to relate to her career. Biographer and subject had a

tense encounter. Kert produced a sympathetic and engaging portrait, but Gellhorn threatened legal action. Kert then realized how
hard Hemingway had it – to have this conscience focused on him all
the time. Gellhorn had a Prussian heaviness that held people to a
strict accounting and made them squirm.

After Kert, Jeffrey Meyers did not let unanswered letters and
phone calls deter him from interviewing Gellhorn. He 'went round
to her flat in Cadogan Square, wrote a letter reminding her that we
had corresponded about Wyndham Lewis' portrait of her mother,
and left it with the porter to slide under her door'. Impressed by his
'dogged enterprise', Gellhorn 'agreed to talk for an hour and a half'.
She was still 'tall and blonde, with a good figure, soft skin, and sharp
tongue', but Meyers had to contend with her suspicions about his
work and her claim that she would get 'stomach pains' if she discussed Hemingway. Yet Meyers elicited a compulsive pouring out of
'venom about [Hemingway's] habits and abusive behaviour'.

Journalists and close friends knew the subject of Hemingway was
verboten. In *Travels with Myself and Another* she refused her publisher's
wish to name Hemingway and instead identified him as UC
(Unwilling Companion). Gellhorn even sued a German paper,
spending £1400 to stop them from printing a footnote identifying
UC. Yet as with Meyers, Gellhorn not only did talk about Hemingway, she often initiated the discussion, providing intimate details
such as he was 'shy in bed'. She believed he had had sex with only
five women, and only one of them, Jane Mason, he did not marry. A
'rotten lover ... sex for him was a necessity, like having vitamins. He
took it regularly every night, but he gave no thought to the woman's
pleasure.' She dismissed their courtship: 'He chased me. I didn't want
to marry him. If I'd said "No" he'd have killed me.' He wrote all
morning and then would have lunch 'when he decided. He wasn't a
great conversationalist. He'd eat lunch in silence, then go out with a
gun to kick up a guinea fowl.' Then he'd play a poor game of tennis.
When she completed *Liana* he remarked, 'Not bad for a Bryn Mawr
girl.' Perhaps her latter-day comments are all true, but they resemble
biography by soundbites. Shortly before her death she burned the
letters he sent to her.

In December 1981 Richard Whalen arranged to interview Gellhorn for his biography of Robert Capa. Martial law had just been

declared in Poland. When he arrived at her flat he was greeted by a Gellhorn dressed entirely in black who announced quite dramatically that she was in mourning for Polish liberty. Throughout their interview the phone rang with calls from editors responding to her requests to cover events in Poland. Gellhorn was quite relaxed and spoke in that rich, cultivated voice of the expatriate, a woman of impeccable breeding and manners, smoking and drinking, and commenting to Whalen that the smoking and drinking had been so much a part of her generation that it was too late to quit now. Her flat was sparsely decorated in a Danish modern motif and had an open, tasteful air to it. For both Gellhorn and Whalen, this seemed to be a most enjoyable interview. After all, Robert Capa was a man she had dearly loved.

At seventy-four, Gellhorn wanted to spend the summer of 1982 in Lebanon, but 'nobody would send' her, thinking she would be killed or taken hostage. At seventy-five she visited El Salvador. A part of the world she knew nothing about, it remained her duty as a citizen to find out. She never could abide people who out of laziness or cowardice claimed they could do nothing about their government. America had become involved in Central America and it would be shameful of her not to confront her country's invasive presence in other lands.

Gellhorn found San Salvador, the capital of El Salvador, one of the most frightening places she had ever visited. In Spain, cities had been bombarded and she had been in danger from an external threat. But at least she could gauge its direction. In San Salvador the indiscriminate terror disabled one internally; no one knew when or where the death squads would strike. Two American advisers had been shot dead in a hotel garden restaurant, an American reporter had disappeared, Archbishop Romero had been killed at the altar during a mass, and people on the streets were silent, grim and in a hurry. As in Vietnam, the rich Salvadorans isolated themselves from the populace, while the army enlisted the poor. Briefings at the US embassy reminded her of Vietnam and the fatuous confidence in America's ability to control small countries. Salvadoran governments had been brutal, with atrocious human rights records and, in the guise of killing guerrillas, waged war on the civilian population. The government practised a torture worse than what the Gestapo had perfected in Europe.

Nicaragua, on the other hand, had a popularly elected government defending itself against the Contra terror raids. Gellhorn conceded that the Sandinista leaders had made several blunders and were disorganized, but she rejected President Reagan's view of them as Communist thugs. That Nicaragua did not submit to US interests is what really bothered Reagan. If loyalty to US policy was the test, then where was the moral distinction to be made between the Soviet Union invading Hungary and Czechoslovakia, and America invading Nicaragua? Gellhorn asked.

The Reagan and Thatcher administrations in the 1980s appalled Gellhorn. To Milton Wolff, a veteran of the Spanish Civil War, Gellhorn wrote of an America that was the 'Bully of the World'. She supported independent organizations like Amnesty International that investigated and recorded the hideous increase in the practice of torture all over the world. An updated edition of *The Face of War* (1988) concluded with a passionate argument against the madness of stockpiling nuclear weapons. Chernobyl, Gellhorn observed, ought to be the definitive warning of nuclear disaster. Large parts of the Soviet Union and of Europe had been contaminated, including her beloved Wales.

On her way to Nicaragua in 1986, Gellhorn decided to visit Cuba for the first time in forty-one years. People were cleaner and better dressed and nourished than the Cubans she remembered from her days with Hemingway. The highly visible black Cubans made her realize that her Cuba had been a segregated country. Castro had made all forms of discrimination illegal. It disconcerted her to be addressed by her first name, but the Revolution had mandated informality and she accommodated to the use of the intimate form of address in Spanish. When the weather turned bad, she had to give up hopes of what she had really come for: snorkelling. Instead, she toured the island seeing things she had never bothered to visit when she had lived there. Cuba was a poor country: crowded buses, unpainted cement in shopping areas, the lack of certain consumer goods such as good clothing, and atrocious food in the restaurants – but she appreciated the equality between men and women. This was no police state marked by fear. Cubans were not suspicious of foreigners – indeed, they were eager to meet her and learn about her life abroad. Yet the country did have political prisoners and it was certainly not a democracy. She cited Amnesty International figures to show torture had been practised in Cuba and that it disgraced the Revolution.

Gellhorn made her obligatory visit to the house, now a museum, she and Hemingway had lived in. She recognized the furniture she had made to order by the local carpenter and was amused by the later addition of stuffed animal heads on the walls. She left quickly, feeling depressed, remembering how elated she had been on her first visit and how empty it all seemed when she had left for good. She judged Cuba a much more decent country for the majority of people than the 'feudal' land in her time. This collectivist state would not do for someone as crustily independent as herself, but in her view Castro's Revolution, whatever its faults, posed no threat to the United States. She made the Castro regime seem like a mild form of tyranny – surely an odd position to take for an Amnesty International supporter. Even Susan Sontag and other staunch admirers of Castro and the Cuban Revolution had denounced him by the mid-1980s.

In her last years, Gellhorn seemed a fiercer critic of democratic governments than of dictatorships. In early 1984 she visited the women of Greenham Common, who protested against the presence of nuclear weapons in their country. Putting up with primitive, makeshift shelters, enduring police harassment and absolutely dedicated to a better future free of nuclear poison, these women reminded Gellhorn of the suffragettes of her mother's generation. These were the women Gellhorn had always taken for granted, yet they were the ones who had provided her with the choices and the liberty she enjoyed. The women of Greenham Common were engaged in nothing less than trying to secure the future of a planet that could easily blow itself up. In their determined non-violence, they were worthy of the memory of Gandhi. They had been beaten up by furious men and vilified by Thatcher's government, yet they refused to leave their camps. Their courage and good humour thrilled Gellhorn. They believed in what they were doing, one of them replied. Gellhorn, now too old to spend a freezing night on Greenham Common, announced to the women by way of tribute that they were a 'fact of history' – a revealing phrase for a woman who had been raised to believe in public demonstrations of conviction, one virtually born with a protest sign in her hand.

At the end of 1984 Gellhorn visited the Welsh miners, whose strike, along with that of the Yorkshire miners, Margaret Thatcher would eventually break. The Prime Minister wanted to privatize the mines, Gellhorn argued. The government cared only for profits. Breaking the strike meant assaulting the working class. Thatcher's victory, Gellhorn feared, would crush the spirit of these gallant people. That there might be another side to the story – Thatcher's effort to modernize an economy and to make Britain competitive in the world market – did not get even the briefest hearing from Gellhorn.

By the late 1980s Gellhorn had reached a stage where many writers produce memoirs – a rather stodgy form of writing in her book: 'I hope I won't become the sort of boring old fart who does reminiscences', she told Victoria Glendinning. Yet as early as the first edition of *The Face of War*, and in much of her fiction, Gellhorn fused her personality and her way of reporting. She wanted to be read both for events she had witnessed and for herself. Her collections of journalism, *The Face of War* and *The View from the Ground*, give decade-by-decade snapshots of her life and career, which are almost coy in their avoidance of the big names in her life, like Wells, Hemingway and Gavin.

She was less coy in private, among her 'gaggle of young chaps'. One of them, the buccaneering Bill Buford, then editor of *Granta*, provided a new venue for publication. 'He did something absolutely terrible to me, and everyone thought I'd never forgive him', Gellhorn alleged to Victoria Glendinning. 'He simply stole something from my book, *The View from the Ground*, which was being published in America. He claims he asked me. But when I do business, I expect a letter or something. He just pinched a part of the book and put it in the magazine. I seriously thought of killing him, but I was too busy.' So she sued? 'Don't be ridiculous!' Gellhorn snapped. 'I called him a monster, a creep, and told everyone I'd never speak to him again. Then came the big bouquet of flowers and the abject letter of apology, full of lies of course. And I was back talking to him within three weeks.' (In fact, a former colleague recalls, Burford had acted with perfect propriety.)

After three tries at marriage totalling sixteen years of her life, Gellhorn preferred living alone. Marriage bored her and most men wanted women to take care of all the domestic arrangements. Couples got to look like each other and a sameness pervaded their lives. Some couples would improve things 'if they shot each other', she told an interviewer.

Bill Buford called Gellhorn a 'loner who loved company'. In the last decade of her life she became, in his words, the 'central figure of something like a literary salon'. To Gellhorn's 'austere flat' in Cadogan Square came Buford, James Fox, Rosie Boycott, Victoria Glendinning, Nicholas Shakespeare, John Simpson, John Pilger, Paul Theroux, Jeremy Harding, John Hatt and other writers, editors and publishers who had 'rediscovered' Gellhorn, a term she despised because it seemed condescending to her. Yet she was always complaining about how her work had been neglected and she had lost her place in the queue of working journalists when she married T. S. Matthews and became a society matron.

Fox has left the most complete record of a visit to Gellhorn, which began with a glass of Famous Grouse and her outrage at current events, and her attacks on American foreign policy. 'We hold shameful passports', she told Fox. Then she inquired about one's 'general condition' – quickly sliding over into the 'unfathomable weirdness of dealings between the sexes'. A guest would hope she would not serve her abominable food – part of an everyday necessity that she found distasteful, the grubby, tedious 'kitchen of life'. To Fox she wrote: 'In my darkest hours I thought of you filling my washing machine for me, and tears of tenderness and gratitude flooded my eyes.' She eagerly took in the details of her friends' romances. Although she confessed to Fox that she had never really experienced a passionate love, she dispensed advice on the subject freely. 'Have you tried an ultimatum?' she asked him. She thought they shared an inability to find the right partner. She 'tutored' Buford on 'matters of the heart' and corrected his manners.

On 22 September 1987 Gellhorn wrote to Victoria Glendinning to praise her biography of Rebecca West. She thought West 'nearly mad' but respected her writing enormously. They had met in the spring of 1981, after Gellhorn wrote to West, then at the top of her form as a reviewer for the London *Sunday Telegraph*. The redoubtable Rebecca had been a role model for Martha, although Martha would have detested the cant term for what in her early days had been that 'one grand person' who would make a difference to her and the world. After completing *The Wine of Astonishment*, Martha had cabled journalist John Gunther: 'PLEASE MAKE BIG FUSS ABOUT ME AS IF I WERE FIFTY PER CENT REBECCA.' Gunther had been West's lover and had remained her close friend. West had written about the atrocity of war in *The Return of the Soldier* (1918), she had been a socialist and feminist, and a glamorous novelist filmed and photographed in Europe and America in the 1920s. She had published major pieces of journalism in the *New Yorker*, a venue that had rejected virtually all of Gellhorn's work, from her early journalism in the 1930s to her fiction in the 1950s.

Rebecca invited Martha for a session of reminiscence. Rebecca, an extraordinary raconteur, received Martha's stories with delight, especially her great scoop – that clandestine interview in French with Chou En-lai. No one raised the subject of Ernest Hemingway at that first meeting, but Rebecca had no doubt that the brute had abused Martha. If they discussed H.G., there is no record of it. Would Rebecca have been upset or amused to learn that the feisty Martha, too, had been his lover?

Sufficiently primed, both women could go on for hours about their battles with the male ego. But Rebecca, whose time with H.G. spanned a decade (it was about the same for G. and H.), grew quite fond of her fitful lover as the years went on. At the funeral of one of his mistresses she turned to another, Odette Keun, and said: 'Well, I guess we can all move one up.' Martha rarely indulged in that sort of wry humour.

When Martha arrived for the first time at Rebecca's Kensington flat, she might as well have been sizing up Rebecca for the role Martha would play when Rebecca died two years later, for Rebecca also had her faithful young chaps who gathered round. Just as West had a sort of court biographer in Victoria Glendinning, so did Martha choose a chronicler – the same Victoria Glendinning (who later declined the honour). Just as West could not abide anyone else characterizing her years with H.G. and would threaten legal action against any writer who dared trespass on her life, so Gellhorn told friends to tell her unauthorized biographer to 'sod off'.

Always sentimental about the Left, Gellhorn never understood why strong women like West and Susan Sontag praised Margaret Thatcher. Gellhorn could only take the side of suffering ordinary people. She did not have West's understanding of bureaucracy and modern government. Neither did she have West's ability to analyse the excesses of labour unions and to see that Thatcher, while certainly deserving of criticism, had a job to do in remaking modern Britain. It would be unimaginable for Gellhorn to say – as West did – that politics was a choice between the party that was thirty per cent right and that which was only fifteen per cent right.

Gellhorn was a childish absolutist, content with pronouncing anathemas on all politicians – except those like Kennedy or Clinton who took her fancy. Like Rebecca, who had an affair with Francis Biddle (FDR's attorney general) and close friendships with many important political leaders in Britain, Gellhorn treasured her connections with higher-ups. Meeting with Kennedy in the White House, he asked her how FDR had eluded the Secret Service and found ways to enjoy his women in private. His cheekiness only made him more appealing.

Gellhorn formed a friendship with Jackie Kennedy, as she had earlier established an intimacy with Eleanor Roosevelt. Indeed, it was Jackie Onassis who suggested that I write Martha Gellhorn's biography. 'Oh.' Victoria Glendinning perked up when I told her the story over dinner. 'I'll tell Martha that. Perhaps she will feel better about your biography.' Alas, she did not.

If West had the better geopolitical sense, Gellhorn was the better reporter. She did not overlay her writing with theorizing and psychologizing. West could be brilliant at dissecting Hermann Goering and the Nuremberg trials, but there was a sense in which everything described was Rebecca West. Gellhorn, for all her crabby prejudices, wrote journalism of the purest clarity. Her first dispatches from Spain and her last dispatches in Vietnam reveal her to be perhaps the finest observer in this century of war's devastating results.

Gellhorn just wanted to look and to show what she saw. West wanted to look and transform what she saw into a vision of Western

history. At Nuremberg, for example, West wrote the more compelling story because she unified the trials with her portrayal of
post-war Germany, which became a provocative tale of Germany's
rebuilding and rise to power (for a third time) in the twentieth
century. But Gellhorn was still the better journalist because she
managed to convey the sense of staring day after day at Goering,
thus presenting an unforgettable image of evil untrammelled by
commentary.

If Gellhorn distrusted biography, it was because the biographer
comes afterwards, working the graveyard shift. She observed life in
motion and that life could not be reproduced – except in her limpid
prose. If West, for all her misgivings, finally gave in to biography, it
was because she saw life as a phenomenon that had to be re-imag-
ined. After all, she wrote a biography herself, turning St Augustine
into a Rebecca West persona. Gellhorn wanted our attention *now*.
Her great gift to modern writing is her sense of immediacy. Even at
eighty-eight and eighty-nine, her sense of the present never
deserted her. Friends half her age came to her for the news; from
Martha Gellhorn they learned to take possession of life in the
moment, never to stop looking.

'For the first time this year I realized that I am very old', Gellhorn
wrote to James Fox on 27 October 1989. She was nearly eighty-one
and unhappy about the recent photographs taken of her. Her seventies had been fine, a sort of 'golden plateau', and she had supposed
she could just go on and on. She abhorred her physical disintegration. She wrote to Milton Wolff:

> Is it not wretched, and the only real reason for objecting to age, that
> the body, once so reliable and useful, begins to spring leaks. Mine is
> exactly like my 11 year old Honda, motor runs a treat, body rusts,
> everything rusts, needs patching ... I took my body for granted,
> knew it would do anything I wanted, and am now thrown into
> depression by not being able to walk without pain.

'I have become ugly', she announced to Victoria Glendinning in a
letter dated 2 February 1992. She could not face the fact with
humour. 'I am becoming like an elephant,' West told Raleigh
Trevelyan, 'my nose is getting longer and my ankles thicker.'

Women and men noticed how carefully Gellhorn managed her appearance and rated others by theirs. 'I think you look awful because you are so white', Gellhorn told a female friend who could not tolerate the sun. The sunworshipping Gellhorn took collagen treatments to smooth out her wrinkles. 'She spent quite a lot of time at the cosmetic surgeons and often talked about it', one of her confidants in Kenya remembered. 'You would ask Martha what was the latest. She talked about anything. She was very open. She wasn't self-conscious.'

In the 1990s Gellhorn managed to write engaging and perceptive articles on Wales, the tragic fate of street children in Brazil and the US invasion of Panama. 'The job gets harder every year, not easier, and now it's close to torture. It took me five weeks, working all the hours of the day and some of the night, to write that simple sounding Panama piece', she confided to Milton Wolff. She returned to Germany for the last time in December 1990. Ardently anti-German, she nevertheless reported on young people who 'speak their own ideas', although she 'missed irony, of which there were only rare sparks'. Then a wave of hostility against Turkish immigrants brought out the 'same kind of young thugs who were Hitler's Brownshirts'. The German government did nothing to counteract this 'revolting old variation on the old Nazi themes'. And the younger generation was silent. 'But where were the students, where were those good kids?' Gellhorn asked.

Like Rebecca West in her last years, Gellhorn struggled with several works of fiction she could not complete. Novelist Pauline Neville remembers visiting Gellhorn at her Cadogan Square flat. 'She wrote on a huge long desk in a top-floor attic room with a skylight. She had taken this flat in order to get silence and peace', Neville remembered. 'She was forever looking for peace and silence and then not doing anything with it.' Gellhorn sulked and smoked and drank – sometimes in a tub which overflowed during her inebriated periods.

Avid movie going and reading thrillers had sustained Gellhorn all her life. An editor/friend persuaded her to publish 'Martha Gellhorn's Thriller Guide' in the *Daily Telegraph* (16 January 1993). She liked the 'jokey tone' of the James Bond series, but she saved her accolades for books with 'elegant prose'. A sucker for melodrama, she remarked of one title: 'Lushly overwritten, but never mind.' She sounded more than a little like Rebecca West when she concluded 'Jack Higgins does not actually write, he just plods on with his talk of the how and why of the mortar attack on Downing Street during the Gulf War. Mr Higgins is in the blockbuster bestseller class. All I can say is, it beats me.'

Until the mid-1990s, Gellhorn restored herself at her Welsh cottage, telling Milton Wolff: 'I live in an agricultural area with nothing around me except fields and a view to the north of the Black Mountains. I have no neighboring house in sight.' Because of her difficulty walking and taking other forms of exercise, she had a pool built with glass walls so that she could swim in the winter. But she detested what the structure did to her view and feared that she had ruined her property.

Nearly blind from a botched cataract operation, Gellhorn had the surgeon 'professionally cursed' by a Malagasy medicine man. On 10 May 1994 she wrote to Wolff: 'My mother perhaps a few years older than I, used to say, "Wouldn't it be wonderful to wake up dead?" That's how I feel now, on a grey cold Welsh late afternoon.' Unable to care for her cottage, she sold it in 1995. She managed a radio report on Wales as late as 1997. But her writing days were over. She even stopped letters, sending out a typed announcement that she had become too 'feeble' to conduct correspondence. Yet she managed a letter to Mrs Clinton, making 'an impassioned statement about Cuba hoping it might reach the President'. But it was Congress that oppressed Cuba, she added. 'Sickening injustice.'

Cancer, the final blow, weakened Gellhorn, but she remained indomitable. Two weeks before she died, Ward Just, one of her colleagues in Vietnam, visited her Cadogan Square flat and found her still 'marvellous-looking' but also in aching misery. He spotted her old Underwood typewriter in a corner. She had only recently given up snorkelling and yet still spoke of a trip to Egypt. He gauged her voice as 'somewhere between snarl and purr' as she recalled her days in Sun Valley with Hemingway. The Soviet invasion of Finland had just been announced. 'He wanted to shoot more birds. So I went alone', she told Just.

Four days before Gellhorn died, she visited an exhibition of

Cartier Bresson's photographs. She found her contemporary's work 'too arty'. He had not looked steadily at human suffering. At any rate, she preferred the pleasures of nature. Two days later she conducted a 'spirited discussion' about Iraq.

The end came swiftly. At four in the morning on Sunday 15 February, her son Sandy awoke at his English countryside home, startled by what sounded like the 'cry of a strange bird'. His mother had, in fact, just died.

Vivid tributes and lengthy reminiscences flowed with pent-up feeling as Gellhorn's friends were released after years of seeing her silence both her allies and enemies when it came to speaking about her own life. She was hailed as the century's greatest war correspondent and a journalism award was established in her honour.

Peter Kurth represented one of the few dissenting voices. Author of a well-received biography of journalist Dorothy Thompson, Kurth called Gellhorn the 'Sacred Cow of combat reporting' and deplored her fussing about Hemingway. Her professed statements about him and about males in general provoked a deeply sceptical response in Kurth, who noted that 'to the end of her life Gellhorn liked to surround herself with the toughest of tough-guy journalists, as if she was, in fact, just one of the boys'.

Even Gellhorn's closest friends did not attempt to smooth away her rough edges – indeed, they provided striking examples of a 'superhumanly irritable' and 'tyrannical' woman. Anger fuelled her energy. Like Rebecca West, she maintained an oppositional nature from her teens to her ninetieth year.

Like West also, it was said that Gellhorn favored and advanced her young chaps and had little use for women. Yet Julie Burchill's testimony deserves quotation: 'I never met Martha Gellhorn or spoke to her on the phone even, but when I was working at the *Mail on Sunday*, some time in the 80s, she sent me the most wonderful postcard from Wales, telling me what a great journalist I was. To say I was knocked out would be to employ classic English understatement.' Burchill had not received this kind of support from other journalists who she thought found her 'less educated, more flashy' and an 'upstart. ... With those few short sentences from someone I considered to be the world's greatest living journalist, I was set up for life.' Burchill's experience was not unique. Martha Gellhorn loved to send fan letters to writers she admired, regardless of their politics and gender.

Yet Gellhorn's difficult personality accounts, in part, for the fitful nature of her career. Constantly rediscovered, she went constantly out of print. When Michael Joseph dropped her as an author, she confessed her bafflement to Raleigh Trevelyan, her editor. She thought she had reached some sort of eminence as a writer and now nobody wanted to publish her. 'It was a bit embarrassing for me', Trevelyan remembered. He liked and admired Gellhorn, but 'she was a bit alarming. I always felt I had to tread carefully. She was one of those writers – like Edith Sitwell or A. L. Rowse – in front of whom one didn't really want to express an opinion on anything literary until you knew that it would be acceptable. If you said the wrong thing, you were out for ever.' People were always curious about her, Trevelyan noted, but she was a difficult person to get to know and to have people to meet. Comparing Gellhorn with his friend Rebecca West, Trevelyan observed: 'I had a cosier relationship with Rebecca and invited her to my flat.' Cosy is not a word that suited Gellhorn – although she used the word in an interview to describe her close friendships. Her fastidious, judgemental temperament flashed out even on social visits. At Pauline Neville's flat Gellhorn noticed a number of exposed wires and said, 'You know, no American housewife would have those out. They would all be behind the wall.' The first time Neville met Gellhorn in Kenya, Gellhorn spent most of the conversation telling Neville 'how awful' Neville's friends were.

West had a gift for meeting and knowing people in a comprehensive way. She sought out biographers of H.G., for example, even if only to quarrel with them. She reviewed and argued with her contemporaries and with later generations. Gellhorn put breaks on her career, so to speak, by refusing to have her story passed around. By denying herself an autobiography and by opposing biographies, she damaged herself by separating from a dialogue with the literary history she had helped to form. Her cherished role as outsider cost her. It is no accident that she built her Kenyan home on Mount Longonot or that her Welsh cottage sat atop a hill called Catscradle, or that her sixth-floor Cadogan Square 'flat in the sky' – as John Simpson called it – gave her nearly a rooftop view of Kensington. It was always something of a climb to reach Gellhorn, who towered over London in her last years, thinking of herself as an 'historic monument'.

Raleigh Trevelyan thought Gellhorn's devotion to 'goggle swimming' (snorkelling) exemplified the sort of 'lonely, mystic world' she created for herself. 'She liked great vistas. Goggle swimming gives you the same feeling. A huge sort of dimension.'

From the Thames Tower Bridge, Gellhorn's stepson, Sandy Matthews, dispatched her ashes as instructed for her 'continuing travels'. A friend asked him if it was an 'outgoing tide'. 'Oh, God,' Matthews replied, 'I hope so.'

NOTES AND COMMENTS

ABBREVIATIONS

AF	Mrs Aaron Fischer
BB	Bernard Berenson
BBP	Bernard Berenson Papers, Villa I Tati, Florence, Italy
BK	Bernice Kert, *The Hemingway Women*, Norton, New York, 1983
BL	Buck Lanham
CB	Carlos Baker, *Ernest Hemingway: A Life Story*, Scribner's, New York, 1969
CC	Charles Colebaugh
CM	Edna Fischel Gellhorn (18 December 1878–24 September 1970.) Commemorative Meeting, 11 October 1970, Graham Chapel, Washington University Archives, St Louis, Missouri
CP	Content Peckham
CR	Carl Rollyson
CS	Charles Scribner
DB	Denis Brian, *The True Gen: An Intimate Portrait of Hemingway by Those Who Knew Him*, Grove Press, New York, 1988
DM	Delia Mares
EG	Edna Gellhorn
EGC	Edna Gellhorn Collection, WUA
EH	Ernest Hemingway
ELN	Emily Lewis Norcross
ER	Eleanor Roosevelt
EW	Emily Williams interview with Martha Gellhorn, St Moritz Hotel in New York City, 20 February 1980, on deposit with the Roosevelt Library, Hyde Park, New York
FDR	Franklin D. Roosevelt Library, Hyde Park, New York
FK	Francis King
FVF	Frederick Vanderbilt Field
FW	*The Face of War*
HGW	H. G. Wells
HOA	*The Heart of Another*

HR   Harold Ross

HWH   Lloyd Arnold, *High on the Wild with Hemingway*, The Caxton Printers, Caldwell, Idaho, 1968

Int.   Interview

JF   James Fox, 'Memories of Martha', *Independent*, 22 February 1998

JFK   Ernest Hemingway Collection, John Fitzgerald Kennedy Library

JG   John Gunther

JM   Jeffrey Meyers, *Hemingway: A Biography*, Harper & Row, New York, 1985

JO   Jacqueline Orsagh, 'A Critical Biography of Martha Gellhorn', Michigan State University Ph.D. dissertation, 1978

JSP   Joseph Stanley Pennell Papers, Special Collections, University of Oregon Library, Eugene, Oregon

KL   Kenneth Lynn, *Hemingway*, Simon and Schuster, New York, 1987

LA   Lloyd Arnold, *High on the Wild with Hemingway*, The Caxton Printers, Caldwell, Idaho, 1968

LH   Lorena Hickok

MG   Martha Gellhorn

MHS   Missouri Historical Society, St Louis, Missouri

MLS   Martha Love Symington

MM   Mary McCarthy

MR1   Michael Reynolds, *Hemingway in the 1930s*, W. W. Norton, New York, 1997

MR2   Michael Reynolds, *Hemingway: The Final Years*, W. W. Norton, New York, 1999

MTH   Mary Taussig Hall

MW   Milton Wolff

NS   Nicholas Shakespeare, 'A Life Less Ordinary', *Independent on Sunday*, 28 June 1998, 12–14

NY   'The Correspondent', a selection of MG's letters published in *New Yorker*, 22 and 29 June 1998, 96–109

NYPL   New York Public Library, Crowell-Collier Collection; *New Yorker Papers*

OA   Martha Gellhorn, 'On Apocryphism', *Paris Review*, Spring 1981, 280–301

OMA   (TSM) *O My America*, Simon and Schuster, New York, 1962

PN   Pauline Neville

PUL   Patrick Hemingway Collection, Hemingway-Lanham Collection, Charles Scribner Collection, Carlos Baker Collection, Firestone Library, Princeton University

RT   Raleigh Trevelyan

RW   Richard Whalen

SLH   Carlos Baker (Ed.), *Selected Letters of Ernest Hemingway 1917–1961*, Scribner's, New York, 1981

SLML   St Louis Mercantile Library

TSM   T. S. Matthews

TWMA   *Travels with Myself and Another*

UL   Rare Books and Special Collections Library of the University of Illinois at Urbana-Champaign

VD   Virginia Deutch

VG   *The View from the Ground*

VGV   Victoria Glendinning, 'The Real Thing', *Vogue*, April 1988, 358–9, 398

WHMC Western Historical Manuscript Collection, Jefferson Library, University of
       Missouri, St Louis
WJP   William Julius Polk
WUA   Washington University Archives

INTRODUCTION

MG's correspondence with Alexander Woollcott can be found in the Special Collections, Houghton Library, Harvard University. A good deal of it is undated.

MG's comment on 'all that objectivity shit' appears in Tim Minogue's profile, 'Martha
Gelhorn, 88, Files Her Last War Report – From Wales', *The Independent*, 27 July
1997, 6.

MG's correspondence with MW: UL.

See NS for his account of efforts to do a documentary on MG's life.

1: THE SPIRIT OF ST LOUIS

For the background of the Gellhorn/Fischel family, see *Notable American Women: The
Modern Period: A Biographical Dictionary*, Barbara Sicherman, Carol Hurd Green,
Ilene Kantrov, Harriette Walker (eds), Harvard University Press, Cambridge, 1980,
268; US Census records; City of St Louis Circuit Court File 09101; *St Louis Missouri
Republican*, 3 March 1878; 'A Sketch of the Life of Mrs Washington E. Fischel',
Central High School Red and Black, St Louis High School Year Book, June 1938;
'Martha Ellis Fischel, 1850–1939', Ethical Society records, WHMC; Marguerite
Martyn, 'A Defender of the Modern Woman', *St Louis Post-Dispatch Daily Magazine*,
30 May 1933, in the Ethical Society Records, WHMC; printed chronology and
handwritten notes in the Ethical Society Records, WHMC; 'Ethical Society Rites
Conducted for Mrs Fischel', *St Louis Star-Times*, 10 January 1939, WHMC; 'Cele-
brates 50 Years of Social Service, Mrs Washington E. Fischel, 88, and Neighborhood
House Still Going Strong', *St Louis Globe-Democrat*, 27 March 1938, WHMC; letter
to author from Melvin S. Strassner, Union of American Hebrew Congregations, 11
October 1988; see also JO, 1.

Edna Gellhorn and her mother, Martha Ellis Fischel, were much beloved figures in St
Louis and memories of their engaging personalities and ambitious projects endure. I
am particularly indebted to interviews with Edna's close friends and associates: AF,
DM and VD. For accounts of Martha Ellis's and Edna's activities, I drew on Olivia
Skinner, 'Edna Gellhorn: Long-Time Civic Worker', *St Louis Post-Dispatch*, undated
clipping, MHS; Clarissa Start, 'Edna Gellhorn at 75: "I have Infinite Faith in the
Future"'. *St Louis Post-Dispatch*, 20 December 1953, MHS; Clarissa Start, 'Edna
Gellhorn – Still on', *St Louis Post-Dispatch*, 15 December 1963, MHS; Mary Kim-
brough, 'Three Decades of Votes for Women', *St Louis Star-Times*, 25 August 1950,
MHS; tape recording of EG at her eight-fifth birthday celebration speaking on the
beginning of women's suffrage, WUA. 'Mrs Edna Gellhorn Dies at 91; Suffragist
Worker, Civic Leader', *St Louis Post-Dispatch*, 25 September 1970, MHS; Press
Release, National League of Women Voters, December 1938, WHMC; 'Mrs
Gellhorn Subject of Life Sketch in Post', undated clipping, WUA; TSM, *Angels
Unawares: Twentieth-Century Portraits*, Ticknor & Fields, New York, 1985, 266; letters
of 9 and 22 December 1921 from M. Carey Thomas to EG, WUA; Avis Carlson,

'Dame Edna of Saint Louis', *Greater Saint Louis Magazine*, November 1968, 21; JO, 5; *OMA*, 14; CM.

George Gellhorn's career is documented in JO, 2–3; 'George Gellhorn, MD', *The History of Missouri, Family and Personal History*, Vol. III, Lewis Historical Publishing Company, New York, 1967, 187; 'The Reminiscences of Walter Gellhorn', Part I, 22 April 1955, Columbia Oral History Project, Columbia University Library; 'Washington Emil Fischel', *The Book of St Louisans: A Biographical Dictionary of Leading Living Men of the City of St Louis*, John W. Leonard (ed.), The St Louis Republic, St Louis, 1906, 192.

For MG's account of her parents' courtship and family life, see JO, 400; BK, 285; VGV, 359.

The Gellhorn household and EG's child-rearing methods are described in Marguerite Martyn, 'A Defender of the Modern Woman', *St Louis Globe-Democrat*, 30 May 1933, WHMC; VGV, 359; JO, 5.

George Gellhorn's view of religion and Sister Miriam are discussed in 'The Reminiscences of Walter Gellhorn', Part I, 22 April 1955, op. cit.; 'Sister Miriam, Last Member of Episcopal Order, Dies', *St Louis Post-Dispatch*, 18 June 1936, 15C; 'In Memoriam: Sister Miriam', *Journal of the Ninety-Eighth Conventions of the Diocese of Missouri*, 12 January 1937.

Martha and Walter in Sunday School: 'The Reminiscences of Walter Gellhorn', Part I, 22 April 1955, op. cit. Martha discusses her early trips abroad in JO, 8.

For memories of MG's childhood and her St Louis milieu, I am indebted to interviews with ELN, MTH, MLS, WJP; newspaper clippings (unidentified) WUA; JO, 9, 11.

For MG's part in her mother's suffragist campaigns, see JO, 5; MG's memorial tribute to her grandmother: Ethical Society Records, WHMC.

2: A WINDOW ON THE WORLD

For my view of Gellhorn's schooling I consulted the Mary Institute Catalogue, 1918–19, 52–4. For descriptions of John Burroughs I relied on interviews with Carol Daniel, DM and ELN and on the following sources: Martin L. Parry, *A Way of Life: The Story of the John Burroughs School, 1923–1973*, John Burroughs School, St Louis, 1973; 'Educator, in Address, Rejects Theory that School Work Must be Distasteful to be of Value, Dr Otis W. Caldwell of Columbia University Declares Pupils Learn Best when Subjects Are Made Engaging, and Not Unnecessarily Hard', undated clipping in the records of the John Burroughs School.

Descriptions of MG and of her early writing appear in the *John Burroughs Review*, May 1924, November 1924, Christmas 1924, February 1925, May 1925, November 1925, December 1925, February 1926, March 1926, June 1926, JSP, Diary, 30 September 1932.

MG's letter to Carl Sandburg and the poems she enclosed for his inspection are on deposit in the Carl Sandburg Collection, University of Illinois at Urbana-Champaign Library; MG describes Sandburg's response in JO, 10.

For accounts of MG and her period at Bryn Mawr I am indebted to CP, ELN and the following sources: 'Interview with Helen Bell de Freitas '31 by Caroline Smith Rittenhouse '52', London, 7 May 1985; *The College News*, 13, 20 October, 10 November 1926, 23 February 1927, JO, 12; *The Lantern*, June, November 1928.

For Kenneth Lynn's remarks on the 1920s, see KL, 336–7.

MG's letters to her mother c. April 1928: EG Papers, WUA.

MG's trip to Germany: Dr Heinz Richard Landmann to CR, 11 January 1992.

3: LIBERATION

On MG's decision to abandon Bryn Mawr, her efforts to support herself and her parents' concerns, I rely on interviews with AF, DM, MTH, ELN, VD, and on Marguerite Martyn, 'St Louis' Young Woman Novelist', *St Louis Post-Dispatch*, 3 October 1936, clipping files SLML; *VG*, 66; BK, 285; VGV, 398.

MG's work at the *New Republic* and the *Albany Times Union*: JO, 12–14 and MG's comments in 'Veteran Correspondent Says Much Has Changed, Except Government's Continuing Fear of the Press', n.d., *The Freedom Forum Online*, www.freedomforum.org/international/1998/2/gellhorn_interview.asp

MG's trip to Europe and her first days in Paris: *VG*, 66–7; BK, 286; JO, 14–15; *VG*, 67–8; Margaret Martyn, 'St Louis' Young Woman Novelist', clipping files SLML; interviews with MLS.

MG's articles on the League of Nations meeting: 'Geneva Portraits, Glimpses of the Women Delegates to the League of Nations', *St Louis Post-Dispatch*, 18 November 1930; 'Geneva Portraits, Glimpses of the Women Delegate to the League of Nations', *St Louis Post-Dispatch*, 20 November 1930. In the *New Yorker* papers, NYPL, there is an undated letter from Gellhorn to editor Harold Ross soliciting his interest in her European reporting.

4: BEAUTIFUL EXILE

Henri de Jouvenel and Bertrand's biography: Rudolph Binion, *Defeated Leaders: The Political Fate of Caillaux, Jouvenel and Tardieu*, Columbia University Press, Morningside Heights, New York, 1960, 120, 123, 136; Joanne Richardson, *Colette*, Franklin Watts, New York, 1984, 48, 85, 100; John R. Braun, '*Une Fidélité Difficile*: The Early Life and Ideas of Bertrand de Jouvenel, 1903–1945', Ph.D. dissertation, University of Waterloo, Waterloo, Ontario, Canada, 1985, 22, 28, 49, 95, 98–101, 130, 132, 146, 203, 205, 260; Genevieve Dormann, *Colette: A Passion for Life*, Abbeville Press, New York, 1985, 224, 227–8, 251, 267. MG on Colette: quoted in Judith Thurman, *Secrets of the Flesh: A Life of Colette*, Knopf, New York, 1999.

MG's travels in Europe with Bertrand de Jouvenel: JO, 15–16; Bertrand de Jouvenel, *Un Voyageur dans le Siècle*, Editions Robert Laffont, Paris, 1980, 125; *FW*, 13. Jouvenel remembers purchasing in New Jersey '*une immense* torpedo' for the sum of $50. In an article published in the *Spectator* (August 1936) MG recalls the sum as $28.50 for an 'eight year-old Dodge open touring car'. Their accounts agree that the back seat was full of fallen leaves.

Bertrand de Jouvenel on HGW: *Un Voyageur dans le Siècle*, 11, 97–101, 112. Wells, Jouvenel and Future Studies: Pierre Hassner, 'Bertrand de Jouvenel', *International Encyclopaedia of the Social Sciences, Biographical Supplement*, David L. Sills (ed.), The Free Press, New York, 1979, 360. Jouvenel and the metaphor of the traveller: Hassner, 358.

MG and JSP: her poems and correspondence are in JSP. I have also drawn on Pennell's autobiography and diary on deposit in JSP.

JSP's letters to EG: EGC.

JSP and MG at Erna Rice's: letter to CR from ELN.

MG and Frederick Vanderbilt Field: int. FVF.

Jouvenel and MG in America: *Un Voyageur dans le Siècle*, 126–8, 132–4; see also *VG*, 3.

MG and Jouvenel in Hollywood: int. MLS.

MG's difficulties in placing *What Mad Pursuit* and Jouvenel's opinion of it: Olga Clark, 'First Novel by Former St Louis Woman Will Appear During Autumn', *St Louis Globe-Democrat*, 11 July 1934, 4C.

The Gellhorn/Jouvenel marriage: undated newspaper clipping, MHC; int. DM, MLS, ELN; Genevieve Dormann, *Colette: A Passion for Life* op. cit., 260. MG told Emily Norcross that she was not sure about the legality of her marriage to Jouvenel, but apparently she did not consider it legal when she married EH, since there is no record of a divorce from Jouvenel. Even towards the end of her life, MG was not willing to give a straight answer about her marriage to Bertrand de Jouvenel. She told Julia Edwards, *Women of the World: The Great Foreign Correspondents*, Houghton Mifflin, Boston, 1988, 128: 'I was never married to Bertrand de Jouvenel. The press married us at some point due to hotel registration. Long ago you could not get a room unless Mr and Mrs and we had no money for two rooms.'

For MG's account of her encounters with young Nazis, see *FW*, 14. Jouvenel's view of the Nazis is explored in John R. Braun, 'Une Fidélité Difficile ...', 368–9, 402–3.

Gellhorn's contribution to *La Lutte*: the journal had begun by advocating a national plan for youth, recommending mandatory retirement at age sixty and the establishment of communes for unemployed young people ('maisons de jeunesse'), which would put them to work on New Deal-type projects. Gellhorn had contributed articles on Diego Rivera's controversial American murals (31 May 1933) and on the conflict in Vienna (25 February 1934) between socialists and the Austrian government.

MG's last comments on Jouvenel appear in NS.

5: A DANGEROUS COMMUNIST

For MG's account of her landing in New York and her employment at FERA I rely on *VG*, 17–20, 24–5, 69–71; EW; 'Girl Investigator Writes of Experiences in FERA', *New York World-Telegram*, 19 September 1936, 19A; 'Glamour Girl', *Time*, 18 March 1940, 92.

MG and Lorena Hickok: MG to LH, 7 January, 1935, FDR. I have also drawn on an interview with Blanche Wiessen Cook, Eleanor Roosevelt's most recent biographer.

During her period working for the FERA, Jouvenel returned to the United States in an unsuccessful effort to regain MG's love. See John R. Braun, 'Une Fidélité Difficile...' 492–3.

On Harry Hopkins, see Arthur M. Schlesinger Jr, *The Age of Roosevelt: The Coming of the New Deal*, Houghton Mifflin, Boston, 1959, 263, 265–6, 271–3; JO, 32.

ER's concerns about MG: Joseph Lash, *Love Eleanor: Eleanor Roosevelt and her Friends*, Doubleday, New York, 1982, 217. MG's letters to ER: 30 January 1936, 23 September 1941, FDR; 7 February 1936, FDR.

The Roosevelts and the White House: VGV, 398; EW; *VG*, 72–73.

MG's comments to Orsagh: JO, 40.

HGW: See David C. Smith, *H. G. Wells: Desperately Moral, A Biography*, Yale University Press, New Haven, 1986, 390, 394. The typescript of what HGW called a 'postscript' to his two-volume autobiography, is on deposit in the Gordon Ray Papers at the

Morgan Library in New York City. Although this postscript was published as *H. G. Wells in Love*, Faber & Faber, London, 1984, the references to MG were eliminated. Wells's involvement in negotiating MG's Hamish Hamilton contract is revealed in a series of letters and memoranda in the HGW Collection, UL, where MG's letters to Gip Wells can also be found. Gellhorn's letter about HGW to Victoria Glendinning was published in NY.

MG's research in Germany and her anti-fascism: 'Ohne Mich: Why I Shall Never Return to Germany', *Granta* 42, Winter 1992, 201–8; BK, 288; *VG*, 69.

ER's praise and reviews of *The Trouble I've Seen*: BK, 288–9; EW.

The source for Ruby: BK, 287; int. MTH.

MG's reaction to 'promotional hoopla': BK, 290.

6: HEMINGWAY HELL OR HIGH WATER

MG's first meeting with EH: BK, 290–1; CB, 297; JM, 298–300; JO, 60; KL, 464; James McLendon, *Papa: Hemingway in Key West*, E. A. Seeman Publishing Co., Miami, Florida, 1972, 164–5; MG to ER, 2 January 1937, FDR; interviews with AF, ELN, MLS, MTH, VD. Michael Reynolds, EH's most assiduous and careful biographer, has not been able to confirm many of the details later used to dramatize the EH–MG encounter, but they are certainly in keeping with his behaviour at the time and there is no reason to doubt that he would be in character for his rendezvous with MG, even as she would prove the equal of hard-drinking men in countless trysts throughout her long life.

Reactions to MG: DB, 102; Leicester Hemingway, *My Brother, Ernest Hemingway*, World Book Company, Cleveland, 1962, 202–3; McLendon, 166;

MG's admiration for EH's work: JO, 61, 63. Her reaction to his attentions: BK, 293–4; JM, 301. MR1 quotes the *Paris Tribune*, 20 November 1933: 'Madame Bertrand de Jouvenel, the former Martha Gellhorn of St Louis, MO, has a first novel, *Nothing Ever Happens*, appearing shortly on London bookstands.'

MG's letter to Pauline: 14 January 1937, PUL.

MG's abandoned novel: *FW*, 14.

MG's pursuit of EH: DB, 111. Archibald MacLeish is quoted in Jeffrey Meyers, 'The Hemingways: An American Tragedy', *Virginia Quarterly Review*, 75, 1999.

MG's entry into Spain and meeting with EH: BK, 296; *FW*, 14–16; JO, 67; CB, 304.

MG's ignorance about war and her efforts to learn about it: *FW*, 16; BK, 296.

EH's effort to help MG: CB, 304.

Other accounts of EH and MG in Spain: Herbert Matthews, *Two Wars and More to Come*, Carrick & Evans, New York, 1938, 205; Peter Wyden, *The Passionate War: The Narrative History of the Spanish Civil War*, Simon and Schuster, New York, 1983, 324; Josephine Herbst, 'The Starched Blue Sky of Spain', *The Noble Savage*, Meridian Books, New York, 1960, 83; Virginia Cowles, *Looking for Trouble*, Harper & Brothers, New York, 1941, 31; DB, 111.

MG's descriptions of living and travelling with EH to the battlefields: Wyden, 323–4; OA, 283, 290; CB, 304; MG, 'Madrid to Morata', *New Yorker*, 24 July 1937, 31.

MG's visits to soldiers: Cecil Eby, *Between the Bullet and the Lie: American Volunteers in the Spanish Civil War*, Holt, Rinehart & Winston, New York, 1969, 74–5; JO, 77.

Matthews on the hub of the world struggle: *Two Wars and More to Come*, 222. On his friendship with EH and MG see Herbert L. Matthews, *A World in Revolution: A*

Newspaperman's Memoir, Scribner's, New York, 1971, 23–5; *The Education of a Correspondent*, Harcourt, Brace and Co., New York, 1946, 95, 117.

The old homestead: Wyden, 334.

EH's assertion of authority and the scene in Sefton Delmer's room: DB, 109–10; Cowles, 19; Wyden, 330.

The near round bullet hole in MG's window: Cowles, 29.

Frederick Voight: Phillip Knightley, *The First Casualty: From Crimea to Vietnam: The War Correspondent as Hero, Propagandist and Myth Maker*, Harcourt, Brace, Jovanovich, New York, 1975, 198; William White (ed.), *Byline: Ernest Hemingway: Selected Articles and Dispatches of Four Decades*, Scribner's, New York, 1967, 294–7.

Ten hard days: CB, 311; BK, 299.

We were all in it together: Knightley, 215, 192.

7: A WINDOW ON WAR

MG's reasons for coming to Spain: *FW*, 15.

EH's and Matthews's role in stimulating MG's war correspondence: JO, 68; MG's response: *FW*, 16; BK, 298.

EH's war dispatches: William White (ed.), *By–Line* ...

Phillip Knightley's discussion of war correspondents: *The First Casualty* ... 10.

The EH/MG collaboration: *My Brother, Ernest Hemingway*, 206.

Joris Ivens: BK, 302.

The Writer's Congress: CB, 313–14; BK, 304; Powell is quoted in MR1, 270. EH's speech: Henry Hart (ed.), *The Writer in a Changing World*, Equinox Cooperative Press, USA, 1937, 63–5, 67, 69, 71; MG to ER, n.d., FDR; Frederick R. Benson, *Writers in Arms: The Literary Impact of the Spanish Civil War*, New York University Press, New York, 1967, 33.

MG's lobbying the Roosevelts on Spain: EW; MG to ER, Wednesday, n.d., FDR. ER on MG's emotionalism: MG to ER, Saturday, n.d., FDR.

MG's meeting with Dorothy Parker: Marion Meade, *Dorothy Parker: What Fresh Hell Is This?*, Villard Books, New York, 1988, 282; sulking company of Lillian Hellman: OA, 289.

MG and the soldiers: JO, 83–4.

EH and MG at Belchite: CB, 319.

The Teruel front: Matthews, *Two Wars and More to Come*, 311.

October: OA, 292.

Madrid: BK, 307; OA, 292: HOA, 123–4, 127.

Dorothy Bridges in *The Fifth Column and Four Stories of the Spanish Civil War*, Scribner's, New York, 1966, 36, 39, 41, 42, 44, 80, 84; see also JM, 323.

Hemingway's impish humour: Wyden, 406; BK, 309.

Stephen Spender: DB, 131–4; OA, 281–6.

The dismal November weather: BK, 310; *FW*, 27, 31.

The trenches: *FW*, 33.

Jeffrey Meyers: JM, 317.

Pauline in Paris: CB, 324.

MG's return to New York: BK, 311–12.

8: THE AGONY OF HER OWN SOUL

Gellhorn at the University of Minnesota: JO, 91; Dan Brennan to CR, n.d. (*c.* 1990).

Gellhorn's lecture tour: MG to ER, 24 January 1938, FDR; 'Martha Gellhorn Sees Spain as Breeding Place for World War', *St Louis Globe-Democrat*, 28 January 1938; JO, 91, MG to ER, 1 February 1938; EG calendar, WUA; MG to HGW, 8 February (1938).

Grace Hemingway: BK, 314; the newspaper account is quoted in MR1, 283.

EH, MG, Sheean and Forbes-Robertson: Wyden, *The Passionate War: The Narrative History of the Spanish Civil War*, 450.

EH's military pretensions: Richard Whelan, *Robert Capa: A Biography*, Knopf, New York, 1985, 150.

MG's imitation of EH: Wyden, 467.

MG and her companions: BK, 314.

MG making love to EH: BK, 315. For a discussion of EH's discarded draft of *The Fifth Column*, see MR1, 279.

MG's letter to her editor: 1 June 1938, NYPL.

EH in Key West: BK, 316.

England as a fine green island: *VG*, 34; see also Virginia Cowles, *Looking for Trouble*, Harper & Brothers, New York, 1941, 124–9. MG wrote to HGW from Prague on 13 June (1938), UL.

MG in France: 'Guns Against France', *Collier's*, 8 October 1938, 13.

Vacation in Corsica: MG to ER, 14 August 1938, FDR.

MG's 2000-word report: MG to ER, 19 October 1938, 'Anti-Nazi Refugees in Czecho-slovakia', FDR.

MG on the Republican army: *VG*, 41.

Last Ditchers: Whelan, 154.

America had failed Spain: MG to ER, n.d., FDR.

MG's opposition to the war: MG to ER, 17 May 1939.

9: TRAPPED

MG at home for Christmas: MG to ER, 1 January 1939, FDR.

Martha Ellis Fischel's death: EG calendar, WUA; MG to ER, Thursday, n.d., FDR.

MG's confiding in ER: MG to ER, 3 February 1939; MG to ER, 8 March 1939, FDR; see also MR2, 30.

EH's promise not to interfere with MG's career: EH to MG, 28 August 1940, JFK. His terms of endearment for MG and his dreams about her: EH to MG, n.d., (*c* 1940); EH to MG, 30 September 1940, JFK.

EH at work on *For Whom the Bell Tolls* and MG's comments on his novel and his influence on her: *SLH*, 477, 479, 480, 482–3; BK, 325; JM, 353; MG to Gerry Brenner, 7 March 1976, JFK.

The Finca: CB, 340–1; BK, 326–7.

Luigi's House: *HOA*, 1–2.

Gellhorn's lack of jealousy: BK, 328.

To All American Foreign Service Officers: JO, 106–7.

Arnold's reminiscence of MG: HWH, 23, 25, 27, 51.

An ecstatic EH and his efforts to please MG: BK, 330; HWH, 52.

Clara Spiegel: BK, 331.

Sun Valley as paradise: BK, 331.

EH as old Indian: HWH, 70.

'Husky as a well-pastured horse': MG to CC, 28 September 1940, NYPL.

EH's praise of MG's courage: BK, 331.

EH as big clown: HWH, 71.

MG's passage to Finland: MG to CC, n.d., NYPL; SLOW BOAT TO WAR: FW (1959 edition), 46, 54.

MG's long emotional letter: BK, 333.

Gellhorn's evacuation: Virginia Cowles, *Looking for Trouble,* 321.

'Fear Comes to Sweden': *Collier's,* 3 February 1940, 20–2.

'Good Will to Men': *HOA,* 186–267.

The war of survival: *FW,* 51.

MG's letters to EH and ER from Finland and on her way home: BK, 334; JO, 113; Joseph Lash, *Love Eleanor,* Doubleday, New York, 1982, 288–9.

Mrs Martha: BK, 338–9.

EH's drinking: CB, 346.

EH's mermaid: Leicester Hemingway, *My Brother, Ernest Hemingway,* World Book Company, Cleveland, 1962, 224.

MG's reluctance to leave Cuba: MG to CC, 13 March 1940, NYPL.

Gregory's memories of the Finca: Gregory Hemingway, *Papa: A Personal Memoir,* Houghton Mifflin, Boston, 1976, 47.

Jack's memories of MG: Jack Hemingway, *Misadventures of a Fly Fisherman: My Life With and Without Papa,* Taylor Publishing Company, Dallas, Texas, 1986, 30–1.

Patrick's memories: BK, 341, 349.

Jacks talks with MG: BK, 341.

MG's 'itch': BK, 343.

MG's visit to EG: MG to CC, n.d., NYPL.

EG's charm: *My Brother, Ernest Hemingway,* 224.

EG's doubts about EH and MG's later reactions to EH's mental state: BK, 343; MR2, 30.

'You can stand me up': CB, 350; EG describes this period in her calendar, WUA.

'Absolutely lamentable females': JM, 349.

MG's fondness for Sun Valley: MG to ER, 20 July 1940, FDR.

MG's hope to marry EH in Cuba: CB, 351–2; BK, 344.

EG's advice not to marry EH: JO, 116.

MG's treatment of Gregory: *Papa,* 41–2; see also JM, 349.

EH on Gary Cooper: *SLH,* 518–19.

The well-barbered EH: JM, 481.

Dorothy Parker: undated letter from Dorothy Parker to Alexander Woollcott, Special Collections, Houghton Library, Harvard University.

EH's request that MG adopt his name: CB, 353.

EG's visit: JO, 117.

Mary Hall: int.

MG's hectic life with EH: HWH, 111.

EH and HG: BK, 348–9. The typescript of HGW's 'Postscript to an Experiment in Biography', Gordon Ray Papers, Morgan Library, contains his comments on EH.

MG's teenage desire to visit China: MG to ER, 5 December 1940, FDR.

Calling MG Mrs Hemingway: MG to ER, 27 December 1940, FDR.

EH on MG's trip to Finland: BK, 354.

The Heart of Another: BK, 347–8.

10: HORROR JOURNEY AND HUSBAND

EH and MG in Honolulu: *TWMA*, 21; CB, 360

MG in Hong Kong: MG to CC, 1 March 1941, NYPL. My account of EH and MG in China is taken from *TWMA*, Matthew J. Bruccoli (ed.), *Conversations with Ernest Hemingway*, University Press of Mississippi, Jackson, 1986, 30, 34; *FW*, 78–9, 83; MG, 'Her Day', *Collier's*, 30 August 1941, 16, 53; *SLH*, 523; MG to CC, n.d., NYPL; EH to CC, 18 June 1941, NYPL. On the meeting with Chou En-lai, see MR2, 38, 43.

EH's endearing love letter: EH to MG, (c. May 1941), JFK.

EH ready for sexual play: int. MLS; on EH's hygiene, see MR2, 50.

Summer in Cuba: BK, 363.

MG on her German soul and housekeeping: MG to Bill and Emily Davis, 1, 17 April, and n.d. 1942, courtesy of Rob and Abby Mouat.

Sun Valley: MG to ER, 1 or 2 November 1941, FDR.

MG's dust jacket photograph: MR2, 51.

MG on HOA: MG to ER, 17 October and 1 or 2 November 1941, FDR.

Reviews of HOA and MG's reaction: BK, 365; Marianne Hauser, 'Noise of Guns', *New York Times Book Review* 2 November 1941, 22; MG to ER, 1 or 2 November 1941, FDR.

'November Afternoon': ER to MG, 10 November 1941, FDR.

Sun Valley-Grand Canyon vacation: CB, 370; *SLH*, 533.

MG as devoted wife and EH as her liege lord: MG to CC, 19 January 1942, NYPL; MG to ER, n.d., FDR.

MG's study of war: MG to ER, 13 February 1942, FDR.

MG's letter to Bill and Emily Davis: this undated letter, as well as several others, courtesy of Robert and Abby Mouat.

Shoot fools: MG to CC, 3 February 1942, NYPL.

Virginia Cowles's visit: MG to ER, 13 February 1942, FDR; JM, 327.

MG's speculation on EH's madness: quoted in Lawrence Graver, *An Obsession with Anne Frank: Meyer Levin and the Diary*, University of California Press, Berkeley, 1995, 192. I'm indebted to JM for calling this item to my attention.

Teaching the Hemingways table manners: MG to ER, 22 June 1942.

EH on MG's obsession with the sanitary: A. E. Hotchner, *Papa Hemingway*, Random House, New York, 1966, 133–4.

Gregory Hemingway: BK, 368; *Papa: A Personal Memoir*, 70–1. On EH's intelligence reports, see MR2, 60.

Bill Walton: DB, 146.

On MG's alleged adultery and EH's response: JM, 354–5.

EH's letters to MG in Miami: EH to MG, 24, 29, 31 May, 1, 2, 24 June 1942, JFK; Gloria Bristol: EH to MG, 24 June 1942, JFK. MG wrote to Katherine White at the *New Yorker* proposing a profile of Gloria Bristol, 'She is a character and runs the most expensive beauty emporium in New York or maybe the world. ... She talks the most amazing pseudo-scientific jargon and performs plain simple unadorned miracles.' MG to KW, Saturday, n.d., NYPL.

MG's Caribbean trip: MG to CC, 10 June 1941; MG to CC, 28 June 1942, NYPL; MG to CC, 16 July 1942, NYPL.

11: THE UNENDING BATTLE

Travelling light: BK, 370.

MG's happiness as journalist/traveller: MG to ER, 2 August 1942, FDR.

Health cure: 'A Little Worse than Peace', *Collier's*, 14 November 1942, 85.

EH to Hadley: *SLH*, 535.

EH's supportive letters: EH to MG, 6 August 1942, JFK.

MG's letters to EH: BK, 371.

MG's dream of picking up survivors: *TWMA*, 66; Chirpy: *TWMA*, 67; patchwork quilt: *TWMA*, 69; de lady: *TWMA*, 70; three hurricane-birds: *TWMA*, 75; youthful unencumbered days: *TWMA*, 82; boat bum: *TWMA*, 85; lovely mulatto: *TWMA*, 86; good giggle: *TWMA*, 93.

EH's bitter letters: EH to MG, 2, 5 September 1942, JFK.

The EH menagerie: MG to ER, 6 October 1942, FDR.

Martha and Gregory in back country: *SLH*, 543.

EH's letters to MG in New York: EH to MG, 13, 18 October 1942, JFK.

Dorothy Parker: EH to HR, 28 November 1942, *The New Yorker Papers*, NYPL.

Visiting the White House: JO, 133–4.

Missing EH: BK, 373.

MG's spot of domesticity: CB, 378.

EH's help with *Liana* and complaints about MG: EH to MG, 16 March 1943, JFK.

EH's behaviour while writing *For Whom the Bell Tolls*: JF, 2.

EH's abuse of MG: CB, 380–2; JM, 377.

Winston Guest: PUL; DB, 144.

MG's work on *Liana*: MG to PH, PUL, 4 July 1943.

MG's longing to be young again: BK, 379–80.

You're the writer: *Papa: A Personal Memoir*, 90–1.

Petty and cruel exchanges between EH and MG: EH to MG, 7 July 1942, JFK.

Browbeating servants: int. FVF; Frederick Vanderbilt Field, *From Right to Left: An Autobiography*, Lawrence Hill & Company, Westport, Connecticut, 1983, 203–4.

EH's lovemaking: BK, 381–2; JM, 355; *Papa*, 91; JF, 2.

I'm leaving: Norberto Fuentes, *Hemingway in Cuba*, Lyle Stuart, Secaucus, New Jersey, 1984, 22.

MG in New York: BK, 383.

The Loing Canal: BK, 383.

The great unending battle: CB, 379.

MG's letter to HGW: 9 June (1942), UL.

Criticism and reviews of *Liana*: D. L. Kirkpatrick, *Contemporary Novelists*, St Martin's Press, New York, 1986, 335; Diana Trilling, 'Fiction in Review: "Liana"'. *Nation*, 22 January 1944, 104–5; Mark Schorer, 'Exotics', *New Republic*, 28 February 1944, 286, 288.

12: WAR

MG's letter to EH inviting him to join her: BK, 385.

MG's articles on the RAF and the civilian populace: *FW*, 85–6, 90; 'Children Are

Soldier's, Too', 14 March 1944.

EH as mythical being: BK, 386.

'German for ever': 'Three Poles', *Collier's*, 18 March 1944, 16.

The Dutch: 'Hatchet Day for the Dutch', *Collier's*, 25 March 1944, 27, 59.

Visiting military hospitals: 'Men Made Over', *Collier's*, 20 May 1944, 32.

MG–EH correspondence over his coming to the war: BK, 388–9.

EH to Archibald MacLeish: 25 December 1943, Archibald MacLeish Papers, Library of Congress.

'Kick her ass good': CB, 386.

MG's report on an English village: 'English Sunday', *Collier's*, 1 April 1944, 60–2.

MG's refusal to return to Cuba: BK, 390.

EG's letter to EH and EH's reaction: EG to EH, 9 January 1944; EH to MG, 13 January 1944; EH to MG, 31 January, 1944, JFK.

Driving in an army jeep: *FW*, 102–8; 'Postcards from Italy', *Collier's*, 1 July 1944, 41.

'Are you a war correspondent': BK, 391.

On 27 February: William M. Stoneman, 'Martha Gellhorn Sets Out to See Cassino; Shot At, Dives into Ditch', *St Louis Post-Dispatch*, 28 February 1944, 1, 6.

André Gide: Philip Ziegler, *Diana Cooper*, Hamish Hamilton, London, 1981, 221.

Jack Hemingway: *Misadventures of a Fly Fisherman: My Life With and Without Papa*, 125.

MG's return to Cuba: BK, 390–2.

EH's decision to work for *Collier's*: MR2, 92.

On 13 May: CB, 391, 393; BK 397.

An uncomfortable Leicester Hemingway: *My Brother, Ernest Hemingway*, 229, 239–40.

D-Day: MG, 'Over and Back', *Collier's*, 22 July 1944, 16; *FW*, 109–10; 'Hangdog Herrenvolk', *Collier's*, 29 July 1944, 24, 40–1.

In Italy with no papers: BK, 410.

Harold Acton: *Memoirs of an Aesthete, 1939–1969*, Viking, New York, 1970, 152.

Carpathian Lancers: *FW*, 121–5.

Florence: 'Treasure City: The Fight to Save Florence', *Collier's*, 30 September 1944, 31.

MG meeting partisans: BK, 410.

The Eighth Army: *FW*, 133.

'When I got to know Marty': DB, 152.

'When head was all smashed': SLH, 571.

Affectionately called madmen: JO, 182.

MG and EH meeting: BK, 411; Richard Whelan, *Robert Capa: A Biography*, 228.

Nijmegen: 'Death of a Dutch Town', *Collier's*, 23 December 1944, 21, 58–9.

General Gavin: 'Rough and Tumble', *Collier's*, 2 December 1944, 70; '82nd Airborne: Master of Hot Spots', *Saturday Evening Post*, 23 February 1946, 40; James Gavin, *On to Berlin*, Bantam Books, New York, 1985, 5; JO, 187–8.

Maxine McClellan and MG: Ernie Sibley to CR, 21, 24 February 1998.

MG in Toulouse: 'The Undefeated', *Collier's*, 3 March 1945, 42.

Christmas and New Year's Eve with the 22nd Infantry: CB, 440–1; DB, 177–8; BK, 415–16.

New Year's day: *FW*, 146–8.

Thunderbolts: *FW*, 153.

MG's passport: BK, 417.

13: POINT OF NO RETURN

Germany's surrender: '82nd Airborne: Master of Hot Spots', *Saturday Evening Post*, 23 February 1946, 44; *FW*, 179.

All God's chillun hid Jews: *FW*, 162.

General Gavin: JO, 203–4.

Dachau: *FW*, 181, 185.

Back in London: *FW*, 188; *VG*, 106–7. MG to HGW: 25 August 1945, UL. See also Gellhorn's descriptions of settling in London in *FW* and *VG*.

Exchanges between MG and EH: Norberto Fuentes, *Hemingway in Cuba*, 376–81.

EH and Buck Lanham: EH to BL, 23 July, 1945; EH to BL, 20 January and 21 February 1946; EH to BL, 25 August 1948; PUL. Lanham's wife thought EH hated all women: Mrs C.T. Lanham to Carlos Baker, 1 June 1964, PUL; see also CB, 452; BK, 421. Yet Mary Hemingway wondered why Hemingway kept so many of his ex-wife's possessions in open view. See Mary Welsh Hemingway, *How It Was*, Knopf, New York, 1976, 177–8.

Mary and MG crossed paths only once in November 1944 at the Hotel Scribe in London. In the dining room Mary walked past MG and Virginia Cowles. According to Capa, Virginia and MG looked daggers at Mary, who later gave a fair, even gracious description of MG to EH: 'very pretty ... the line of her nose was quite different from mine, and her skin nicer. It made me wish I were a tall slim sultry brunette ... for you must be a little tired of blondes. And knowing she is very slim and straight-legged and lovely, I was terribly conscious of my damned old can. There was no face-to-face nonsense or anything stupid like that.' Mary is quoted in MR2, 120.

Love Goes to Press: *VG*, 107; Gellhorn wrote an introduction to the play, first published by the University of Nebraska Press in 1995; 'St Louisan's Play Given Warm Greeting in London', *St Louis Globe-Democrat*, 19 June 1946, MHS; *New Yorker*, 11 January 1947, 47; *Theatre Arts*, March 1947, 18; 'Martha Gellhorn Co-Author of Play Opening in New York', *St Louis Post-Dispatch*, 2 January 1947, MHS; 'Martha Gellhorn's Play to Close after Four Days', *St Louis Post-Dispatch*, 4 January 1947, MHS.

EH's wartime sketches: item 525a, Untitled Sketch, JFK.

'Cry Shame': See *VG* where the article is reprinted; *SLH*, 630–1.

EH to Lillian Ross: *SLH*, 642–3.

EH and Lanham correspondence: EH to BL, 17 November 1947, PUL; BL to CB, 21 October, 1968; 'Incidental Notes, Hemingway–Lanham Chronology 1944–45', n.d., 17–18, PUL.

EH on James Gavin: EH to BL, 27 November 1947; EH to BL, 25 August 1948, PUL.

EH to CS: *SLH*, 623.

EH's campaign against MG: EH to BL, 2 March and 24 November 1948, PUL.

EH and Stanley Pennell: Maxwell Perkins letter to Joseph Stanley Pennell, 6 June 1944, JSP; *SLH*, 669.

The editor of the *US Infantry Journal*: BK, 433.

Age-conscious MG: EH to BL, 25 August 1948, PUL.

EH's attacks on MG's war novel and her other fiction: EH to BL, 8, 12 November 1948, PUL.

Jeffrey Meyers: JM, 414.

MG's decision to remain abroad: *VG*, 110.

MG's reports on Dachau and Nuremberg are included in *FW* 85–7 and *VG* 106–7.

14: A PRIVATE GOLDEN AGE

MG and *New Yorker*: NYPL; for MG's complaints about *Collier's* see MG to HR, 18 March 1946, NYPL; MG to KW, 28 June (1948).

Private golden age: *VG*, 111; MG to JG, n.d., John Gunther Papers, University of Chicago Library, Special Collections; see also *FW*, 222; *VG*, 111; 'Strange Daughter', *Saturday Evening Post*, 23 August 1952, 21. Descriptions of the Mexican setting are from *The Lowest Trees Have Tops*, 14, 48, 55–6, 81.

Eight-point scheme and plans for schooling 'babies': MG to EG, 28 May (1949), Edna Gellhorn Collection, Schlesinger Library, Radcliffe College; MG to ER, 22 June 1949, FDR.

MG on David Gurewitsch: MG to ER, 14 and 16 July 1949, FDR.

EH's post-war comments on MG: *SLH*, 669; EH to CS, 27 August, 4 October 1949, PUL; *Across the River and Into the Trees*, Scribner's, New York, 1950, 212–13, 251, 273; EH to Buck Lanham, 14 April 1950, PUL; JM, 356; BK, 458. See also JM, 'The Hemingways: An American Tragedy', *Virginia Quarterly Review* 75, April 1999.

MG's child-raising: 'Little Boy Found', *Saturday Evening Post*, 15 April 1950, 168; MG to ER, 14 December 1949; 12, 28 February 1950, FDR; MG to BB, 1 January 1950, BBP.

Dorothy Parker's visit: MG to ER, 29 March 1950, FDR.

Bernard Berenson: MG to BB, 7 March, 2, 23 April, 9, 19 May, 31, 18 June 1950, BBP.

'Not some sort of dried seed pod': MG to EG, 28 May (1949), Edna Gellhorn Collection, Schlesinger Library, Radcliffe College.

David Gurewitsch and Eleanor Roosevelt: Joseph Lash, *A World of Love: Eleanor Roosevelt and Her Friends, 1943–62,* Doubleday, New York, 1984, 239, 241–3; 246, 248–50, 254, 259, 263, 283, 303, 337, 341–9, 356–7, 363–4, 370, 373; EW 29.

EH and BB: *SLH*, 789; JM, 414–15; BK, 468–9; EH to BB, 27 May 1953, BBP.

'There's my beautiful Martha': JM, 415.

15: OPEN MARRIAGE

MG in Italy: MG to ER, 8 September and 1 March 1952, FDR.

EG's calendar, WUA; Int. MLS.

'That ugly slave life': MG to BB, 27 July 1953, BBP.

'Silence': MG to ER, 28 June, n.y., FDR.

TSM: MG to BB, 27, 31 December 1953; MG to BB, n.d., BBP; Int. CP, MTH, MLS, WJP and several TSM friends; 'The Reminiscences of Max Gissen. Elisabeth Freidel interview with Max Gissen in New York City, 1962–1963, for the Oral History Research Office', Columbia University Library, Transcript, 155. For my portrait of TSM I also draw on his autobiographical writings and poetry: *Name and Address*, Simon and Schuster, New York, 1960, 3, 166, 202–4, 297; *The Worst Unsaid*, Anthony Blond, London, 1962, 98; *Jacks or Better: A Narrative*, Harper & Row, New York, 1977, 16–17, 20, 22, 26–7, 71; TSM to Allen Tate, 16 January 1942, Allen Tate Papers, PUL.

First phase of the marriage: MG to BB, n.d.; MG to BB, 30 March 1954, BBP.

MG on EH: MG to BB, 30 March, 14, 26 April 1954, BBP.

EH on MG: EH to BB, 9 July 1955; 18 August 1956, BBP.

Establishing a pattern for the marriage: EG's calendar, WUA.

Urbane, attractive couple: Int. Stanley Flink.

TSM on *Time* and Edmund Wilson: TSM interview with Joan Pring in London, 20 Chester Sq., 1958–9, Columbia University Library, Transcript, 24; *Jacks or Better*, 124.

TSM and women: *Jacks or Better*, 245; Gissen.

Matthews's sense of doom: *The Worst Unsaid*, 68.

MG on McCarthyism: *VG*, 119.

MG's access to Adlai Stevenson: Adlai Stevenson Oral History Project, Columbia University Library, tape recording; MG to BB, 7 September 1954, BBP.

MG's missing TSM: MG to BB, n.d., BBP.

MG on England and no McCarthyism: *VG*, 120–8, 131; 'Good Old London', *Harper's*, October 1959, 79.

Diana Cooper: MG quoted in Philip Ziegler, *Diana Cooper*, Hamish Hamilton, London, 1981, 15.

Perfectibility of man: *FW*, 1.

A special type of war profiteer: *FW*, 2.

Form of honourable behaviour: *FW*, 3.

Reviews of *FW*: Herbert Mitgang, 'A Message for Today', *New York Times*, 22 March 1959, Section 7, 10; Nigel Nicolson, 'A Woman at the Wars', *New Statesman*, 17 October 1959, 517.

Martha was always talking pacifism: Int. MLS, MTH, ELN.

The MG/TSM/EG American tour: *OMA*, 70–1.

MG's Germanic blood: MG to BB, n.d., BBP.

I never thought of: JO, 356.

MG and ER: EW.

'Married to quite a rich man': EW; Gellhorn makes similar disparaging remarks about TSM and his 'albatross house' in MG to BB, 14, 27 January and 14 March 1956, BBP.

MG's fondness for Poles: *VG*, 167–82.

The acid TSM and his last wife: int. FK.

16: HEART'S DESIRE

MG in Poland: *VG*, 169, 291.

MG in Israel, the Eichmann trial, and German women: *VG*, 230, 242, 254.

MG on JFK: MG to JFK, 8 April, 6 November 1961, JFK; MG to James Gavin, JO, 325, 433.

Sandy's American citizenship: 'Miss Gellhorn's Adopted Son May Become Citizen', *St Louis Post-Dispatch*, 28 March 1961, Vertical File, MHS.

For MG's African travels I draw on *TWMA*, 111, 114, 118, 137–8, 185, 190, 197, 210, 232.

MG's meeting with CB and her comments on his biography of EH: PUL; see also JO, 325. Her comment that EH seems 'quite insane' is quoted in Lawrence Graver, *An Obsession with Anne Frank*, op. cit., 192.

17: A NEW KIND OF WAR

'Good Americans': JO, 336.

For my account of MG's reportage on Vietnam and her later assessment of it I draw on *FW*, 230, 233, 238, 242, 262, 270, 274, 279–80 and *VG*, 284, 296, 298.

American streets 'bombed by poverty': *FW*, Virago Press, London, 1986, 250.

'Fuck Nixon': *VG*, 308.

18: HOPE AGAINST HOPE

My description of MG's reports on the Six Day War derives from: *FW*, 283–7, 291, 295, 298, 302; 'The Israeli Secret Weapon', *Vogue*, October 1967, 192.

MG's house on Longonot: MG to RT, 26 December 1967, courtesy of RT; *VG* 260–8; I rely on interviews with PN and others who do not wish to be identified.

MG's letters about Sandy: each one became more negative on the subject of her son. MG to EG, 15 and 29 June, 24 July and 9 August, EGC.

TSM's letter to EG about Sandy: 3 June 1968, EGC; TSM's poem, 'Old Girl', is copied out longhand in WHMC files.

EG's death: int. MLS, MTH, WJP, AF.

'Stupid internecine offspring bits: MG to EG, 24 July 1968, EGC.

MG's 'paralysis': *VG*, 328.

A. S. Knowles: A. S. Knowles to MG, courtesy of A. S. Knowles; A. S. Knowles to CR, 25 August 1988.

For MG's visit to Nadezhda Mandelstam, I consulted *TWMA*, 239, 243–4.

'Thank you, my blossom': *TWMA*, 272.

MG campaigning for McGovern: JO, 380; int. Martha Kessler.

MG's 'last hurrah': JO, 380–1.

19: THE LEGEND OF MARTHA GELLHORN

James Gavin: JO, 381.

Attacking Nixon's peace with honour: JO, 381.

'Lesson for future generations': JO, 381.

MG's suddenly expansive world: *VG*, 329.

MG's London flat: JO, 384.

MG never getting close enough to Africa: *TWMA*, 235.

Markham's sturdy settler furnishings: quoted in Mary Lovell, *Straight On to Morning: A Biography of Beryl Markham*, St Martin's Press, New York, 1987, 312.

MG on Isak Dinesen: MG to RT, 26 December 1967, courtesy of RT.

MG's car accident in Africa: JM, 'The Hemingways: An American Tragedy', 267. An African visiting London also told novelist Francis King a similar story about Gellhorn's accident and that he had helped her to leave Kenya afterwards. Int. FK.

VG on *The Weather in Africa*: 'Colonials', *New York Times Book Review*, 30 March 1980, 9.

MG's FBI file: I obtained her FBI file under the Freedom of Information Act.

MG interviewed about the Roosevelts: EW.

MG on LH: EW; Int. Blanche Wissen Cook, ER's most recent biographer.

Apocryphiars: OA, 281, 292–3; MG to MM, 6 April 1983, courtesy of Marion Meade; MG to CR, 23 May 1986; MG to Mary McCarthy, 29 May (n. y.), Mary McCarthy Papers, Vassar College Library, Special Collections.

Immobilizing rage attacks: 'My Private Anti-Anger War in This Mad, Mad World', *The Times*, 1 October 1975, 12a.

'Not quite so angry': 'Interview with Helen Bell de Freitas '31 by Caroline Smith Rittenhouse '52, 12, Special Collections, Bryn Mawr College Library.

Sybille Bedford: NS.

'This conversation is so boring': Rick Lyman, 'Martha Gellhorn, 89, a Pioneering Female Journalist', *The New York Times*, 17 February 1998.

'Playing chicken with oneself': MG to JF, 20 January 1988, NY.

'Virago has put me off women publishers': MG to Bill Buford, NY.

'Feminists nark me': NS.

Richard Whalen: Int. RW.

MG's Danish modern flat: Int. BK.

Pacts with MG: Int. BK.

JM, 'The Quest for Hemingway', *Virginia Quarterly Review*, Autumn 1985, 592–3.

Suing a German publisher: Bill Buford, 'Martha Gellhorn Remembered', *Los Angeles Times*, 22 February 1998, 2.

MG's desire to report on Lebanon: Julia Edwards, *Women of the World: The Great Foreign Correspondents*, Houghton Mifflin, Boston, 1988, 133.

MG on Nicaragua and Cuba: *FW*, 326; *VG*, 384.

MG on America as the 'Bully of the World': MG to MW, 5 December 1993, UL.

Women of Greenham Common: *VG*, 349, 351, 353.

MG on doing memoirs: VGV, 398.

MG on Bill Buford: Michael VerMeulen, 'Bill Buford, *Granta's* Bad Boy', *Vanity Fair*, November 1980, 140.

John Gunther: MG to JG, 14 February 1949, John Gunther Papers, University of Chicago Library.

MG and the *New Yorker*: MG's letters to Harold Ross and to Katherine White are in the *New Yorker* archive at the New York Public Library.

MG's meeting with Rebecca West: Int. Alison Selford.

'Sod off': VGV, 359.

MG on growing old: MG to MW, 1 April 1992, UL.

MG on Clinton: 'Cry Shame', *New Republic*, 23 June 1994, 14–15, attacking the press for what she deemed its disgraceful treatment of Clinton, especially its unprecedented probe of his private life. 'For the first time in forty-nine years I believe that we have a president and his wife who are the spiritual heirs of the Roosevelts.'

MG's articles in the 1990s: 'The Invasion of Panama', *Granta* 90, Spring 1990: 203–29; 'The Killings in Brazil', *London Review of Books*, 18, 22 August 1996, 3–7. MG on Panama piece: MG to MW, 25 July 1990.

MG's Welsh cottage, her announcement that she could not answer letters, and her writing to Mrs Clinton: MG to MW, 11 January 1991; 19 April 1995; 10 June 1997, UL.

MG's last two weeks: Ward Just, 'War: From Both Sides', *New York Times Magazine*, 3 January 1999, 35. See also Mary Blume, 'Martha Gellhorn: A Life of Wit and Rage: An Appreciation', *International Herald Tribune*, 19 February 1998; Clare Longrigg, 'War Reporter Gellhorn Dies at 89', *Guardian*, 17 February 1998, 18; 'Pioneering Woman War Correspondent Dies', *BBC News*, 16 February 1998 <http://news2.thls.bbc.co.uk>

Peter Kurth: letter to *Salon*, 12 March 1998, <salon.com>

'Superhumanly irritable': NS.

Julie Burchill: JB to CR, 12 November 1999.

Raleigh Trevelyan: Int.

'Historic monument': VGV, 359.

Sandy Matthews: NS.

A CHRONOLOGY OF
MARTHA GELLHORN'S
WRITINGS

A. ARTICLES AND STORIES

'Rudy Vallee: God's Gift to Us Girls', *New Republic*, 7 August 1929, 310–11.

'Toronto Express', *New Republic*, 30 April 1930, 297–8.

'Geneva Portraits, Glimpses of the Women Delegates to the League of Nations', *St Louis Post-Dispatch*, 18 November 1930.

'Geneva Portraits, Glimpses of the Women Delegates to the League of Nations', *St Louis Post-Dispatch*, 20 November 1930.

'Mexico's History in a Film Epic', *St Louis Post-Dispatch*, 9 August 1931, 2, 6.

'La Plume et l' Epée', *La Lutte des jeunes*, 10 June 1934.

'The Federal Theatre', *Spectator*, 10 July 1936, 51–2.

'Justice at Night', *Spectator*, August 1936. Reprinted in *Living Age*, November 1936, 155–8 and *The View from the Ground*.

'Returning Prosperity', *Survey Graphic*, 26 February 1937, 103.

'Only The Shells Whine', *Collier's*, 17 July 1937, 12–13, 64–5. Reprinted as 'High Explosive for Everyone' in *The Face of War*.

'Madrid to Morata', *New Yorker*, 24 July 1937, 31.

'Exile', *Scribner's Magazine*, September 1937, 18–23. Reprinted in *The Honeyed Peace*.

'Visit to the Wounded', *Story Magazine*, October 1937, 58–61.

'Writers Fighting in Spain' in *The Writer in a Changing World*, ed.

Henry Hart. USA: Equinox Cooperative Press, 1937.

'Men without Medals', *Collier's*, 15 January 1938, 9–10, 49.

'City at War', *Collier's*, 2 April 1938, 18–19, 59–60. Reprinted as 'The Besieged City' in *The Face of War*.

'Come Ahead, Adolf!', *Collier's*, 6 August 1938, 13, 43–4.

'The Lord Will Provide – for England', *Collier's*, 17 September 1938, 16–17, 35–8. Reprinted in *The View from the Ground*.

'Guns Against France', *Collier's*, 8 October 1938, 14–15, 34–6.

'Obituary for a Democracy', *Collier's*, 10 December 1938, 12–13, 28–9. Reprinted in *The View from the Ground*.

'Slow Boat to War', *Collier's*, 6 January 1940, 10–12.

'Blood on the Snow', *Collier's*, 20 January 1940, 9–11.

'Bombs from a Low Sky', *Collier's*, 17 January 1940, 12–13.

'Fear Comes to Sweden', *Collier's*, 3 February 1940, 20–2.

'Death in the Present Tense', *Collier's*, 10 February 1940, 14–15, 46.

'Flight into Peril', *Collier's*, 31 May 1941, 21+.

'Time Bomb in Hong Kong', *Collier's*, 7 June 1941, 13+.

'These, Our Mountains', *Collier's*, 28 June 1941, 16–17, 38, 40–1, 44. Reprinted in *The Face of War*.

'Fire Guards the Indies', *Collier's*, 2 August 1941, 20–1.

'Her Day', *Collier's*, 30 August 1941, 16, 53.

'Singapore Scenario', *Collier's*, 9 August 1941, 20–1, 43–4.

'The Love Albert L. Guerard Spurns', *New Republic*, 10 August 1942, 173–5.

'A Little Worse than Peace', *Collier's*, 14 November 1942, 18–19, 84–6.

'Holland's Last Stand', *Collier's*, 26 December 1942, 25–8.

'Children Are Soldiers, Too', *Collier's*, 4 March 1944, 21, 27.

'Three Poles', *Collier's*, 18 March 1944, 16–17. Reprinted in *The Face of War*.

'Hatchet Day for the Dutch', *Collier's*, 25 March 1944, 27, 59.

'English Sunday', *Collier's*, 1 April 1944, 60–2.

'Visit Italy', *Collier's*, 6 May 1944, 62+. Reprinted in *The Face of War*.

'Men Made Over', *Collier's*, 20 May 1944, 32, 74–6.

'The Bomber Boys', *Collier's*, 17 June 1944, 58–9. Reprinted in *The Face of War*.

'Postcards from Italy', *Collier's*, 1 July 1944, 41, 56.

'Over and Back', *Collier's*, 22 July 1944, 16.

'Hangdog Herrenvolk', *Collier's*, 29 July 1944, 24, 40–1.

'The Wounded Come Home', *Collier's*, 5 August 1944, 14–15, 73–4.

'Treasure City', *Collier's*, 30 September 1944, 22, 30–1.

'The Wounds of Paris', *Collier's*, 4 November 1944, 72–3.

'Rough and Tumble', *Collier's*, 2 December 1944, 12, 70.

'Death of a Dutch Town', *Collier's*, 23 December 1944, 21, 58–9. Reprinted as 'A Little Dutch Town' in *The Face of War*.

'The Undefeated', *Collier's*, 3 March 1945, 42, 44.

'Night Life in the Sky', *Collier's*, 17 March 1945, 18–19, 31. Reprinted as 'The Black Widow' in *The Face of War*.

'We Were Never Nazis', *Collier's*, 26 May 1945, 13+.

'Dachau: Experimental Murder', *Collier's*, 23 June 1945, 16+. Reprinted in *The Face of War*.

'The Russians' Invisible Wall', *Collier's*, 30 June 1945, 24, 54. Reprinted as 'The Russians' in *The Face of War*.

'You're On Your Way Home', *Collier's*, 22 September 1945, 22, 39.

'82nd Airborne: Master of Hot Spots', *Saturday Evening Post*, 23 February 1946, 22–3+.

'Java Journey', *Saturday Evening Post*, 1 June 1946, 11+. Reprinted in *The Face of War*.

'The Paths of Glory', *Collier's*, 9 November 1946, 21, 74–6. Reprinted in *The Face of War*.

'They Talked of Peace', *Collier's*, 14 December 1946, 19, 83–5. Reprinted in *The Face of War*.

'Miami–New York', *Atlantic Monthly*, May 1947, 48–56.

'Journey Through a Peaceful Land', *New Republic*, 30 June 1947, 18–21. Reprinted in *The View from the Ground*.

'An Odd Restless, Beautiful Country', *New Republic*, 4 August 1947, 26–8. Reprinted as 'Journey Through a Peaceful Land' in *The View from the Ground*.

'Cry Shame … !', *New Republic*, 4 October 1947, 20–1. Reprinted in *The View from the Ground*.

'The Honeyed Peace', *Atlantic Monthly*, August 1948, 48–55. Reprinted in *The Honeyed Peace*.

'Lonely Lady', *Saturday Evening Post*, 6 November 1948, 18, 70–9.

'Grand Passion', *Woman's Home Companion*, April 1949, 17.

'Everybody's Happy on Capri', *Saturday Evening Post*, 8 October 1949, 29, 148, 150, 152, 154.

'Party Girl in Paradise', *Saturday Evening Post*, 7 January 1950, 24–5, 76, 78.

'Little Boy Found', *Saturday Evening Post*, 15 April 1950, 29, 167–8, 170–2.

'Alone', *Good Housekeeping*, May 1949, 38–9.

'Children Pay the Price', *Saturday Evening Post*, 27 August 1949, 17–19+.

'Dream from the Movies', *Good Housekeeping*, August 1950, 52–3.

'The Kids Don't Remember a Thing', *Saturday Evening Post*, 23 December 1950, 20–1, 56–7.

'There's Nothing Else Like Eton', *Saturday Evening Post*, 10 March 1951, 33, 114–16.

'Are the British Willing to Fight?', *Saturday Evening Post*, 21 April 1951, 32–3, 161–3.

'Paco's Donkey', *Good Housekeeping*, April 1951, 60–1.

'Weekend at Grimsby', *Atlantic Monthly*, May 1951, 391–400. Reprinted in *The Honeyed Peace*.

'The Long Journey', *Good Housekeeping*, June 1952, 53, 120, 123–4, 126, 128–9.

'Strange Daughter', *Saturday Evening Post*, 23 August 1952, 21, 42, 44, 46, 50, 52.

'A Psychiatrist of One's Own', *Atlantic Monthly*, March 1953, 30–8. Reprinted in *The Honeyed Peace*.

'It Takes Two', *McCalls*, August 1953, 26–7.

'Mysterious Lady in Black', *Saturday Evening Post*, 13 June 1953, 40–1.

'The Good Husband', *Collier's*, 4 February 1955, 25, 66–9.

'It Don't Matter Who Gets in, Dear', *New Republic*, 6 June 1955, 7–10. Reprinted in *The View from the Ground*.

'Kind Hearts vs. Coronets', *New Republic*, 31 October 1955, 7–8.

'The Smell of Lilies', *Atlantic Monthly*, August 1956, 41–54. Reprinted as 'In Sickness and in Health', in *Two by Two*.

'Weekend in Israel', *New Republic*, 29 October 1956, 14–15; 5 November 1956, 16–17. Reprinted in *The View from the Ground*.

'Spies and Starlings', *New Republic*, 28 November 1955, 14–15.

'You Too Can Be a Pundit', *New Republic*, 18 February 1957, 11–12.

'The Queen's Justice is Quick', *Saturday Evening Post*, 16 February 1957, 40–1, 120, 122.

'The Tacopatli Passion Play', *Atlantic Monthly*, November 1958, 100–6. Later incorporated into *The Lowest Trees Have Tops*.

'Home of the Brave', *Atlantic Monthly*, March 1959, 33–9. Reprinted in *The View from the Ground*.

'Good Old London', *Harper's*, October 1959, 78–81.

'Tanganyika: African New Frontier', *Atlantic Monthly*, 40–5.

'Town No Scandal Can Shake', *Vogue*, 15 November 1963, 144–5+.

'I Have Monkeys on My Roof', *Ladies Home Journal*, July 1964, 26, 30–1. Reprinted in *The View from the Ground*.

'Animals Running Free, Two Weeks in the Serengeti', *Atlantic Monthly*, February 1966, 70–6.

'A New Kind of War', *Guardian*, 12 September 1966, 8. Reprinted in *The Face of War*.

'Open Arms for the Vietcong', *Guardian*, 15 September 1966, 10. Reprinted in *The Face of War*.

'Real War and the War of Words', *Guardian*, 19 September 1966, 10. Reprinted in *The Face of War*.

'Orphans of All Ages', *Guardian*, 23 September 1966, 12. Reprinted in *The Face of War*.

'The Uprooted', *Guardian*, 26 September 1966, 8.

'Saigon Conversation Piece', *Guardian*, 29 September 1966, 10. Reprinted in *The Face of War*.

'Casualties and Propaganda', *Guardian*, 24 July 1967, 6. Reprinted in *The Face of War*.

'Why the Refugees Ran', *Guardian*, 25 July 1967, 6. Reprinted in *The Face of War*.

'Thoughts on a Sacred Cow', *Guardian*, 26 July 1967, 8.

'Arab Coffee Break', *Nation*, 23 October 1967, 395–7.

'The Israeli Secret Weapon', *Vogue*, October 1967, 192–3, 235.

'The Indomitable Losers: Spain Revisited', *New Yorker*, 2 February 1976, 42–7. Reprinted in *A View from the Ground*.

'The Vietcong's Peacemaker', *The Times* (London), 27 January 1969, 11. Reprinted in *The Face of War*.

'My Private Anti-Anger War in This Mad, Mad World', *The Times* (London), 1 October 1975, 12a.

'Doomed to the Dole', *Observer*, 2 January 1977, 9. Reprinted in *A View from the Ground*.

'On Apocryphism', *Paris Review*, Spring 1981, 280–301.

'Testament of Terror', *New Statesman*, 1 July 1983, 15–17. Reprinted in *A View from The Ground*.

'Frontier Spirit', *Observer*, 12 February 1985, 8–12.

'We Are Not Little Mice', *New Statesman*, 3 May 1985, 19–20.

'The Face of War', *New Statesman*, 21 March 1986, 23–5. Reprinted in *A View From The Ground*.

'The Invasion of Panama', *Granta* 90, Spring 1990, 203–29.

'Ohne Mich: Why I Shall Never Return to Germany', *Granta* 42, Winter 1992, 199–208.

'Martha Gellhorn's Thriller Guide', *Daily Telegraph*, 16 January 1993, 18.

'Cry Shame', *New Republic*, 23 June 1994, 14–15.

The Killings in Brazil', *The London Review of Books* 18 (22 August 1996): 3–7.

B. COLLECTIONS (JOURNALISM)

The Face of War (1959), Atlantic Monthly Press, New York, 1988; Granta Books, London, 1993.

The View from the Ground, Atlantic Monthly Press, New York, 1988.

C. BOOKS (FICTION)

What Mad Pursuit (novel), Frederick A. Stokes Company, New York, 1934.

The Trouble I've Seen (stories), Morrow, New York, 1936.

A Stricken Field (1940) (novel), With a new Afterword by the Author, Virago Books, London, 1986.

The Heart of Another (stories), Scribner's, New York, 1941.

Liana (novel), Scribner's, New York, 1944. With a new Afterword by the Author. Virago Books, London, 1987.

The Wine of Astonishment (novel), Scribner's, New York, 1948.

The Honeyed Peace (stories), Doubleday, New York, 1953.

Two by Two (stories), Simon and Schuster, New York, 1958.

His Own Man (novel), Simon and Schuster, New York, 1961.

Pretty Tales for Tired People (stories), Simon and Schuster, New York, 1965.

The Lowest Trees Have Tops (novel), Dodd, Mead, New York, 1967.

The Weather in Africa (stories), Dodd, Mead, New York, 1978; (paper-back), Avon Books, 1981.

The Short Novels of Martha Gellhorn, Sinclair-Stevenson, London, 1991.

The Novellas of Martha Gellhorn, Knopf, New York, 1993.

D. NONFICTION

Travels with Myself and Another, Dodd, Mead, New York, 1978; Allan Lane, London, 1978; (paperback), Eland Books, 1983.

E. DRAMA

Love Goes to Press: A Comedy in Three Acts, Lincoln, University of Nebraska Press, 1995.

INDEX